PUBLICATIONS OF THE BUREAU OF BUSINESS AND ECONOMIC RESEARCH

Previously published in this series:

A TREATISE ON WAR INFLATION
by William Fellner (1942)

BREAD AND DEMOCRACY IN GERMANY
by Alexander Gerschenkron (1943)

THE ECONOMICS OF THE PACIFIC COAST PETROLEUM INDUSTRY
PART 1: MARKET STRUCTURE
by Joe S. Bain (1944)

LAND TENURE PROBLEMS IN THE SANTA FE RAILROAD GRANT AREA
by Sanford A. Mosk (1944)

NATIONAL POWER AND THE STRUCTURE OF FOREIGN TRADE
by Albert O. Hirschmann (1945)

THE ECONOMICS OF THE PACIFIC COAST PETROLEUM INDUSTRY
PART 2: PRICE BEHAVIOR AND COMPETITION
by Joe S. Bain (1945)

CALIFORNIA BUSINESS CYCLES
by Frank L. Kidner (1946)

MONETARY POLICIES AND FULL EMPLOYMENT
by William Fellner (1946)

The Structure of Transcontinental
Railroad Rates

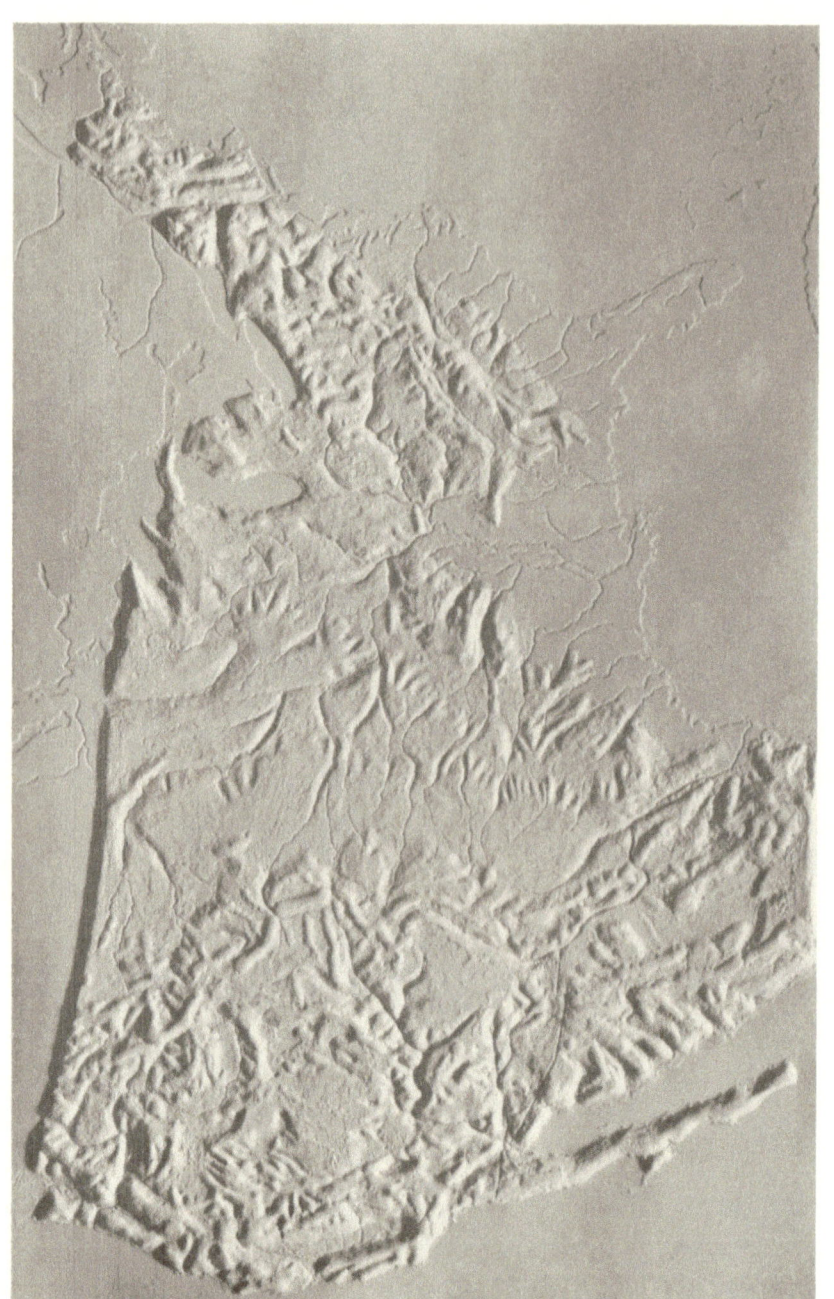

Topographical Map of the United States

*Publications of the
Bureau of Business and Economic Research
University of California*

The Structure of Transcontinental Railroad Rates

By

STUART DAGGETT

AND

JOHN P. CARTER

UNIVERSITY OF CALIFORNIA PRESS
BERKELEY AND LOS ANGELES
1947

UNIVERSITY OF CALIFORNIA PRESS
BERKELEY AND LOS ANGELES
CALIFORNIA

◇

CAMBRIDGE UNIVERSITY PRESS
LONDON, ENGLAND

COPYRIGHT, 1947, BY
THE REGENTS OF THE UNIVERSITY OF CALIFORNIA

BUREAU OF BUSINESS AND ECONOMIC RESEARCH

WILLIAM FELLNER, CHAIRMAN

ROBERT A. BRADY

MALCOLM M. DAVISSON

LEONARD A. DOYLE

ROBERT A. GORDON

EWALD T. GRETHER

MELVIN M. KNIGHT

FRANK L. KIDNER, DIRECTOR

◇

The opinions expressed in this study are those of the authors. The functions of the Bureau of Business and Economic Research are confined to facilitating the prosecution of independent scholarly research by members of the faculty.

Preface

MOST LARGE *aggregations of persons are principally occupied, first, in extracting and forming local materials for their own use; secondly, in storing and distributing these products; and thirdly, in providing a great variety of services. Such communities usually supplement their local activities, however, by trade with other areas, bringing in goods in different degrees of completion and exporting their own specialties in return. They also introduce raw materials and partly processed commodities for reëxport after enhancing the value of these articles by operations conducted in the importing state.*

The purpose of the present monograph is to describe the railroad rate system which is applied to, and which in a measure controls, the export of goods from California to eastern states and the importation of eastern commodities in exchange. This is part of a larger study in which the effects of the railroad rate structure on the economy of California will be considered in some detail. The advantages of prompt publication of descriptive material, along with some analysis from the point of view of transport pricing, are believed, at the moment, to justify issue of the preliminary portion of the work. The authors have in mind the fact that transcontinental rate making is imperfectly understood except by a small number of technicians, and that this is unfortunate because large plans for reconversion of war industries and for the future development of the resources of the Pacific Coast depend for their realization upon railroad rates. There are also problems of rate technique which can be more intelligently discussed with more general knowledge of basic facts.

Most of the information used in this study has been collected directly from published railroad tariffs as of 1943 and 1944. This has, at least, been possible in working with local western and transcontinental rates. Requests have been made on the railroads for other material, which has been used in chapter vii for comparisons between western and eastern rates. The promptness and courtesy with which the carriers have honored these requests is here acknowledged. Special thanks are extended to J. P. Haynes, of the Pacific Freight Tariff Bureau, whose friendly coöperation has been most helpful.

Weaknesses in the procedure followed are of two sorts. In the first place, there may be errors in quoting rates, and, also, in comparing rates which are not really comparable because of differences of one sort or another in conditions of application. Very immediate experience shows that railroad traffic men can make mistakes in rate quotation; outside students are very likely to do this also. A second observation is that conclusions arrived at depend upon sampling. This is inevitable. The only question then is whether the samples chosen are numerous enough and significant enough to provide an ample base to support the conclusions reached. Perhaps a third weakness is that many suggestions of causal connection in the study are suggestions only and not statements which are demonstrably true. The authors are conscious of these difficulties, but cannot avoid them. They believe that in spite of them, and in spite of other limitations to which this and any similar rate study is subject, the picture presented in the following chapters is essentially correct.

THE AUTHORS

Contents

CHAPTER	PAGE
I. Physical Characteristics of Western Territory	1
II. Mechanics of Transcontinental Rate Making	21
III. Western Termini	35
IV. Rate Groups on Eastbound Traffic	50
V. Rate Groups on Westbound Traffic	76
VI. Rate Profiles on Eastbound Traffic	88
VII. Class Rate Levels	108
VIII. Commodity Rate Levels	117
IX. Summary and Conclusion	140
Index	163

CHAPTER I

Physical Characteristics of Western Territory

WE MAY reasonably begin consideration of the transcontinental rate structure with the statement and elaboration of two facts. The first of these is that railroads carry most of the commodities which are exported from the Pacific Coast to other parts of the continental United States or are imported into Pacific Coast communities from eastern continental points of origin. The second is that this rail carriage of goods between the East and the West takes place through long distances and over a peculiar terrain. These are obvious but not necessarily simple facts, and they deserve discussion.

Let us, therefore, commence our study by examining the distribution of transcontinental traffic between available transport agencies—that is, between intercoastal water, highway, air, and railroad lines.

Of the agencies just mentioned, the share of the air lines may be dismissed as at present insignificant, although it will doubtless increase in future years.

The division of traffic between railroad, intercoastal, and highway carriage is, on the contrary, of real importance, although there are difficulties in ascertaining exact amounts. An estimate which seems reasonable is shown in table 1.[1]

---

[1] The table shows, for a typical prewar year, the distribution by type of carrier of traffic moving between California and destinations east of California. Traffic moving to or through the Pacific Northwest has been excluded. In the text estimate, railroad figures are based on statistics supplied by the carriers for 1941, showing business handled at gateways on the different routes. These figures are exact and pertinent, although not all statements give direction, and this, when not reported, has to be estimated.

The data on highway traffic are taken from traffic counts conducted by the California State Highway Department and from a study of interstate and intrastate transportation of commodities published by the Arizona Highway Department in 1941. There is a difficulty here in that the California report, although available for every year, supplies information only on the number of vehicles passing central points, without segregation by direction or, in detail, by type of carrier, and only for two selected days. The Arizona study supplies

The conclusion from the table is that railroads handled 72 per cent of the eastbound and 81 per cent of the westbound traffic, or a total of 76 per cent of the total tonnage exchanged in 1941 between California and eastern states.

In comparison, water lines carried 20 per cent and highway carriers 4 per cent of the same business. An estimate supplied by one of the larger western railroads and referring only to the division of traffic between rail and intercoastal lines is to the effect that in 1940

TABLE 1
ESTIMATED PREWAR DISTRIBUTION OF TONNAGE BETWEEN CALIFORNIA AND THE EAST BY TYPE OF CARRIER

Class of carrier	Eastbound	Westbound	Total
	(per cent)	(per cent)	(per cent)
Water (intercoastal)	22.2	16.2	19.5
Rail	72.4	80.9	76.2
Highway	5.4	2.9	4.3
Total	100.0	100.0	100.0

the railroads carried 53 per cent of the eastbound, 32 per cent of the westbound, and 45 per cent of the total business between the Pacific Coast and destinations in Atlantic and Gulf states. These figures are

loading information on traffic passing between California and Arizona during a full year, but does not, of course, cover traffic between California and Nevada. The distribution of freight vehicles by type and the average loading at these two boundaries may not be the same, although it is assumed that they are identical. Neither highway nor railroad statistics, it may be added, classify shipments according to final destination. Most railroad business which leaves California travels a considerable distance; but a large proportion of highway traffic crossing the Nevada and Arizona state lines terminates in Nevada and Arizona. This difference is important.

Water statistics are as difficult to interpret as are highway figures. The War Department publishes statistics of coastwise tonnage by ports. The Maritime Commission reports total intercoastal traffic, but does not distinguish California shipments from other Pacific Coast business. We do know, however, from the War Department's figures, California's proportion of all coastwise (including intercoastal) cargo tonnage. This percentage can be used to break down the total of Pacific Coast intercoastal traffic, but, of course, with a large margin of error. Available data do not separate, for water carriers, weight tons and measurement tons. The selection of a typical year for the water movements is particularly difficult. In fact, there is no typical year for water transport, that is, no year in recent history in which overwhelmingly important special factors were not at work. The years 1937 and 1938 were depression-affected. By 1939 the war in Europe had begun, with its concomitant diversion of tonnage to foreign flags. Diversions in 1940 were even more marked. With 1941 began the wartime statistical blackout. From the foregoing comments it is clear that the degree of estimate in the figures is substantial.

PHYSICAL CHARACTERISTICS: WEST

below the text estimates for the reason that they deal with traffic to competitive destinations only.

The conclusion that railroads handled from 70 to 80 per cent of the commodities interchanged between California and other states, excluding the Northwest, before the war, indicates well enough that their services are in major volume. This brings us to the second fact mentioned at the beginning of this chapter, and to a brief discussion of some of the conditions under which transcontinental movements occur.

The obstacles to railroad transport between California and eastern points are, first, distance, and second, topography. In the third place, it as arguable that the sparse population and slight industrial and agricultural production of the territory which lies between the Pacific seaboard and large centers of the Mississippi Valley and the Atlantic States handicap transcontinental transport. Something can be said with respect to these conditions, and the discussion may occasionally be expanded to include air and water as well as railroad routes.[2]

Air-route distances.—The principal air-line companies which now connect California with eastern states are the United Air Lines, Transcontinental and Western Air, and the American Air Lines. Table 2 gives the distances and the time schedules of the first two companies between San Francisco and Los Angeles in the West and selected points in eastern territory.

Distances in table 2 approximate direct distances by air, but do not express these distances exactly. The reasons for the variation are, principally, two. First, airplanes do not travel directly from San Francisco to every conceivable point of destination. They follow, instead, a system of main and branch lines which resembles the route system of roads and railways, though simpler in its form. And second, even the main lines do not trace the shortest course from point of origin to ultimate destination, but are controlled by the distribu-

---

[2] It is not implied in the following discussion that railroad rates should be adjusted with sole or even with principal attention to cost. Later chapters will develop the extent of competition which affects the level and form of transcontinental railroad rate structures; and there are elements of public policy which should, perhaps, be considered also. Nevertheless, the obstacles to transcontinental railroad transport which distance and, especially, topography present are factors which must always and obviously be taken into account.

tion of population and by the necessity of serving intermediate points of industrial concentration.

Rail distances.—The rail distances from San Francisco and Los Angeles to selected eastern points are set forth in table 3,[a] presented on the following page.

TABLE 2

AIR-ROUTE DISTANCES AND TIME SCHEDULES, SAN FRANCISCO TO NEW YORK

Station	Mileage	Time[a]
United Air Lines		
San Francisco	0	Lv. 7:30 A.M.
Salt Lake City	658	Ar. 12:47 P.M.
Denver	1,088	Ar. 3:54 P.M.
Omaha	1,481	Ar. 8:14 P.M.
Chicago	1,905	Ar. 10:53 P.M.
Cleveland	2,225	Ar. 2:13 A.M.
New York	2,657	Ar. 4:56 A.M.
Transcontinental and Western Air		
Los Angeles	0	Lv. 3:10 P.M.
Albuquerque	902	Ar. 8:10 P.M.
Amarillo	1,181	Ar. 11:00 P.M.
Wichita	1,478	Ar. 12:40 A.M.
Kansas City	1,667	Ar. 1:55 A.M.
St. Louis	1,896	Ar. 3:35 A.M.
Cincinnati	2,217	Ar. 6:35 A.M.
New York	2,809	Ar. 12:10 P.M.

[a] Figures show local time of departure or arrival. In calculating time in transit, allowance must be made for local time variations.

The short-line distance from San Francisco to Chicago and New York is by way of Omaha. In fact, from origins in central and northern California the central route is shorter to most eastern points than the southern one. From Los Angeles the short-line route, according to destination, runs either northwest from Los Angeles to Salt Lake and thence east, or from El Paso northeast to Memphis and St. Louis, or from El Paso east and then northeast to points beyond. Slight

[a] Distances in this and in succeeding tables have been taken from the Official Guide and apply to routes over which a share of the traffic may be expected to move. They are not necessarily the shortest routes.

PHYSICAL CHARACTERISTICS: WEST 5

differences in mileage have little practical importance in hauls of this length.[4]

It will be observed that the rail distances to Chicago and New York are longer than the air-route distances. Thus, the distance from San

TABLE 3
RAIL MILEAGES BY SELECTED ROUTES

Point of origin	Point of destination	Distance	Route
		miles	
San Francisco....	Ogden.........	786	Southern Pacific
	Omaha.........	1,776	Southern Pacific–Union Pacific
	Omaha.........	2,233	Western Pacific–Denver & Rio Grande Western–Union Pacific
	Kansas City....	1,893	Southern Pacific–Union Pacific
	St. Louis.......	2,171	Southern Pacific–Union Pacific–Wabash
	Chicago........	2,264	Southern Pacific–Union Pacific–Chicago & Northwestern
	New York......	3,184	Southern Pacific–Union Pacific–Chicago & Northwestern–Elgin, Joliet and Eastern–Pennsylvania
Los Angeles......	El Paso........	814	Southern Pacific
	New Orleans....	2,004	Southern Pacific
	Memphis.......	2,022	Southern Pacific–Chicago, Rock Island and Pacific
	Chicago........	2,299	Union Pacific–Chicago & Northwestern
	Charlotte, N. C..	2,786	Southern Pacific–Southern

Francisco to Chicago is 1,905 miles and the rail distance 2,264 miles. To New York the corresponding figures are 2,657 and 3,184.

Water distances.—Water distances may be added to the foregoing for the sake of completeness and because water routes compete with land routes in transcontinental transport.

Water distances from California to eastern points are longer than any of the land routes, and the time they require is greater. More-

---
[4] There are a number of ways by which distance may be measured. The Interstate Commerce Commission measures distance over the shortest route, regardless of ownership, over which carload freight may be handled without transfer of lading. It need hardly be said that such routes rarely correspond with routes authorized in railroad tariffs.

But, even when authorized routes are used, a number of problems remain. Distances shown in the Official Guide are distances between passenger stations. At large terminals, freight stations may be miles from passenger stations, and industrial spurs within switchover, the destinations which can be reached by a water haul without transshipment are limited; they include only points on the Gulf and Atlantic seaboards and such additional destinations as lie on inland waterways that are accessible from either of these coasts.

The intercoastal route is served in normal times by a number of lines which differ among themselves in time between ports and in the distances which the ships traverse. The differences in time are related, of course, to the speed of the vessels used and the time spent in ports along the way. The variations in distance depend partly upon the number and location of the intermediate ports visited, and partly upon the order in which these destinations are arranged. An example of the second situation may be found in the fact that the distance from Los Angeles to Philadelphia, so far as the American-Hawaiian Steamship Company is concerned, is greater than the distance to New York, for the reason that the American-Hawaiian ships go first to New York and then return to Philadelphia, a port which they have passed on the direct voyage out. On the other hand, by the Luckenbach service the distance is less to Philadelphia than to New York because the Luckenbach ships call in what may, perhaps, be termed a more natural order. Speaking again of the American-Hawaiian, the distance which ships travel between Los Angeles and Norfolk is less than that between Los Angeles and Charleston because Norfolk is on a direct line whereas the only ships that serve Charleston touch at Puerto Rico and Jacksonville on the way.

Table 4 sets forth the distances in statute miles between Los Angeles and San Francisco and ports mentioned, and the time required by certain intercoastal steamship companies for intercoastal service to these eastern destinations in the period shortly before the United States entered the war.

Topography.—The second obstacle to traffic between California and eastern states is topography. There are four railroads and five routes which enter California from the East. These railroads are the

---

ing limits even farther. Even for line hauls, exact figures are difficult to determine. The operating department in operating timetables, the engineering department in profiles, and the traffic department in mileage tariffs, all may show minor differences for apparently identical hauls. With double-track operation a still further difficulty arises when grades are separated in mountain territory: the easier ascending grades involve greater distances—a difference which is only coincidentally canceled out by the same phenomenon on the other side of the summit.

TABLE 4
INTERCOASTAL STEAMSHIP SERVICE

Company	Port of destination	Distance (statute miles)	Time (days)
	From Los Angeles		
American-Hawaiian[a]	New York	5,804	17
	Philadelphia	6,080	21
	Norfolk	5,477	16
	Charleston	6,240	24
Luckenbach[b]	New York	5,683	17
	Philadelphia	5,645	20
	New Orleans	5,023	17
	From San Francisco		
American-Hawaiian[a]	New York	6,228	21
	Philadelphia	6,504	25
	Norfolk	5,890	20
	Charleston	6,665	28
Luckenbach[b]	New York	6,059	19
	Philadelphia	6,027	22
	New Orleans	5,397	21

[a] Sailing Schedule No. P.C. 47, effective May 1, 1939.
[b] Sailing Schedule P.C. Card No. 150, issued September 22, 1941.

TABLE 5
CENTRAL AND SOUTHERN TRANSCONTINENTAL ROUTES, MAXIMUM ELEVATIONS ABOVE SEA LEVEL

Company and route	Distance	Maximum elevation
	miles	*feet above sea level*
Southern Pacific:		
Oakland to Ogden	782	6,884[a]
Oakland to Tucumcari	1,611	6,724
Union Pacific:		
Los Angeles to Council Bluffs	1,814	8,013
Western Pacific and Denver and Rio Grande Western:		
Oakland to Salt Lake City	924	5,907
Salt Lake City to Denver[b]	745	9,257
Atchison, Topeka and Santa Fe:		
Oakland to Chicago[c]	2,540	7,310

[a] Westbound, the peak is 7,017 feet.
[b] Via the Moffat Tunnel.
[c] Via Amarillo.

Santa Fe, the Union Pacific, the Western Pacific, and the Southern Pacific. The last-named carrier operates two routes. Two more routes to the East pass through the Pacific Northwest.

Elevation.—The special fact which confronts California railroads is the presence of two great mountain ranges—the Sierra Nevada and

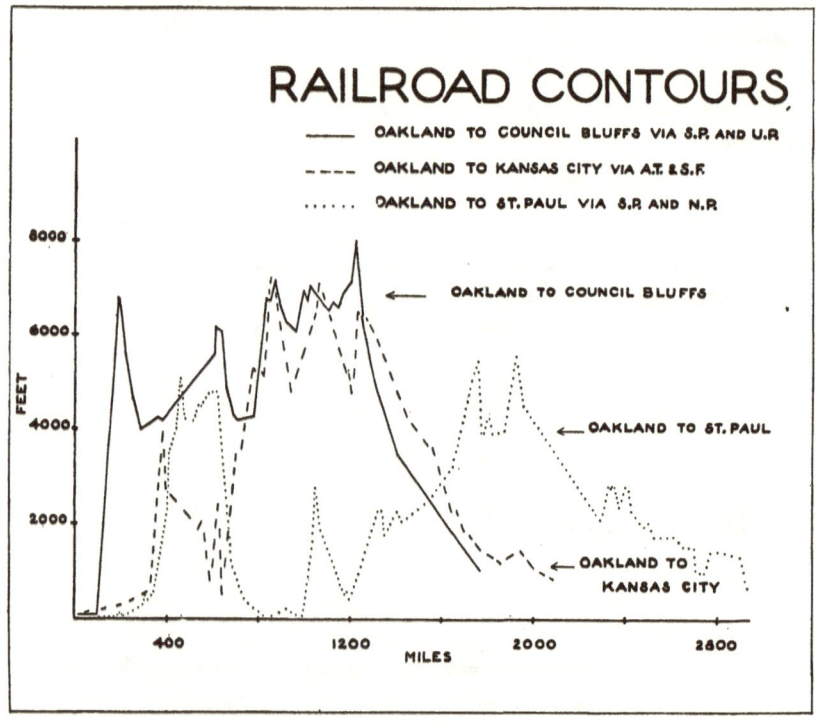

Chart 1. Contours of railroad lines between Oakland and Council Bluffs, Kansas City, and St. Paul.

the Rocky Mountains—and certain inferior, yet important, divides between the Pacific Ocean and the western plains. Table 5 shows maximum elevations on three transcontinental routes.

Attention is directed to the profiles shown in chart 1, supplementing the figures of maximum elevation given in table 5.

On the central route via Ogden, the Sierra summit is passed just west of Truckee, California, at an elevation of 6,884 feet. The next major elevation is encountered east of Wells, Nevada, at 6,165 feet,

PHYSICAL CHARACTERISTICS: WEST

and then, east of Odgen, the railroad climbs the Continental Divide, reaching elevations of 7,230 feet near Evanston, Wyoming, and 8,013 feet between Laramie and Cheyenne.

On the Santa Fe route the elevations are lower, but the major obstacles are likewise encountered at two points. First, over the Tehachapi between Bakersfield and Mojave, the line rises from a moderate altitude of 414 feet at Bakersfield to a maximum of 4,031 feet. After an irregular decline to Needles, the route then ascends again from 482 feet at Needles to 7,310 feet at a point between Williams and Flagstaff, Arizona, in the course of 240 miles. Farther on it has to surmount two additional elevations, of which one, at 7,244 feet, is on the Continental Divide and the other, at 6,491 feet, is in the Sandia Mountains east of the Rio Grande. From this last point the railroad descends steadily to the plains of Kansas.

The northern route from Oakland to St. Paul, by way of the Southern Pacific and Northern Pacific, crosses a peak of 5,106 feet in the Klamath range and then, turning east, after a descent to the Columbia River and to Puget Sound, passes over the Cascades in Washington at 2,837 feet and the Rockies in Montana at elevations of 5,548 feet at Blossburg and 5,565 feet near Bozeman.

The process of attaining elevation is expensive, both because of the capital cost of construction in mountainous country and because of certain characteristics of operating expense, three of which should be considered here.

In the first place, steep ascent usually requires curvature, and this lengthens the route which trains traverse. Thus the line of the Union Pacific between Cheyenne and Los Angeles turns ninety-three complete circles in a road length of 1,303 miles. The air-line mileage from San Francisco to Denver is 1,088 miles, but the route by way of the Western Pacific and the Denver and Rio Grande Western through the Moffat Tunnel is 1,673 miles, or more than half again as great a distance traveled to connect the same points of origin and destination.

A second disadvantage of rise and fall in transport results mainly from the increased power required to pull a train uphill and the increased wear and tear on track and equipment, both in ascending and in descending operations. The greater power demanded includes

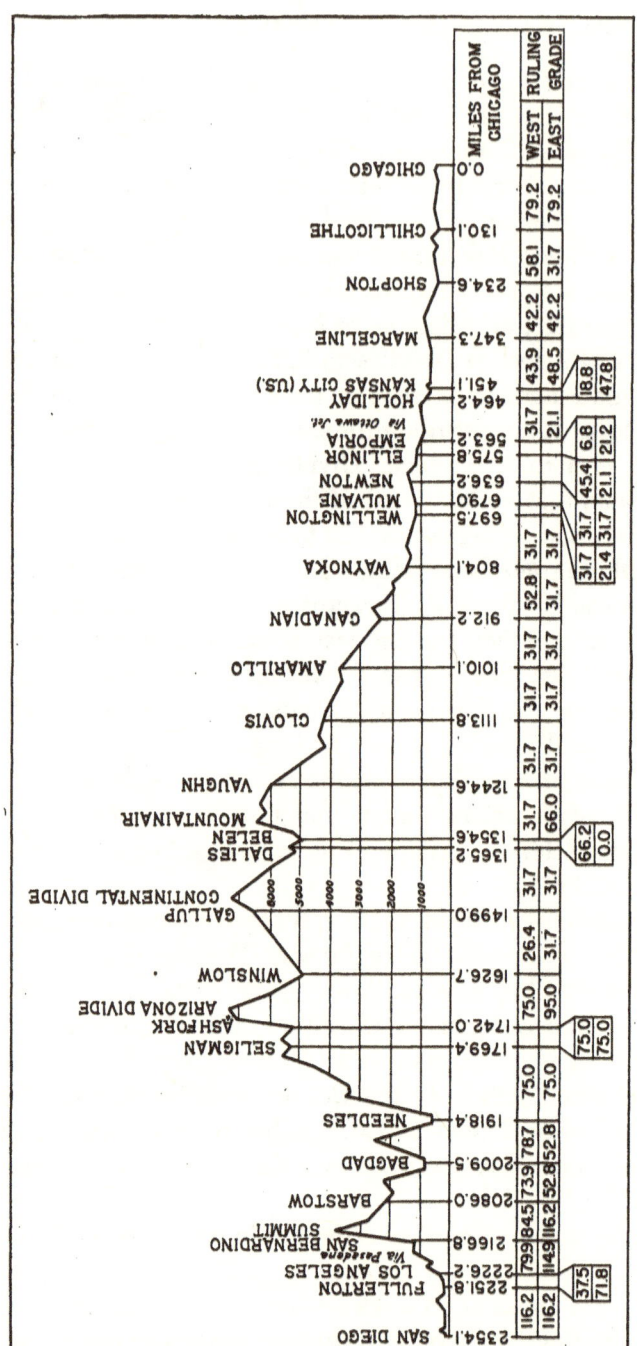

Atchison, Topeka and Santa Fe elevations, ruling grades, and distances, Chicago to San Diego via Pasadena.

that required simply to raise the weight of train and content from a lower to a higher altitude, and this is independent of the length or steepness of the grade. But, in addition, there are effects produced by descending grades which vary with the degree of gradient. On minor descents the fact of fall is expressed merely in increased speed; on medium grades power is shut off, and on major grades brakes must be applied.

The disadvantages of increased fuel consumption and of greater wear and tear are most noticeable when the grades require the full power of the engine in ascending and the vigorous use of brakes in descending. C. C. Williams has estimated that the total increase in rail operating expense may be as much as 8.92 per cent for every 0.3 per cent or 15.84 feet rise per mile.[5]

In this connection, mention should be made of ruling grades. A ruling grade is the grade which determines the maximum weight, including the weight of the equipment, which can be assigned to locomotives over a given segment of line. Limitation of tonnage to suit the ruling grade is expensive, because the power of the locomotive that is needed at this critical point is incompletely utilized on all other sections of the line.

The accompanying condensed profile of the Atchison, Topeka and Santa Fe between Chicago and San Diego shows ruling grades on successive parts of the route, along with elevations above sea level.

On the chart, the extreme ruling grades eastbound are to be found in the first 200 miles out of San Diego, where the elevation nowhere exceeds 1,100 feet, and over the San Bernardino Mountains, where the maximum elevation is 3,821 feet. In each of these sections the maximum ruling grade eastbound is 2.2 per cent. In contrast, the ruling grade over the Arizona Divide at 7,310 feet and over the Continental Divide at 7,244 feet are 1.8 and 0.6, respectively. The ruling grade between Chillicothe and Chicago is 1.5 per cent, or more than on any other part of the route except those just mentioned, while the ruling grade of 0.6 per cent is found equally, eastbound, in northern Illinois between Shopton and Chillicothe, and between Winslow and Needles where the railroad crosses the Arizona Divide. High ruling grades are not, evidently, necessarily associated with high moun-

---

[5] C. C. Williams, *The Design of Railway Location* (New York: Wiley, 1917), p. 263.

tains, but this is frequently because large sums have been spent to eliminate sudden steep ascents in mountainous terrain.

A comparison of maximum ruling grades on certain transcontinental routes is shown in the accompanying table.

COMPARISON OF MAXIMUM RULING GRADES

Company	Route	Maximum ruling grade	Location	Distance from San Francisco
		per cent		*miles*
Southern Pacific	San Francisco to Ogden			
	Eastbound......	2.4	Colfax to Norden....	145
	Westbound.....	1.8	Truckee to Summit...	211
Southern Pacific....	San Francisco to El Paso			
	Eastbound......	2.2	Santa Margarita to Summit..........	232
	Westbound.....	2.2	San Luis Obispo to Summit..........	248
Atchison, Topeka and Santa Fe.....	San Francisco to Chicago			
	Eastbound......	2.6	Bena to Tehachapi...	335
	Westbound.....	2.3	Mojave to Eric......	389
				Distance from Los Angeles
Union Pacific......	Los Angeles to Council Bluffs			
	Eastbound......	2.2	San Bernardino to Summit..........	69
	Westbound.....	1.6	Victorville to Summit	114

On the Western Pacific, between Oakland and Salt Lake, the ruling grade nowhere exceeds 1 per cent.

This problem of ruling grades is probably less important in Mountain-Pacific territory than elsewhere in the United States, becaused long, sustained grades are a characteristic of the Far West. Carriers have been able to establish large terminal yards at either end of grades in this section, so that freight trains characteristically may be assembled and tonnaged to suit the peculiarities of the motive power available at such points. Recent practice on at least one carrier in the West, however, has been to operate diesel-powered freight trains, without switching or retonnaging, from points west of the mountains in California to points east of the Continental Divide. Helpers are used, by this carrier, on one or two grades only. Freight operation here presents the same features that characterize passenger operation, and the difficulty of less than full utilization of motive power is real.

Labor costs are also higher in the intermountain territory. Wage costs per mile for train-service personnel are higher in mountain service. Rates in mountain operations exceed base rates by variously contrived arbitraries, sometimes in the form of a flat addition to the minimum rate for the division or subdivision and sometimes in the form of the addition of constructive mileage to the actual division mileage. On any one division the two methods may be combined, or still other methods may be employed which also have the end result of increasing wage rates.

In addition, costs are higher because more labor is required in train service per unit of output. It may be physically necessary that trains be smaller in mountain territory, owing to limitations in motive power, although this does not usually seem to be the case. But it is true that in California the law requires that the number of cars which each brakeman tends be reduced as the grade over which the train operates is increased. This means that, for a train of any given length, more men must be employed while that train is moving over mountains than while it is running on a level.

Finally, wages and salaries paid to station, yard, and shop employees on the desert are often somewhat above those paid for the same work in less isolated areas.

Curvature has some of the same effects as rise and fall. Thus, the Union Pacific between Cheyenne and Los Angeles is not only longer than it would be if the line were straight, but its trains have to encounter an extra resistance because of curves equivalent to a rise of 678 feet in addition to elevations which the profiles show.[6]

---

[6] This is on the assumption that one degree of curvature is equivalent to 0.04 feet of rise. In calculating the saving from an improvement by tunnel construction on 23.1 miles of Canadian Pacific line at Rogers Pass, B. C., company engineers estimated that a shortening of line of 4.42 miles with a reduction of 547.8 feet in rise and of 1,222 degrees in curvature would, with a total eastbound and westbound tonnage of 6,473,378 tons, reduce

14 TRANSCONTINENTAL RAILROAD RATES

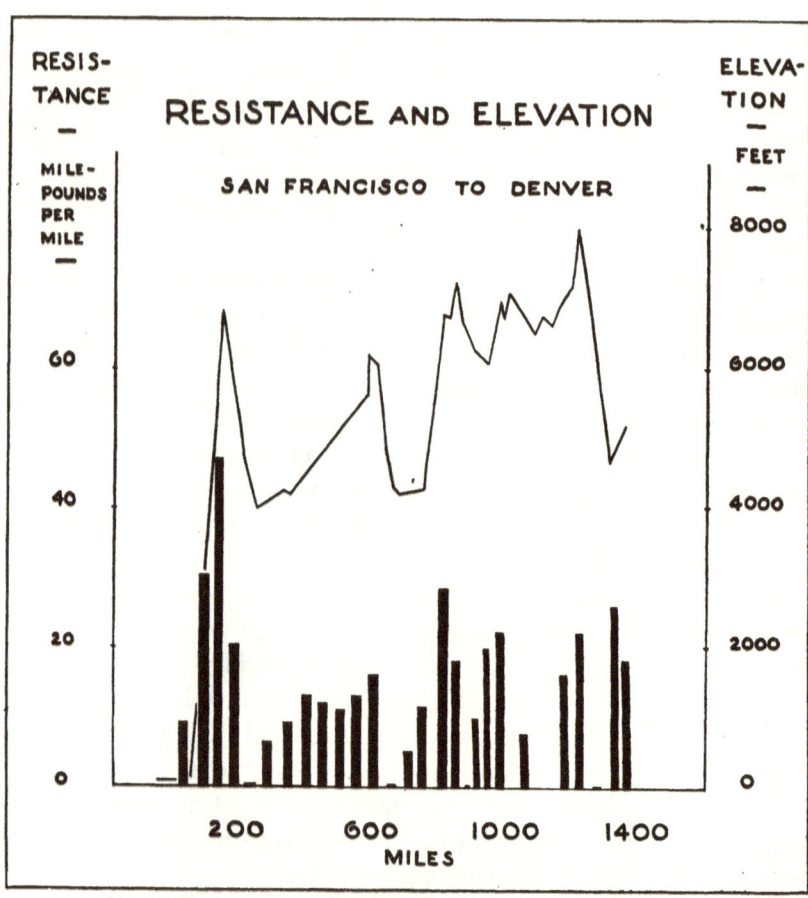

Chart 2. Resistance and elevation—San Francisco to Denver via the Southern Pacific and Union Pacific railroads.

Resistance summarizes the effect of rise, fall, curvature, and internal friction. It is difficult to calculate resistance accurately because of many variables, but chart 2 gives the result of simplified computations, this time on the Southern Pacific–Union Pacific route from San Francisco to Denver.

In chart 2 the columns indicate the average resistance in mile-

---

operating costs by $170,635.61 annually, without any change in ruling grades. This particular calculation included economies due to elimination of snowsheds. The calculated savings amounted to 2.6 cents per ton. (*Railway Age Gazette*, 58:194–195, January 29, 1915.)

pounds per mile which a locomotive has to overcome, computed for each of the segments of approximately fifty miles on the Southern Pacific–Union Pacific route from San Francisco, eastbound, to Denver. The continuous line follows elevations on the same route, expressed in thousands of feet above sea level. It is to be observed that resistance is greatest when elevations change, but that it is not affected by altitude in and of itself. This is a conclusion which one should expect.

Density of traffic.—California railroads transport transcontinental traffic across an area which originates little freight. The states which are unproductive, in the sense in which the word is here used, are Nevada, Utah, Arizona, New Mexico, Wyoming, and Colorado. These constitute, with Idaho and Montana, the group known as the Mountain States, and to them may be added Oklahoma and western Texas, through which traffic from the Coast also moves. The Mountain States are rich in certain mineral resources, but they offer limited possibilities for intensive agriculture, and their manufacturing industry is undeveloped. They are sparsely settled, and their income and purchasing power per square mile are low. Likewise, and for the same reasons, the number of tons of railway freight per square mile which originates in the area is also low.

Chart 3 (which is presented on the next page) illustrates the statements just made by depicting the varying number of tons originated for railway shipment per square mile of territory in the states which the Southern Pacific and connecting lines traverse between California and Illinois.

Government figures show that the number of tons originated per square mile of territory in the year 1941 were 216 in California, 10 in Nevada, 80 in Utah, 52 in Wyoming, 26 in Arizona, 22 in New Mexico, 100 in Nebraska, 126 in Texas, and 176 in Oklahoma. The figure for Illinois was 1,660, which in turn was comparable with still higher figures reported for Ohio and New York, farther east.[7] The number of tons per square mile in the Mountain District is low throughout.

---

[7] Interstate Commerce Commission, Bureau of Transport Economics and Statistics, Statement No. Q-550 (SCS), *Tons of Revenue Freight Originated and Terminated*. . . . 1941; Bureau of the Census, *Statistical Abstract of the United States* (Washington, D. C., Government Printing Office, 1944), p. 1.

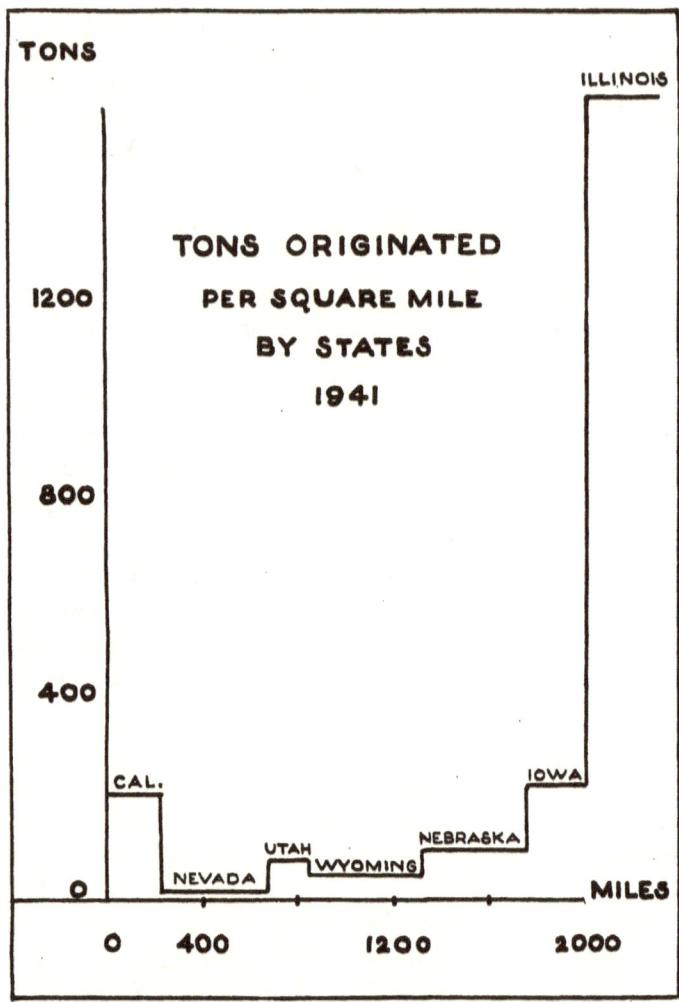

Chart 3. Tons originated per square mile by states, along the line of the Southern Pacific, Union Pacific, and Chicago and Northwestern railroads, between California and Illinois.

The ordinary assumption appears to be that transcontinental carriers are handicapped in handling through business by the lack of originations in intermountain territory and in the western plains. This may be true, but it must be remembered that absence of originating traffic in the states between California and eastern Kansas and

PHYSICAL CHARACTERISTICS: WEST

Nebraska may be consistent with a high degree of intensity of utilization of the railroads in the western district.

According to the Federal Coördinator of Transportation, the annual net ton-miles per mile of line was greater, in 1935, in Nevada, Utah, Arizona, and Wyoming than it was in California, and in New Mexico and Nebraska the difference was only moderate. The reason for this was, of course, the small amount of branch-line and secondary mileage in the states referred to.

This matter may be looked at in another way. It can be shown, and the fact is worth demonstrating, that there is no variation in density of traffic per mile of main line between divisions ranged in order from west to east that is comparable with variation in originations in successive states. Three illustrations will make this clear.

First, we may examine the direct line of the Southern Pacific and Union Pacific from San Francisco to Omaha. On this route the Southern Pacific reported 4,557,000 net ton-miles per mile of main line on the Sacramento Division in 1941, and 5,405,000 net ton-miles on the Salt Lake Division, which includes Ogden. At Ogden, traffic is transferred to the Wyoming Division of the Union Pacific. From Ogden east, the density of traffic on the Wyoming Division is 11,685,000 net ton-miles per mile of main line. The increase is due to the fact that the Union Pacific handles freight to and from its own line to California on the southwest, the Western Pacific on the west, and the Oregon Short Line on the northwest, as well as freight interchanged with the Southern Pacific. East of the Union Pacific's Wyoming Division is the Nebraska Division. The density here becomes 11,443,000 net ton-miles per mile of main line. This is still high, though less than the density in the relatively barren Mountain District. There is certainly no slump to be attributed to the lack of originating traffic.

A similar regularity occurs in density of traffic over the Atchison, Topeka and Santa Fe. Table 6 shows density of Santa Fe traffic in net ton-miles per mile of main line, by divisions arranged from west to east on its route from San Francisco to Chicago, in 1941.

The lowest density on the Santa Fe was on the Middle Division, in Kansas; the highest was on the Pecos Division, in New Mexico. There was, evidently, no depression in the mountain and desert

TABLE 6

ATCHISON, TOPEKA AND SANTA FE—NET TON-MILES PER MILE OF MAIN LINE, BY DIVISIONS, SAN FRANCISCO TO CHICAGO, 1941

Division	Net ton-miles per mile of main line
	thousands
Valley (California)	2,800
Arizona (California–Arizona)	4,800
Albuquerque (Arizona–New Mexico)	5,165
Pecos (New Mexico)	5,973
Plains (Texas–Oklahoma)	5,162
Panhandle (Texas, Oklahoma, Kansas)	4,702
Middle (Kansas)	3,679
Eastern (Kansas)	4,010
Missouri (Missouri)	5,950
Illinois (Illinois)	5,608

TABLE 7

SOUTHERN PACIFIC LINES—GROSS TONNAGE HANDLED AT DIVISION POINTS, 1941

Division point	Eastbound	Westbound
	thousands	*thousands*
Los Angeles (California)	8,773	.....
Indio (California)	8,427	7,370
Yuma (Arizona)	8,872	6,882
Tucson (Arizona)	7,677	6,707
El Paso (Texas)	4,042	5,815
Valentine (Texas)	3,931	3,534
Sanderson (Texas)	3,952	3,531
Del Rio (Texas)	4,369	3,560
San Antonio (Texas)	4,311	3,990
Englewood (Texas)	3,859	2,632
Echo (Louisiana)	3,506	3,155
Lafayette (Louisiana)	3,888	2,787
New Orleans (Louisiana)	.....	3,097

states. In fact, the lowest density in any section of the main line was in California, where traffic was abundant but where railroad competition was comparatively great and alternative main-line routes were numerous.

Finally, attention may be drawn to the Southern Pacific lines between Los Angeles and New Orleans. Pertinent Southern Pacific figures of tonnage upon this route differ from those referred to in preceding paragraphs, first, because they relate to gross and not to net ton-miles; second, because they distinguish eastbound and westbound movements; and third, because they record tonnage forwarded from division points rather than tonnage handled per mile of main line. They show, however, a similar result.

Table 7 shows a sharp drop in density at El Paso, which is due to the fact that the line here divides; part of the traffic is delivered to other carriers, part goes north by way of Tucumcari, and part continues toward New Orleans. The small westbound movement out of Englewood, Texas, is the result of a multiplicity of routes between this station and San Antonio. Except for these variations, the density of traffic is well maintained over the entire Southern Pacific route.

The general conclusion which we may draw from the facts presented is that transcontinental carriers are able to preserve a reasonably uniform density of main-line traffic across the western mountains and deserts in spite of the paucity of originating business in this area. This is possible, of course, because most of the traffic which originates in California is destined to the central Mississippi Valley or the Atlantic Coast. Consignments travel, that is to say, the entire way.[8] The density attained is, however, considerably less than that reported by major lines in eastern territory. Thus, in 1941 the net ton-miles per mile of main line on the through route of the New York Central Railroad between Chicago and New York ranged on the various divisions from 4,688,000 to 20,836,000. And the net ton-miles per mile of line on the Pennsylvania, including main and branch lines between Chicago and New York, were from 6,560,000 to 11,870,000 on the different divisions. This lower density is regarded by railroad men as a handicap to the western roads, and it may be so, although the truth of the assumption is not certain. It is evident that a railroad which is built to handle twenty million net ton-miles per mile of line per year and which actually transports only five million net ton-miles will operate inefficiently. It is not evident that a rail-

---

[8] With respect to unit cost, uniformity of traffic density over different sections of a line is important only on the assumption that the capacity of railroad facilities on successive divisions cannot be readily fitted to a flow which is heavy at one point and light at another. Seasonal fluctuations and the balancing of eastbound and westbound traffic may be factors even more significantly affecting costs.

road which is constructed to accommodate five million net ton-miles per mile of line and does, in fact haul that amount is mechanically inefficient, nor, in fact, that it operates at higher unit costs. The problem here is that of determining an optimum size for railroad enterprise; we cannot speak confidently of economies of scale until that optimum is known.[9]

---

[9] This is not to say that large volume of business may not permit economies in operation. Thus a road equipped to handle a heavy tonnage may, more easily than a route with less tonnage, assemble men and material to meet emergencies. On the other hand, light tonnage due to absence of local business may result in more economical operation of through business.

CHAPTER II

Mechanics of Transcontinental Rate Making

A REALISTIC study of western rate structures will keep in mind the problems presented by physical conditions confronting railroads in their conduct of trancontinental business, but the pricing system which has been set up in the light of these conditions has still to be discussed and understood. This system is framed and administered by the carriers, subject to Interstate Commerce Commission control of rates affecting interstate shipments, and to such control of intrastate rates as state commissions can and do exert.

The present chapter will begin the description and analysis of transcontinental rates with certain preliminary observations upon the mechanics of western rate making. It is not intended here to dwell upon routine procedures in the compilation, printing, filing, and utilization of tariffs, but to consider a few questions of acknowledged importance.

For rate-making purposes the carriers have separated the Pacific Coast into two segments, which are known as "South Coast" and "North Coast." The segments correspond roughly to California and the Northwest, respectively. Discussion in this study is limited to the South Coast, but neither the pattern nor the level of rates to and from the North Coast differs significantly from the structure here considered.

Rates in, into, and out of California are mostly published by two agencies: the Pacific Freight Tariff Bureau, with headquarters in San Francisco; and the Transcontinental Freight Bureau, with headquarters in Chicago. For certain movements railroad companies publish their own rates.

The dividing line between the activities of the Pacific Freight Tariff Bureau and of the Transcontinental Freight Bureau, in publishing rates to and from California, is shown in map 1.[1] The line runs from the international frontier at the junction of Montana and North Dakota to the Rio Grande just east of El Paso.

The first-named agency publishes most, but not all, rates on shipments (1) between stations in California, and (2) between stations in California and stations west of the designated line.

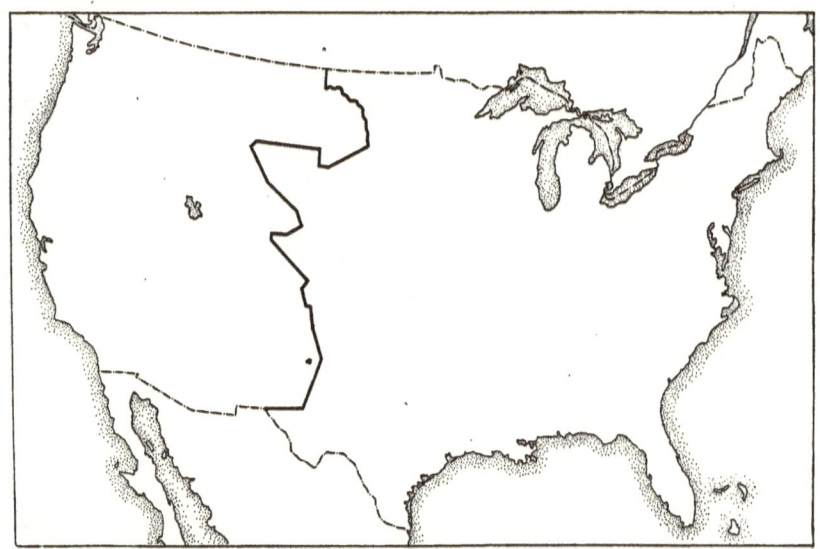

Map. 1. Division of territory between the Pacific Freight Tariff Bureau and the Transcontinental Freight Bureau.

The second agency publishes tariffs covering shipments between stations in California and stations east of the designated line. The same tariffs provide rates between stations in states immediately east of California and stations east of the designated line.

[1] An exact delineation of the line separating Pacific Coast Tariff Bureau and Transcontinental Freight Bureau publishing territories is as follows:

Beginning at the international frontier at the Montana-North Dakota state line; thence via the Montana-North Dakota state line to the Yellowstone River; thence southeast to the Little Missouri River; thence down the Little Missouri and Missouri rivers to the Cheyenne River; thence up the Cheyenne River to the Wyoming-South Dakota state line; thence north along the Wyoming-South Dakota state line to the meeting point of that line with the southern boundary of Montana; thence west on the Wyoming-Montana state line to a point west of that stretch of the Burlington Railroad which connects Cody and Frannie, Wyoming, and Billings, Montana; thence south to a point southwest of Lander, Wyoming; thence east to a point just west of Cheyenne on the Union Pacific; thence southwest to a point south of Coalmont, Colorado; thence west

Both agencies publish still other rates, which are not germane to the discussion in the present study.[2]

The types of rates issued by the Pacific and Transcontinental bureaus are those in use by American railroads generally. They are, that is to say, class rates and commodity rates. The differences between the two are well known. Class rates constitute a more or less integrated rate structure throughout the country. Tariffs called "classifications" list almost all conceivable commodities and classify them into a number of classes. For any article it is always possible, though perhaps not without effort, to find a class rate, in appropriate tariffs, for shipment between any two stations in the United States. But that class rate may not be the rate to be applied, because a lower commodity rate may be available over part or all of the journey.

---

to a point north and west of Craig, Colorado; thence in a general southeasterly direction and running south of all stations on the Denver and Salt Lake Railroad to a point just west of Denver; thence along a line west of the Denver and Rio Grande Western–Atchison, Topeka and Santa Fe joint track to Trinidad; thence south to the Colorado–New Mexico state line at a point west of the Santa Fe between Raton and Trinidad; thence east along the Colorado–New Mexico state line to a point east of the Santa Fe Railroad between Raton and Trinidad; thence southeast to a point just east of Tucumcari on the Chicago, Rock Island and Pacific; thence continuing southeast to the New Mexico–Texas state line between Clovis and Farwell; thence southwest to the Pecos River at the New Mexico–Texas state line; thence southwest to a point between El Paso and Ysleta, Texas.

[2] There are, however, some exceptions or variations from these generalizations which should be noticed. These result from the imperfect fitting of the two areas concerned or from certain exceptions. The following modifications are to be mentioned, and could be traced upon a detailed map:

1. Bismarck, North Dakota, and Mobridge, South Dakota, are included in both Pacific Freight Tariff Bureau and Transcontinental Freight Bureau publishing territories.

2. A few points along the line described are in neither Pacific Freight Tariff Bureau nor Transcontinental Freight Bureau territories. Rates to and from such points are made by combination. Among these stations are the following:

a) Stations on the Whitehall branch of the Soo Line in North Dakota and Montana.

b) Stations on the Chicago and Northwestern east of Rapid City and west of Pierre, South Dakota.

c) Stations on the Chicago, Milwaukee, St. Paul and Pacific east of Rapid City and west of Murdo Mackenzie, South Dakota.

3. J. P. Haynes, agent of the Pacific Freight Tariff Bureau, publishes most rates within California and most rates between California and points west of the line shown in map 1. However:

a) Rates between California points and destinations on the former Los Angeles and Salt Lake Railway in Nevada and Utah, short of Utah common points, are generally published by the Union Pacific Railroad. Utah common points are clustered about Ogden, Salt Lake City, and Provo. (Common points consist of a group of stations the rates to all of which are usually identical. They differ from the usual groups, or blanket, in the

Commodity rates are specialized rates developed to cover movements of individual commodities or groups of commodities between particular stations or groups of stations. They are typically, but not always, lower than class rates; but they do not typically provide, for any particular commodity, an integrated nation-wide rate structure. They tend, on the contrary, to be localized and specialized.[a] A third possibility, the all-freight rate, is less widely used and will be mentioned presently. With rare exceptions not here relevant, all these rates are quoted in cents per hundred pounds.

All rates to, from, and within California are governed by the Western Classification, but they are subject to exceptions stated in the various tariffs. R. C. Fyffe, at Chicago, is agent for the lines in Western Classification territory. J. P. Haynes, of the Pacific Freight Tariff Bureau, however, publishes "Exceptions to the Western Classification" which control certain of his tariffs. Each individual class tariff contains its own list of exceptions to the classification and to the exception sheets.

In class tariffs subject to the Western Classification, rates are quoted upon five numbered and five lettered classes, along with seven classes which are multiples of first class and twelve so-called column classes or rates which are percentages of first class. To each column class, with one exception, is assigned a percentage of first class which is less than 100, ranging from 77½ to 35. The highest group recognized in the classification is four times first, or 400 per cent of first

---

respect that the groups are used on movements to and from most other parts of the country instead of to and from certain parts only.)

b) Individual carriers publish some rates on shipments of perishables between points in California. These rates are used when they are lower than class rates published at the same time by the Pacific Freight Tariff Bureau.

c) Shippers are sometimes able to employ combinations of rates for movements between California points and destinations in the North and East which are usually governed by rates published by the Pacific Freight Tariff Bureau. These combinations may use variously published rates as factors. They are serviceable, of course, only when the combination is less than the through rate.

4. L. E. Kipp, agent of the Transcontinental Freight Bureau, publishes all through rates between points in California and points east of the line shown in map 1. But through rates are not published upon all commodities between California and all transcontinental lettered groups. When there are no through rates, actual rates are built by combination, and this may require the use of tariffs which the Transcontinental Freight Bureau does not publish. Combination rates are sometimes lower than through rates.

[a] Specialized services such as refrigeration involve an additional charge. Rates discussed herein exclude such charges, and cover transportation only.

class, and the lowest is 35, or 35 per cent of first class. There are carload, less-than-carload, and any-quantity ratings.

According to a study published by the Board of Investigation and Research in 1943, 66.2 per cent of the carload ratings in Western territory[4] in 1937 were then in classes 4, A, and 5, or 55–60, 50, and 45–50 per cent of first class, respectively. Of the less-than-carload ratings, 72 per cent were in classes 1, 2, and 3, and 90 per cent were in classes 1, 2, 3, and 4, or 100, 84, 70, and 55–60 per cent of first class, respectively. In 1937, the distribution of all class ratings was as indicated in table 8.

The figures presented in the text and in table 8 suggest that the distribution of class ratings in Western territory was slightly more favorable to shippers than the distribution in Official territory, in 1937, but less favorable than that in Southern territory.[5]

The discrepancies mean, probably, very little, if only because we do not know the volume of movement under different ratings, and because the levels of first-class rates in the different territories are not the same.[6] Moreover, there is another reason, and this is disturbing, for caution in basing conclusions of any sort upon the relationships between, and the distribution of, class ratings in the West. The reason is that the relationship of classes to each other in Transcontinental Freight Bureau territory and in some parts of Mountain-Pacific territory varies with the origin and destination

[4] Western territory includes Western Trunk Line, Southwestern, and Mountain-Pacific territories. This is, substantially, the area west of the Mississippi River.
[5] Board of Investigation and Research, Transportation Act of 1940, *Report on Interterritorial Freight Rates*, 1943, pp. 27–30.
[6] It is also true that the relation of Official, Southern, and Mountain-Pacific ratings varies with the point of division selected in illustration. The following table, supplementing that given in the text, makes this clear:

DISTRIBUTION OF CLASSIFICATION RATINGS IN OFFICIAL, SOUTHERN, AND MOUNTAIN-PACIFIC TERRITORIES, 1937 (From the *Report* cited in the preceding footnote)

Distribution	Territory		
	Official	Southern	Mountain-Pacific
Percentage of carload ratings which were 55 per cent of first class or higher................	35.8	43.2	45.2
Percentage of carload ratings which were 60 per cent of first class or higher................	23.7	22.9	23.4
Percentage of less-than-carload ratings which were 70 per cent of first class or higher............	83.6	79.8	82.0
Percentage of less-than-carload ratings which were 75 per cent of first class or higher............	56.6	55.9	56.1

of the shipment. This irregularity does not, it is to be presumed, characterize scales which the Interstate Commerce Commission has prescribed. It is, however, a feature of many western class arrangements, as the following facts will indicate:

Table 9 sets forth the percentage relationship to class C in the Western Classification of each class in transcontinental tariff No. 39-G, governing class rates between California and points in Transcontinental Freight Bureau territory. The point of origin is taken as San Francisco.

Table 9 makes it evident that the relationship of the class C rate is not the same to destinations in Colorado as it is to destinations on the Atlantic seaboard. Nor is the relationship uniform for shipments to intermediate cities. The variations are not large, but they are noticeable.

For traffic forwarded from San Francisco to points in the territory covered by publications of the Pacific Freight Tariff Bureau the contrasts are both noticeable and large. If we take, for instance, the relation between classes 5 and A for purposes of illustration, it appears that class A rates in California exceed fifth-class rates. But to part of Wyoming, the rates on fifth class are higher than those on class A, and in shipments to Utah and Colorado common points both classes are equal. To destinations on the Denver and Rio Grande Western, fifth class is higher than class A for shipments to some points, on a parity for shipments to other points, and lower for those to still other points.

Class rates between San Francisco and stations in Pacific Freight Tariff Bureau territory along the Overland route show variations in the relations of other class rates to class C rates such as those displayed in table 10.

Truckee, Ogden, and Laramie, the three destinations mentioned in table 10, are stations which succeed each other, in the order given, on the central route from San Francisco to the East. On this route the first-class rate is approximately twice the class C rate on shipments to Truckee; at Ogden it is two and three-fourths times, and at Laramie it is more than three times the class C rate.

Examination of the tariffs suggests that class relationships are less regular on traffic from California to other western states than they

TABLE 8
DISTRIBUTION OF CLASSIFICATION RATINGS IN OFFICIAL, SOUTHERN, AND WESTERN TERRITORIES

Distribution	Territory		
	Official	Southern	Western
	per cent	per cent	per cent
Percentage of carload ratings which were 50 per cent of first class or higher............	46.9	44.1	45.8
Percentage of less-than-carload ratings which were 60 per cent of first class or higher......	83.7	79.8	82.0

TABLE 9
INDICES OF CLASS RELATIONSHIP—RATES FROM SAN FRANCISCO TO POINTS IN TRANSCONTINENTAL FREIGHT BUREAU TERRITORY

Destination	Class									
	1	2	3	4	5	A	B	C	D	E
New York...................	309	267	221	188	159	160	127	100	87	69
Cleveland..................	306	264	221	187	157	159	126	100	86	68
Detroit.....................	304	264	219	187	153	158	123	100	81	64
Chicago....................	308	268	222	188	156	161	126	100	83	65
St. Louis...................	313	271	226	190	156	163	126	100	82	65
Kansas City.................	315	273	231	193	166	168	130	100	88	69
Dallas......................	310	268	228	189	162	166	128	100	85	67
Denver.....................	312	271	228	192	168	168	129	100	94	78

TABLE 10
INDICES OF CLASS RELATIONSHIP—RATES FROM SAN FRANCISCO TO POINTS IN PACIFIC FREIGHT TARIFF BUREAU TERRITORY

Destination	Class									
	1	2	3	4	5	A	B	C	D	E
Truckee, Calif.................	198	179	158	140	119	129	108	100	90	79
Ogden, Utah.................	273	233	206	171	141	141	110	100	71	60
Laramie, Wyo................	313	271	229	193	168	168	129	100	94	79

are in California itself, and they are obviously less regular on transcontinental business than in areas where the relationships of lower classes to first class have been prescribed by the Interstate Commerce

Commission. The differences do not, it is believed, invalidate any general conclusions which the text presents, but they are to be kept appropriately in mind.

Class rates are important historically and because of their influence upon the entire rate structure. Thus, many of the characteristic features of transcontinental rate making have taken form in class-rate tariffs, and even today the zone boundaries set in class tariffs are often used in commodity-rate construction, although particular zones may be grouped in commodity tariffs in combinations which the class tariff does not recognize. Class tariffs may, moreover, carry lower minima than commodity tariffs; they always provide for less-than-carload shipments, which the commodity tariffs sometimes neglect; and sometimes, apart from these peculiarities, the class rate is lower than the commodity rate. Such divergencies occur, for example, in California, where the Railroad Commission has prescribed a uniform system of first-class minimum rates based upon constructive highway mileage which the railroads adopt as a measure of their actual charge. These California class rates are sometimes above, but also sometimes below, commodity rates which are also available in the State.

Yet, in spite of exceptions, class rates are usually higher than commodity rates. The extent of the difference between class and commodity levels in tariffs applicable to transcontinental shipments is shown in table 11. In this table, especially on westbound shipments, the class ratings chosen govern most, but not all, of the items covered by the stated commodity rates.

The average of commodity rates on the articles listed in the table ranges from 25 to 75 per cent of the rates which would be chargeable if these articles were shipped under the Consolidated Classification. The over-all average is 43 per cent.

Fundamentally, however, the question at issue is one of procedure. Class tariffs can be made to provide low rates, especially if column rates are used. When class rates govern transport, they often establish a degree of unity of policy between scales. Of course, they are indispensable for the wide range of goods which move in small quantities. On the other hand, commodity tariffs can be more finely tailored to the traffic needs of a given article or group of related articles.

TABLE 11

COMPARISON OF CLASS AND COMMODITY RATES BETWEEN CALIFORNIA TERMINI AND EASTERN POINTS OF ORIGIN OR DESTINATION

(Rates are in cents per 100 pounds)

Commodity	Point of origin or destination	Class (carload)	Class rate	Commodity rate
Eastbound				
Oranges	New York	3	438	135
Grapes	New York	3	438	150
Lettuce	New York	A	317	184
Canned fruits	Cleveland	5	305	96
Wine	New York	4	372	99
Dried fruits and vegetables	St. Louis	5	271	121
Sugar	Chicago	5	284	70
Westbound				
Automobile bodies	Detroit	A	300	176
Beverages (beer)	Milwaukee	5	284	99
Canned vegetables	Chicago	5	284	88
Clothing	New York	2	528	307
Dry goods	Boston	1	611	206
Fertilizers	Nashville	E	122	75
Tin articles	Chicago	5	284	77
Steel articles	Chicago	5	284	110
Vehicles	Detroit	1	578	450
Wine	Buffalo	4	363	182

This means, especially, that points of origin and destination can be grouped in ways appropriate to special situations, particularly to competitive situations, that routing can be easily controlled, and that the level of rates, as we have seen, can be set low with minimum repercussion on other rates and movements where no similar reason for rate reduction exists.[7]

The practice in the western area has been, definitely, to rely upon commodity tariffs rather than modified class tariffs in developing an appropriate system of rates. Comparatively little western traffic now

---

[7] Commodity rates on transcontinental traffic are less closely related to distance than are class rates. This independence of distance is a kind of adjustment which can be defended when applied to particular commodities, but less easily when suggested for the multiplicity of articles covered by the railroad classification.

moves on class rates. A recent estimate by the Board of Investigation and Research, based on reports for a single day in 1942, is to the effect that, of the intraterritorial carload business, only 1.7 per cent in Mountain-Pacific, 6.8 per cent in Southwestern, and 0.8 per cent in Western Trunk Line territories moved on classification ratings (including exceptions to the classification). The details of the Board's estimate are set forth in table 12.

TABLE 12

Estimated Proportion of Intraterritorial Carload Traffic in Each Territory, Originating on September 23, 1942, Which Moved on Regular Classification Ratings, Exception Ratings, and Commodity Rates

Territory	Classification ratings	Exception ratings	Commodity rates
	per cent	per cent	per cent
Official	5.8	17.6	76.7
Southern	1.8	6.0	92.2
Western Trunk Line	0.6	0.2	99.2
Southwestern	2.4	4.4	93.2
Mountain-Pacific	1.7	....	98.3

Source: Board of Investigation and Research, Transportation Act of 1940, *Report on Interterritorial Freight Rates*, table 31, p. 57. See also I.C.C., *Class Rate Investigation*, 262 I.C.C. 447, 564, 1945.

It is clear from the figures given that carriers in Official territory make considerable use of class rates, but that carriers in other parts of the United States prefer to adjust by separate tariff publications, and that the proportion of class traffic in the Far West is especially small.

Interesting enough, in view of the foregoing, is the fact that attention has been given in the West, as indeed elsewhere in the United States, to the possible use and development of all-freight rates which are neither class nor commodity rates but a simplification of both.

An "all-freight rate" is a charge which covers articles of different descriptions included in a single consignment without distinguishing them from one another and without raising or lowering the rate in accordance with the description of the items shipped.

The "all-freight rate" is one of a series in which the mixed-carload rate, the container rate, and the full-truck rate have their place.

Under Rule 10 of the Consolidated Classification it is possible to combine consignments and to ship them at a carload rate, even

TRANSCONTINENTAL RATE MAKING 31

though each element in the combination is offered in small amount. The carload rate used will be the highest rate applicable to any article in the combination, under the Western Classification; or, under the Official and Southern classifications, each consignment will be charged the carload rate which the tariff separately provides.

For goods shipped in containers, the Interstate Commerce Commission first approved a flat third-class rate on the weight of container and contents, with the provision that the charge should not be less than the highest carload class rate for any article in the container or less than the class rate next lower than the amount specified as an "any-quantity" rate for any article in the container.[8] Subsequently the Commission suspended its order to permit carriers to quote container rates that were lower than third class and which did not conform to the prescribed limitations.[9]

So-called "ferry trucks" are operated in carrying freight between Chicago industries and railroad freight stations. The goods transported are loaded in closed trailer or truck bodies locked and sealed by the shipper, and are moved on specially constructed flatcars. There is a flat charge of 30 cents with a minimum of 10,000 pounds and of 20 cents with a minimum of 20,000 pounds.[10]

These three techniques set up systems of rate making which depart from or modify the generally recognized principles of rate quotation. Likewise the all-freight rate constitutes such a modification because it is a charge applied to the weight of shipments without reference to their kind or even, in "ferry-truck" operation, to the type of container in which they are enclosed.

All-freight rates have been used in the West since 1940, with Interstate Commerce Commission approval. The traffic mentioned in the pertinent Commission decisions is that from transcontinental rate territories D to N to Pacific Coast terminals all the way from Seattle to San Diego and to interior points.[11] All-freight rates may also be used on shipments from the Gulf to California points if these shipments

---
[8] 173 I.C.C. 377, 1931.
[9] 185 I.C.C. 787, 1932.
[10] 182 I.C.C. 653, 1932.
[11] Zone N is an eastern group used in quoting rates between eastern points and North Coast territory, including termini such as Portland and Seattle. It is not recognized in connection with rates to South Coast territory.

originate at New York piers. And they are specifically permitted on business from Chicago, St. Louis, St. Paul, Duluth, and some other western points to Salt Lake City and to other destinations in Utah.[12] Finally, all-freight rates are quoted, within California, on traffic from San Francisco to points in the Central Valley and from Los Angeles as far as San Diego, Santa Barbara, and the Imperial Valley. These local rates are extremely low for very short hauls—lower than the lowest class rates; but they grade upward rapidly as distance increases, so that, for fairly long hauls such as that from San Francisco to Bakersfield, they are only slightly less than the first-class rate. The all-freight rates of 1940 are also low if one compares them with the charges which shippers would have to pay on the same articles under standard class rates. According to the Interstate Commerce Commission, these interstate charges were, in 1940, 49 per cent of the first-class rate from Chicago to the Pacific Coast and 50.4 per cent of the rate from St. Louis. This was approximately the level of fifth class. Using twenty-two articles which moved in quantity under all freight rates, the Commission calculated that the weighted average less-than-carload charge upon these goods would have been 99.2 per cent of first class if they had been shipped under the standard tariff. The difference was, obviously, material.

The all-freight method of rate making was introduced to meet the competition of motor and water lines. It was expected that rate practice would be adjusted, also, to present-day methods of merchandising by enabling a larger number of small shippers to obtain the benefit of carload rates or their equivalent. Retail merchants like the method because it reduces their shipping costs. Motor-vehicle operators, on the other hand, protest, and there is some opposition in government circles. This is based upon the contention that all-freight rates make for poor utilization of railroad cars, and that, in addition, they disregard sound and tested principles of classification. Up to the present time the volume of western traffic moving under all-commodity rates has been small, but the railroads believe that much of this business, in the absence of such rates, would have been handled by motor lines.

Tariffs are complex and difficult for the layman to interpret. That

---
[12] 238 I.C.C. 327, 1940; 248 I.C.C. 73, 1941.

this should be so is, in part, inevitable, because the very great number of distinguishable services rendered by a railroad company requires an unusually extensive price list and leads to groupings, cross references, and special arrangements which need practice to understand and to apply. The only alleviating fact in this situation, so far as the shipper is concerned, is that most business firms or branches of firms specialize in comparatively few articles and market their products in limited areas, so that their representatives need be interested in only a few of the many tariffs which the railroads publish.

There are, however, some difficulties which deserve special mention.

1. *Commodity descriptions.* The reference here includes not only classification items, but commodity descriptions also. It is frequently impossible to state a rate conclusively because two descriptions, carrying different rates, may, so far as the English language or industrial practice is a guide, apply to a single article which the carrier undertakes to transport. These are not difficulties such as that made famous by Gelett Burgess in *Pigs Is Pigs*, but duplications or confusions which cannot be eliminated by research. Nor is it a solution to say that the description resulting in the lowest rate should be used, for this may lead to error by carrier employees and puts upon the shipper a burden which he should not bear.

2. *Long- and short-haul provisions.* Carriers are subject to penalty if and when they quote lower rates without authority from the Interstate Commerce Commission to more distant than to less distant stations over the same line from any given point of origin. Tariffs usually contain a general clause stating that, if unauthorized violations of Section 4 of the Interstate Commerce Act are discovered, carriers will immediately endeavor so to adjust their rates that the violations will be removed as soon as possible after their discovery. Violations of Section 4 are fairly frequent although, presumably, carriers do attempt to remove them upon discovery. The end result is that rather greater geographical sophistication and tariff familiarity are required of a shipper, if he wishes to protect himself, than he can reasonably be supposed to possess.

3. *Aggregate of intermediates.* Section 4 of the Interstate Commerce Act also forbids carriers to charge more for a through haul

than the sum of the local rates on the segments composing that haul without the permission of the Commission. Carriers generally save themselves from violating the law in this fashion by publishing general clauses in their tariffs to the effect that if, in any tariff or tariffs, there are class or commodity rates or combinations of class and commodity rates which provide a lower aggregate than the through rate quoted in the tariff under discussion, such lower aggregate will apply. Rates built up by the aggregation of intermediate rates will fairly frequently—although not, of course, usually—yield totals which are less than the published through rate.

It is to be observed, in such circumstances, that a shipper does not need to make a series of local shipments in order to benefit by a combination of local charges. If the aggregate of intermediates shown in the tariff makes a rate less than the through rate, that aggregate applies under the general rule. Indeed, the rule is so broad that a carrier's through rate between named points is sometimes superseded when an aggregate of intermediates is less upon a different and competing route. With such a rule the burden upon the shipper and the likelihood of error by railroad employees is maximized.

The difficulties in the use of tariffs to which this discussion refers would seem to be due, except for the first mentioned, to excessive simplification of statements, and sometimes to the failure of carriers to work out rate quotations adequately in all their implications. The current method of publication permits carelessness in tariff compilation without penalty, increases the uncertainty of rate quotation, and probably produces a number of unpublicized situations in which some shippers pay more than the legal rate and more than other shippers, who are able to afford elaborate traffic departments, are required to pay. It is true, on the other hand, that publication of tariffs in which all rates have been checked against intermediate combinations would be a substantial and expensive task, the costs of which must be balanced against the benefits.

CHAPTER III

Western Termini

WHEN WE deal with transcontinental rate structures directly, there are three features upon which a description should be based. The first of these is the list of western termini that are used; the second is the extent and form of rate groups which are to be found in eastern territory; and the third is the kind and amount of change that can be observed in the total charge as shipments move from west to east. These features are interdependent, but they are also in some degree distinct. In any case, they can be separately examined.

The present chapter will discuss the subject of western termini. The western terminal problem was, originally, simple. This was because there was only one railroad and one or two terminal points—at Oakland and at San Francisco. But it became more complicated when the number of termini on transcontinental business multiplied. The controlling though not the only influence in this development was, of course, the presence of water transport. Because of water competition, for one thing, the rates to all termini were kept the same, since the intercoastal water rates were the same to all harbors served by ships. Partly also, though not entirely, because of the practices of shipping companies, the list of termini was extended to include population centers not on the coast. There were two principal reasons for this. The recognition of Los Angeles as a terminal was due to the wish of the Atchison, Topeka and Santa Fe to build a distributing center in southern California in order to balance the importance of San Francisco in the north.[1] Other interior cities were named as termini because steamship companies absorbed the local freight rate from the port to the interior destination. This was true, for example, of San Jose, which was accepted as a terminal although not physically accessible to ships.[2] By 1914 there were 193 cities to which the rail-

[1] Holdskon v. Michigan Central, 9 I.C.C. 42, 1901.
[2] Santa Rosa Traffic Association v. Southern Pacific, 29 I.C.C. 65, 1914.

roads charged or desired to charge terminal rates,[a] for the most part in the vicinity of the few major ports, such as San Francisco, Seattle, Portland, Los Angeles, and San Diego.

Rates between Pacific Coast termini and eastern points were less, during many years, than the rates between these same eastern points and intermountain cities. This is a well-known fact, and we shall refer to it again in another connection. But it should be mentioned here because it probably intensified the desire of California cities to be ranked as termini. On the other hand, rates from Coast cities to near-by points were always independent of terminal ratings and unaffected by them, and it is probable that the differences between rates to and from adjacent California cities on business to the East would have been slight, in any case, on the long transcontinental hauls. Probably here as elsewhere, also, there would have been some grouping of competitive points on outbound business, if only to avoid complaint or because of the business rivalry of the railroads concerned. It is likely that in this matter the influence of the old, formal, transcontinental structure has been overstressed.

At any rate, terminal groupings continued when the railroads ceased the contentious practice of charging less between the Pacific Coast and eastern destinations than between intermediate, intermountain cities and these same eastern zones. There are such groupings today, and although they are not difficult to understand, some explanation is required.

We shall consider first the grouping of terminal points on class traffic originating at San Francisco. Under the current class tariffs the following practices apply.

1. Rates from San Francisco to points in California and to stations on the Union Pacific in southern Utah and Nevada are generally quoted from San Francisco only. On traffic between Los Angeles and San Francisco, however, there are groups bounded by a line passing through and including the following stations:

San Francisco group		*Los Angeles group*	
San Miguel	Stockton	Saugus	Los Angeles Harbor
San Jose	Sacramento	Van Nuys	Long Beach
Los Banos	Martinez (but not Suisun)	Los Angeles	Pasadena
Merced	San Francisco	Santa Monica	Lamanda Park

[a] U.S. v. Merchant Traffic Association, 37 Sup. Ct. Rep. 24, 1916.

2. To southern Oregon the content of the San Francisco group varies with destination. San Francisco, Oakland, and Alameda and, usually, all stations intermediate to Niles and Pittsburg are included in all groups.

3. To destinations in Nevada and Utah, west of the Utah common points, rates apply alike from San Francisco, Oakland, Alameda, Hayward, and San Leandro.

4. To Utah common points, to points intermediate between Utah common points and Colorado common points,[4] and also to stations on the Los Angeles and Salt Lake Railway which are related to Tintic, Utah, identical rates are published from a zone bordered by and including San Jose, Tracy, Stockton, Newcastle, Keddie, Biggs, Woodland, Vacaville, Napa, and Vallejo.

5. To southern Idaho via Wells, rates apply from a zone bounded by and including San Jose, Livermore, and Richmond.

6. To Montana and to territory in the Dakotas subject to tariffs published by agent Haynes, identical rates are quoted from a zone which is bounded by and includes San Jose, Tracy, Stockton, Reno, Stacy, Alturas, Strongknob, and Rupert (but not points on the Western Pacific or on the Great Northern north of Keddie), Chico, Marysville, Knights Landing, Davis, and Napa.

7. To destinations in Arizona and New Mexico, rates apply from a zone bounded by and including Bradley, San Jose, Tracy, Lathrop, Avenal, Stockton, Sacramento, Davis, and Suisun-Fairfield.

8. To Deadwood, Hot Springs, Lead, Piedmont, Rapid City, South Dakota, and points intermediate thereto, rates apply from a zone bounded by but excluding El Paso, Belen, and Albuquerque, and including Reno, Wendel, Portola, Alturas, Bieber, Redding, and Willits.

9. To transcontinental territories, rates apply from a zone bounded by the Colorado River on the Southern Pacific and the Santa Fe, Cima on the Union Pacific (but excluding the Owens Valley line of the Southern Pacific), Colfax on the Southern Pacific, Keddie on the Western Pacific, Dunsmuir on the Southern Pacific, and including all points on the Northwestern Pacific.

---

[4] On transcontinental traffic to and from South Coast territory, Colorado common points include Cheyenne, Fort Collins, Greeley, Boulder, Denver, Colorado Springs, Pueblo, Trinidad, and Dalhart.

Map 2 outlines the western terminal area on transcontinental class traffic between points in South Coast territory and transcontinental groups.

The terminal zone defined in map 2 includes practically all the inhabited area in California from the Mexican border on the south

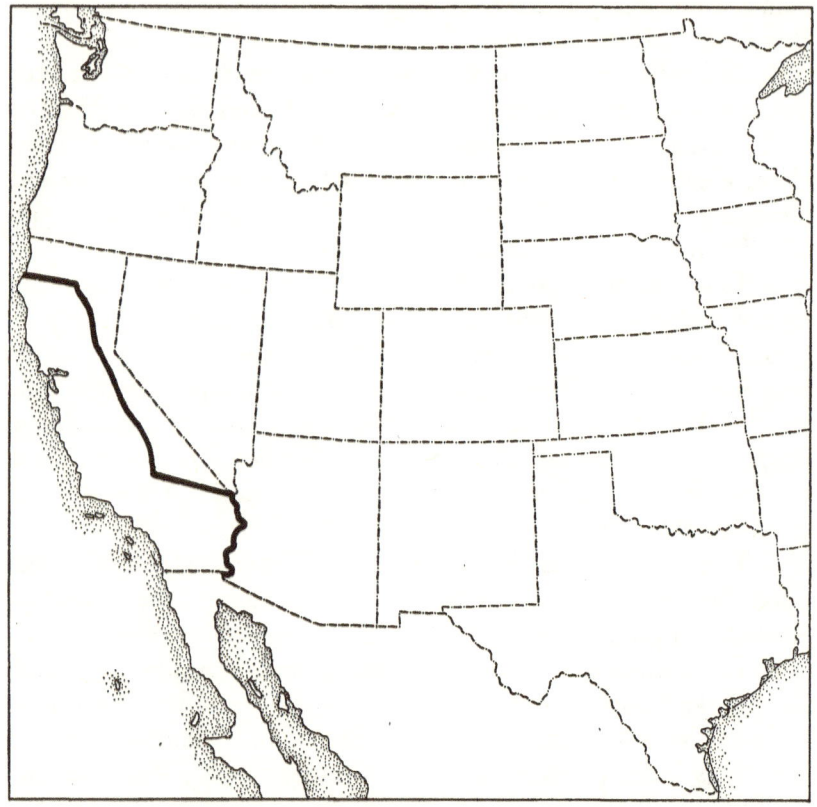

Map 2. Grouping of points of origin and destination on class traffic between points in South Coast territory and points in Transcontinental Freight Bureau territory.

to Dunsmuir and Arcata on the north. The part of the State omitted consists of mountain, forest, and desert. Within its boundaries, for instance, lie Yosemite, Lake Tahoe, and Lassen National Park—sections which, however beautiful and attractive to the tourist, have little significance to production. Except on its western side, the shape of the terminal zone is not determined by anything connected with the sea. Its existence and its form are due to the fact that slight differences in distance are unimportant on hauls which extend over several thousand miles, while railroads at the same time find it convenient to place competing industrial and commercial centers in California on an equality with respect to transcontinental rates. The terminal zone also permits railroads which enter California from the north, south, and east to compete with one another at all points without violating the law which declares it illegal for a carrier to charge a higher rate for a shorter than for a longer haul.

A proper generalization with respect to the grouping of stations in class rate making in California is that rates on short hauls are quoted from single points of origin. As destinations become more remote and the importance of slight differences in distance becomes less, the same rates are charged, initially from stations adjacent to the first starting point, and then from points of origin in groups which become larger and larger, though not regularly so, until, for traffic to transcontinental territories, the same rates are charged from almost all stations in California. Water competition exerts little discernible influence in the arrangement of origin stations under present practice, although the competition of water routes and sometimes of highways still affects the general level of rates which terminal shippers must pay.

Since much the greater part of the traffic handled by rail lines moves on commodity rates rather than on class rates or other types of quotation, the former must necessarily receive most attention. Commodity rates apply on specific commodities only. The commodities chosen as representative of eastward movements are citrus fruits, fresh grapes, dried fruits and vegetables, sugar, canned goods, beverages (specifically, wine), and green vegetables (specifically, lettuce). Although those commodities move in volume, it is not possible, owing to deficiencies in the data, to set forth accurately either the volume of movement of a given commodity between particular stations or the proportion of the total movement which it represents. It can be said, however, that the selected commodities represent, under peacetime conditions, some 20 per cent of the total tonnage originating in California. Many of the items which go to make up total originations are items which also terminate in California; that is, their movement is wholly local. Gravel, sand, and sugar beets are good examples of articles which contribute substantially to tonnage totals but are quite localized in movement. It is a fairly safe assumption, then, that even though some portion of our selected list of commodities terminates within California, they constitute something more than 20 per cent of the total business flowing from California. It is less clear what share of the total inbound traffic is represented by the

TABLE 13
PERCENTAGE OF CARS ORIGINATING IN MOUNTAIN-PACIFIC TERRITORY CONSIGNED TO VARIOUS TERRITORIES

Commodity	Official territory	Southern territory	Western Trunk Line territory	Southwestern territory	Mountain-Pacific territory	Canada and Mexico
Citrus fruits................	50	7	14	8	10	12
Other fresh fruits............	54	3	14	4	20	5
Other fresh vegetables........	44	4	18	9	17	7
Dried fruits and vegetables....	33	11	17	4	29	6
Sugar, syrup, and molasses....	25	6	19	6	45	..
Beverages...................	20	4	4	3	68	..
Canned food products, n. o. s...	35	4	7	4	49	..

commodities we have selected. Almost certainly the proportion is less than in the eastbound sample. It can be said, however, that in both samples the patterns of rates presented by the commodity samples may be considered typical, and that most of the traffic to and from California moves on rates the geographical pattern and level of which are both not dissimilar to the samples.

A Commission study shows, for a truncated classification of commodities, something of the nature of their interterritorial flows.[5] The study is based on an analysis of movements on two days in 1942, and shows movements within and between six geographical regions of the North American rail system. The unit of measurement is the carload. The dominance of Official territory as recipient of traffic originating in Mountain-Pacific territory is clear from table 13.

Lack of refinement in commodity classification again limits statements on traffic terminating in the West. The same study does show,

[5] Beatrice Aitchison, *Territorial Movement of Carload Freight on May 27 and September 23, 1942*, Interstate Commerce Commission, February, 1943.

however, that of the cars of manufactures and miscellaneous consigned to Mountain-Pacific territory, 34 per cent originated in Official territory and 53 per cent in Mountain-Pacific territory.

Commodity terminal groupings are not the same in both directions, and for this reason, as well as because different commodities are treated differently, it will be necessary to distinguish several separate arrangements as we proceed.

Points of origin are grouped for hauls of moderate length, with respect to commodity rates as in the case of class rates, but the groups here, too, are small, and they vary according to destination. We may take the tariff on grapes as an illustration, using Stockton, California, as the specific point of origin.

1. To Bakersfield, California, Stockton rates apply from all stations between Tracy and East Stockton, inclusive.

2. To other points in California, and to Nevada destinations as far as Flanigan and Fernley, rates are quoted from Stockton only.

3. To the rest of Nevada, identical rates are charged from Stockton, Lodi, and intermediate points of origin.

4. To stations in Utah, Colorado, and Wyoming, the Stockton rate applies from all points in a group bounded roughly by a line drawn through Stockton, San Jose, San Francisco, Oroville, and Colfax.

5. To destinations in Arizona and New Mexico the Stockton rate is extended to all stations east of Tracy and south of Sacramento, California, as far south as, but not including, Fresno, and including branch railroad lines. On the Atchison, Topeka and Santa Fe Railway the Stockton group begins at the first station east of Antioch.

6. To points in Oregon, Washington, and Montana the Stockton rate applies from all points in California north of Stockton and San Jose.

Commodity terminal groups are larger for shipments to destinations in Transcontinental Freight Bureau territory, and are appreciably standardized. There are, however, some distinctions.

Map 3 depicts the more usual terminal grouping for eastbound commodity shipments, including grapes, to transcontinental destinations.

Shipments of citrus fruits, grapes, dried fruits and vegetables, canned goods, wine, and some other commodities each take the same rates from all stations within the territory outlined on the map, when consigned to destinations in transcontinental territory. This is the most usual eastbound grouping.

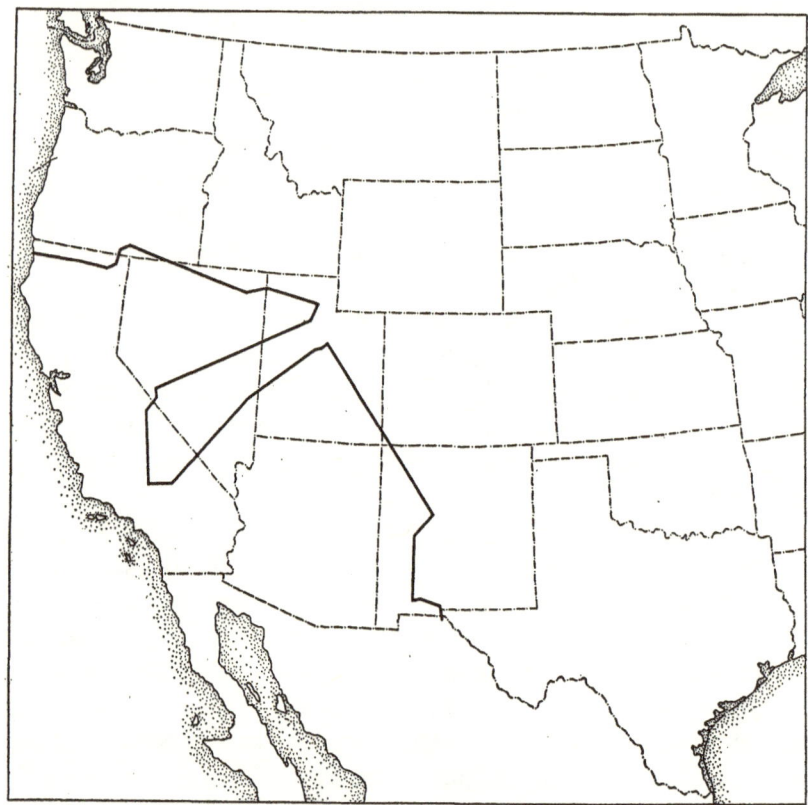

Map 3. Grouping of points of origin on eastbound commodity shipments from South Coast territory to points in Transcontinental Freight Bureau territory. Grapes, citrus fruits, dried fruits and vegetables, canned goods, and wine.

In examining the map we may neglect the long finger extending from northern Utah into southern California. This special feature of the terminal zone, as here drawn, is principally due to the circumstance that the Southern Pacific does not quote terminal rates to stations upon its Owens Valley branch.[6]

[6] The Owens Valley line begins at Mojave, California, and runs north, past Owens Lake, to a terminus near the California-Nevada state line. It does not connect with the Nevada railroad system. Freight consigned from points on the Owens Valley branch to points in

Omitting the finger, it is apparent that the blanket zone on eastbound commodity shipments mentioned provides all the important shipping stations in the Southwest up to but not including Ogden, Salt Lake City, Albuquerque, and El Paso, with opportunity to ship at equal rates. More particularly, it puts Pacific Coast shippers on an equality with their competitors in Arizona, Nevada, and southwestern Utah. This is not an advantage to such competitors. In former years, when terminal rates were lower than those from intermountain origins, towns like Phoenix would have benefited by being ranked as termini. Now, when the terminal rate cannot be less and may be more than the intermediate rate—and this is true with respect to most shipments,—such towns lose by assimilation with the Coast termini, while Coast cities gain. The actual delimitation of the terminal zone will be influenced by the weak bargaining position of shippers in sparse traffic territory; the railroads may also, sometimes, be willing to simplify their rates by widening existing blankets when no great revenue is at stake, without too great attention to minor interests.

A second map (map 4) shows the terminal grouping which controls the rates on eastbound shipments of lettuce and green vegetables. The terms "lettuce" and "green vegetables" refer to a long list of articles including lettuce, beans, melons, tomatoes, celery, and peas.[7]

The chief difference between the origin group used for fresh vegetables and that employed for dried vegetables is that the boundaries for the former exclude Arizona and certain parts of southern California, Utah, and New Mexico. The important areas excluded are those in southern California and in and around Phoenix, Arizona. The important district retained is the Central Valley of California

---

transcontinental territory must be routed south to Mojave before it starts in the direction of its ultimate destination. For this haul to Mojave an addition to the "terminal rate" is charged—a practice which causes the rates between points on the branch and eastern transcontinental groups to become higher than the rates between California termini and these same destinations. This is possible because no traffic from California termini is, or can be, routed by way of Owens Valley points. Most of the remaining area enclosed within the "finger" is desert with no railroad service of any sort.

Ordinarily, rates between eastern groups and points east of South Coast termini are the same as, or less than, terminal rates; the fact that rates to and from points in the finger are higher than terminal rates constitutes an exception.

[7] See p. 59.

and especially, for lettuce, the vicinity of the principal shipping center, Salinas, California.

The contrast just referred to reflects the outcome of a controversy between producers. Prior to September 5, 1936, the same rates

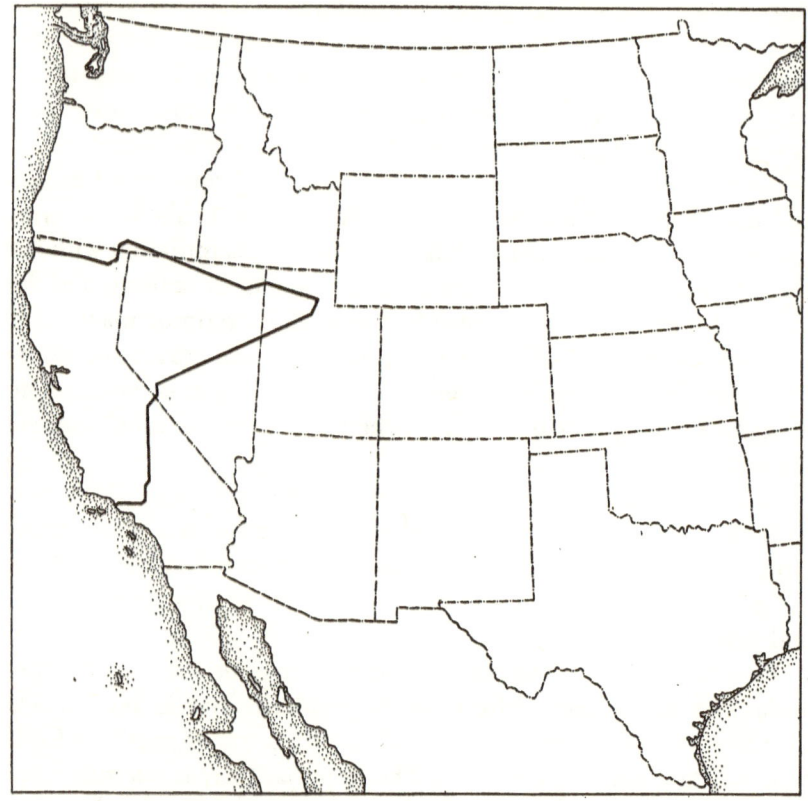

Map 4. Grouping of points of origin on eastbound commodity shipments from the northern and central parts of South Coast territory to points in Transcontinental Freight Bureau territory, lettuce and green vegetables.

applied on fresh fruits and on lettuce and other vegetables from California and Arizona origins to a wide range of destinations. On the date mentioned, the railroads, in compliance with an Interstate Commerce Commission order, established rates from the Phoenix district which were only 90 per cent of the rates applicable from points farther west. Subsequently, the Commission held that rates on lettuce, melons other than watermelons, carrots, and cauliflower would be prejudicial to the Phoenix, Yuma, and Imperial Valley districts to the extent that they were less than 10 cents per 100 pounds lower than the rates from other California territory. It refused, however, to require a rate differential on potatoes, asparagus, broccoli, peas, and cabbage.[8] This rivalry between producing districts and the demand of the southwestern producers for rates which should be lower than those from central California is sufficient to explain the restriction of the list of western termini for shipments of lettuce and green vegetables so as to permit a lower level of rates from the Imperial Valley and the Phoenix area than is charged from Salinas in central California. Under present arrangements the railroad may, and generally does, quote such rates.

Still a third zone of transcontinental eastbound business is that provided in the tariffs on sugar.

Map 5 shows the coastal zone in which are points which enjoy equal rates on sugar shipments to Transcontinental Freight Bureau territory.

Transcontinental rates on sugar do not apply from a zone or group, but only from particular stations—apparently those at or near which refineries are situated, or which are accessible to water transport. It is not necessarily true that all places within the area demarcated upon the map are stations from which transcontinental rates are quoted. It may be, however, that transcontinental sugar rates have intermediate application.[9] In that event, shipments from stations farther east would take terminal rates as maxima, and the influence of the zone would be extended. The map differs in this respect from drawings showing the grouping of transcontinental points of origin which characterize other commodity rate structures.[10] The limitations in

---

[8] 235 I.C.C. 511, 527, 1939.

[9] The exact terms under which departures from the long-and-short-haul clause of the Interstate Commerce Act have been authorized are not publicly available.

[10] Equal transcontinental rates are quoted from the following stations within the zone of origination:

Alameda	Los Angeles	Sacramento
Alvarado (Alameda County)	Los Angeles Harbor	San Diego
Betteravia	Manteca	San Francisco
Clarksburg	Oakland	Spreckels
Crockett	Oxnard	Stockton
Dyer	Pinedale	Sugarfield
Hamilton (Glenn County)	Port Costa	Tracy
Long Beach	Richmond	West Sacramento

the listing of sugar originations are, however, of no practical importance, because all refineries find their place within the zone.

We may now conclude our description of the grouping of terminal rates on the South Coast by a reference to westbound movements.

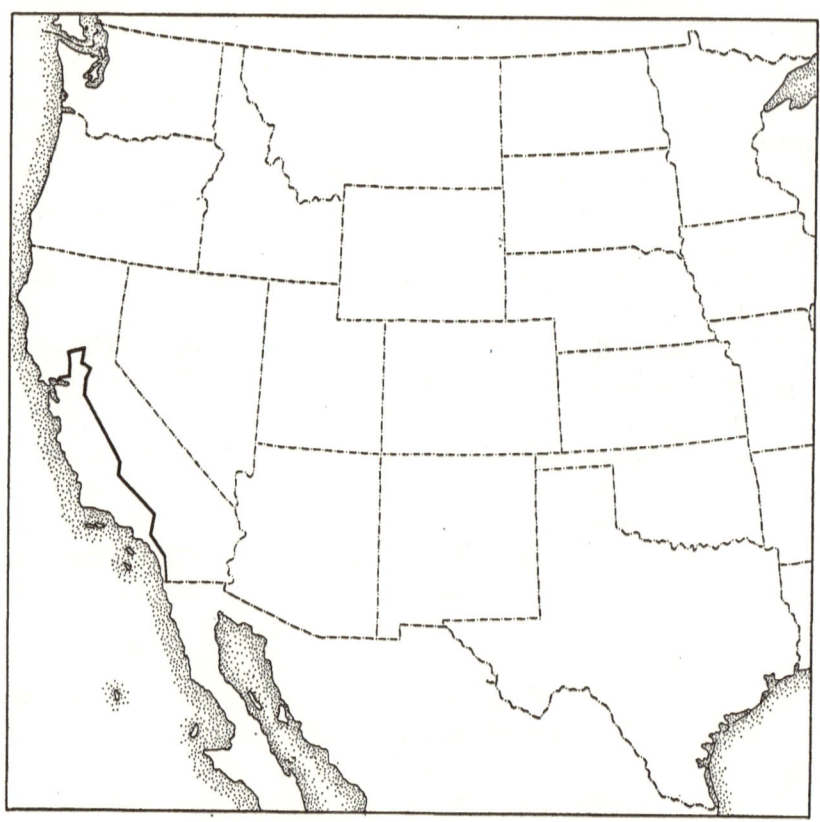

Map 5. Grouping of points of origin on eastbound sugar shipments from South Coast territory to points in Transcontinental Freight Bureau territory.

Points of destination are grouped for westbound shipments much as points of origin are grouped for those eastbound.

On class traffic the destination groups for westbound and the origin groups for eastbound business are identical.

On commodity traffic, carriers group destinations in quoting rates on westbound movements much as they group points of origin in quoting eastbound rates on grapes, citrus, dried fruits and vegetables, canned goods, and wine; but there are some differences.

Map 6 shows the terminal grouping which controls westbound rates on canned goods, clothing, dry goods, steel, tin and tin articles,

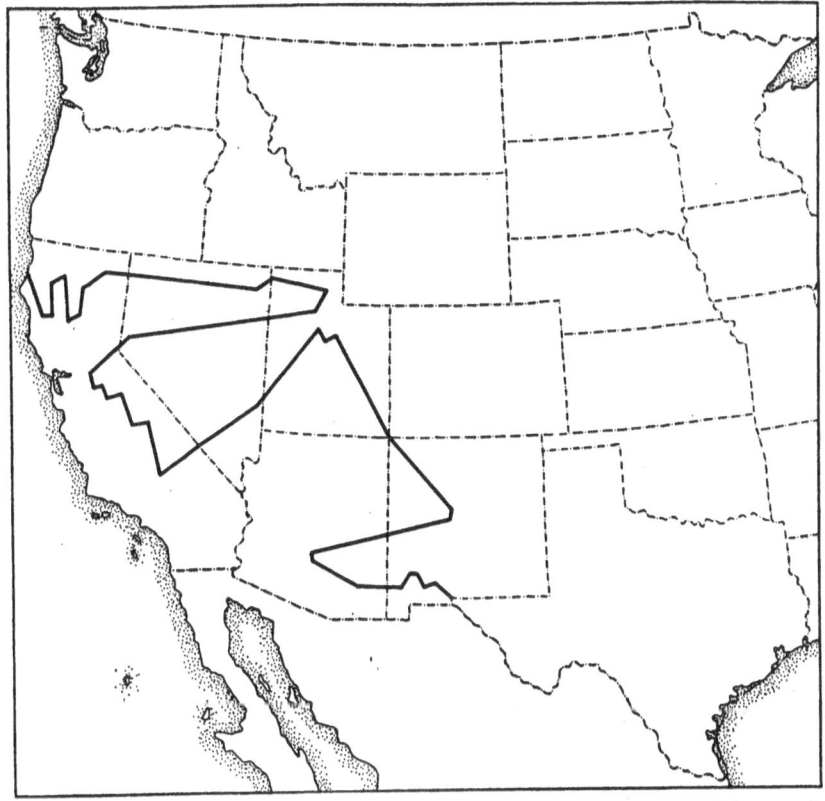

Map 6. Grouping of points of destination on westbound shipments from Transcontinental Freight Bureau territory to South Coast territory. Canned goods, clothing, dry goods, steel, tin and tin articles, and wine.

and wine. A second map (map 7) depicts the terminal grouping which controls the westbound rates on automobile bodies and parts, beverages, vehicles, and fertilizers.

Maps 6 and 7 cover, perhaps, a large enough number of commodities to be representative. The boundaries of the two drawings differ slightly, in central and southern California, but not significantly.

An important difference, most evident in northern California, is due to the fact that certain small branches are excluded from terminal territory in the first case, while they are included in the second. The reasons for the difference are not clear.

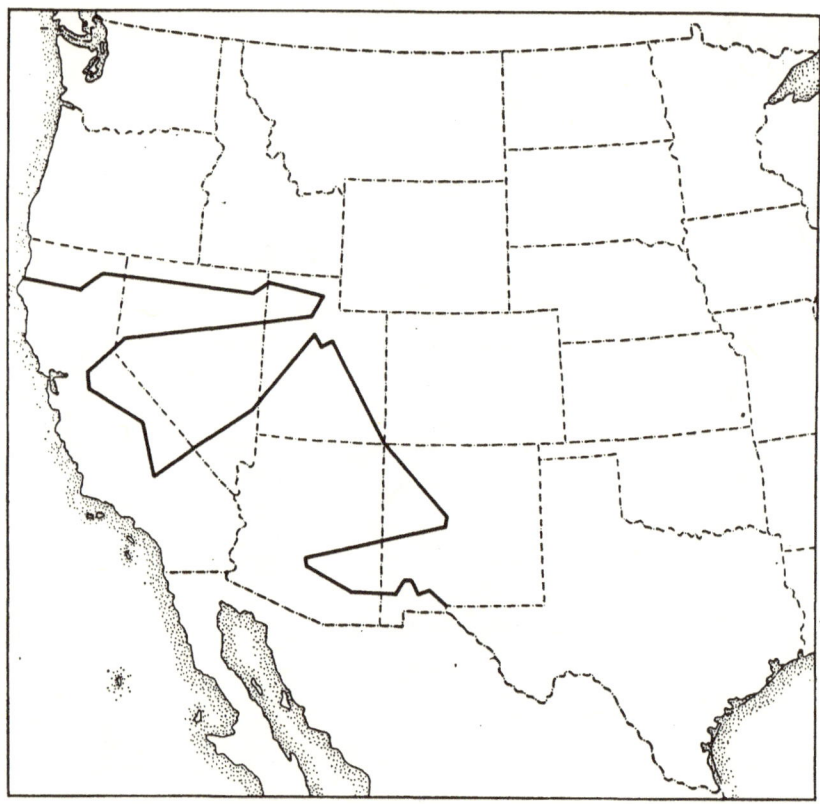

Map 7. Grouping of points of destination on westbound shipments from Transcontinental Freight Bureau territory to South Coast territory. Automobile bodies and parts, beverages, vehicles, and fertilizers.

Comparison of both westbound terminal groups with the more important of the eastbound zones drawn on an earlier map shows that westbound and eastbound groups are almost congruent, except that the finger which extends from northern Utah into east-central California is broader. This is because carriers exclude from terminal territory, in westbound movements, stations on short lines running south from Hazen, Nevada, as well as stations on the Owens Valley branch, which is farther to the south. There is no direct connection with the first-named branches from eastern points of origin. Goods shipped to destinations on these branches must, therefore, travel through Hazen, in terminal territory on the main line, and for the service from Hazen south an extra charge is made. The conditions on the Owens Valley branch have already been explained.[11]

The grouping of western points of origin and of destination in South Coast territory, in its present form, is a moderate example of a practice long used by rail carriers in the United States. We shall discuss other groupings in the chapters which are to come.

---
[11] Terminal rates cannot be lower on traffic to and from Transcontinental Freight Bureau stations than on traffic to or from intermediate points. They may, however, be the same to intermediate as to terminal points, and where they are the same the effect of the terminal adjustment is extended beyond the limits of the terminal area. Rates to and from branch-line stations east of the terminals may, however, be higher than terminal rates if these stations are not technically "intermediate" and so subject to the restrictions of Section 4.

CHAPTER IV

Rate Groups on Eastbound Traffic

THE MATTER next before us is the arrangement of eastern termini characteristic of transcontinental rates—a technique that is even more significant than the grouping of western termini which we have just described.

On shipments from California to points covered by publication of the Pacific Freight Tariff Bureau, class rates progress without the use of significant zones or groups, but ranges are indicated in map 8. Lines on the map do not separate zones in the sense in which this term is used in transcontinental rate making, but they do divide the western area into sections, in each of which rates range within limits of 10 cents.[1] The boundaries of these sections are reasonably concentric on San Francisco for the shorter distances, especially within California, where the California Railroad Commission's scale influences the rate. The influence of water competition is apparent at the ports of the Columbia River and Puget Sound, to which the Interstate

---

[1] Lines on the illustrations are drawn to show the locus of points taking the lowest and the highest rates within selected ranges. Thus the zone marked 60–69½ in map 8 is an area within which no class C rate from San Francisco is less than 60 cents or more than 69½ cents. When a single rate is given, however, that rate applies to all stations in the area bounded by the lines which surround the number. As we have already pointed out, freight rates are expressed in cents per 100 pounds. Rates to points on independent local carriers, only some of which are parties to Pacific Freight Tariff Bureau and Transcontinental Freight Bureau tariffs, have been ignored in the construction of rate intervals. Rates to points on the lines of such carriers tend to be substantially higher than rates to main-line points.

Rates to branch-line stations on lines which are parties to Bureau tariffs may, also, be substantially higher than rates to main-line points. Such stations may be regarded as rate "islands" within the broader zones. It would be inconvenient and possibly confusing to indicate such detail on zone maps, and the "islands," too, have been ignored.

When more than one rate is available, depending upon the minimum weight required, the lowest rate at the heaviest minimum has been used. Effort has been made to discover combinations of intermediate rates that yield totals which are less than the published through rate, and these combinations have been used when found. It is impossible, of course, to state with certainty that the lowest combination has always been ascertained.

Where there are route restrictions in the tariff, it has been assumed that shippers will select the route over which the rate is lowest.

RATE GROUPS ON EASTBOUND TRAFFIC 51

Commerce Commission has authorized lower rates than to intermediate stations. Fourth Section rates are usual on traffic to ports of the Pacific Northwest. Beginning with the zone which takes class C rates of 60 to 69½ cents per 100 pounds, however, present group

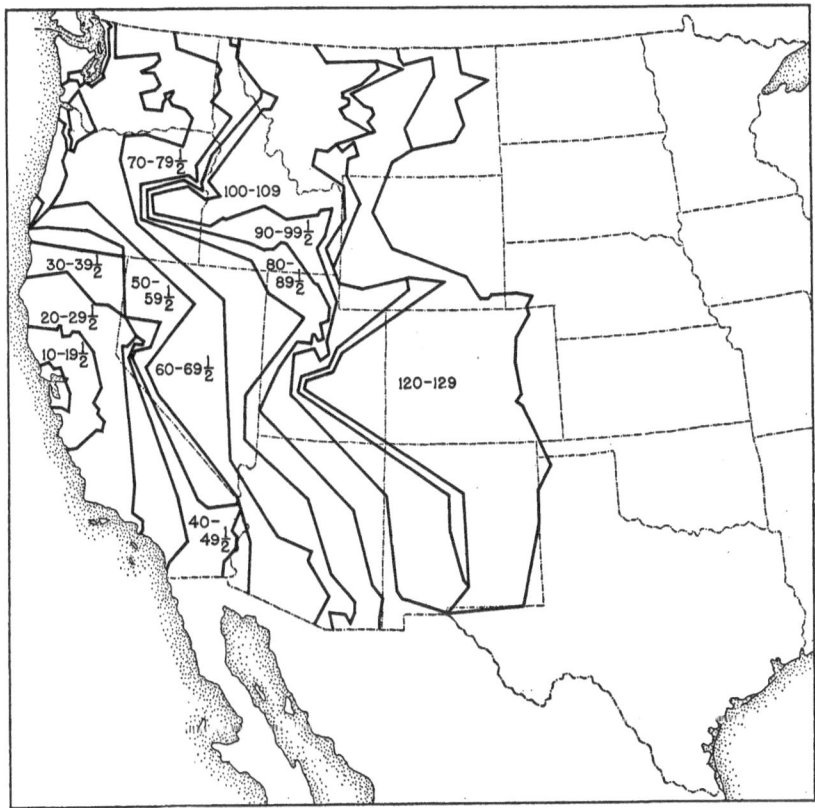

Map 8. Class C rates from San Francisco to points in Pacific Freight Bureau territory.

boundaries in the West tend to straighten out and to assume a direction from NNW to SSE, losing their reference to point of origin. There are, probably, two reasons for this independence of mileage. The first is that cheap water competition up and down the Pacific Coast permits Portland and Los Angeles to compete with San Francisco and, in doing this, to push back the northern and southern limits of rate zones toward the east, and so to straighten the zonal lines.

This must occur, in fact, in order to avoid conflict with the aggregate-of-intermediates provision of Section 4 of the Interstate Commerce Act. The other influence is the pull of market competition between distant consuming and distributing centers. This, together with the accompanying railroad competition, tends to reduce the rate per mile to relatively remote markets by relatively circuitous routes. The full effect of this second factor is not felt within the territory of the Pacific Freight Tariff Bureau, but some results are already there discernible.[2]

Between California stations and destinations beyond the line that separates the jurisdiction of the Pacific Freight Tariff Bureau from that of the Transcontinental Freight Bureau, rates are quoted to or from rather large areas, in each of which the amount charged at all points is the same. These are the so-called "lettered groups." They begin, for traffic from California, with group J on the west and end with groups A and K or K-1 on the Atlantic seaboard.[3] The location and extent of these zones are indicated in map 9.

The history of these lettered zones deserves a moment's attention.

The first attempt of the transcontinental lines to establish a general system of transcontinental rates was made in 1887, when carriers published tariffs fixing rates to Missouri River common points, Mis-

[2] A characteristic of the market for transportation service to and from California and, no doubt, elsewhere is the fewness of buyers and sellers. We have already pointed out that there are only four railroad companies in California selling the service. Shippers of California agricultural products are typically organized into no more than a few closely knit associations. It is probable that at any one station there are very few shippers of any one homogeneous industrial product. This kind of competition has been much discussed by economists in the past decade. It is unnecessary at this point to cite their writings in detail; the doctrines which have emerged indicate, at any rate, that imperfect competition does not necessarily lead to the optimum allocation of resources, and that it is often productive of marked rigidities over time.

[3] There is an M group, not indicated in the text, which has some significance. The boundaries of this group are nearly coterminous with those of group C-1, south of the Ohio River, except that the limits of the M group on the east extend to the western boundary of L territory, whereas the eastern boundary of the C-1 group, in a few places, is not the same as the western boundary of group L. The resultant differences are too small to be represented on the map.

Transcontinental rates on direct hauls to points in C-1 territory take C-1 rates. These are sometimes lower than C or M rates. When, however, shipments are so routed that a north–south or south–north movement is required east of the Mississippi, then, to the same destinations, M rates are applied south of the Ohio and C rates north of that river. M and C rates are charged, in any case, on consignments which move directly to destinations in M and C territories which do not take alternative C-1 rates.

sissippi River common points, Chicago common points, and New York common points. St. Paul, Minneapolis, Galveston, and Houston were at that time charged the same rates as those quoted for the Missouri River.⁴ It does not appear, exactly, what cities were included in the various groups.

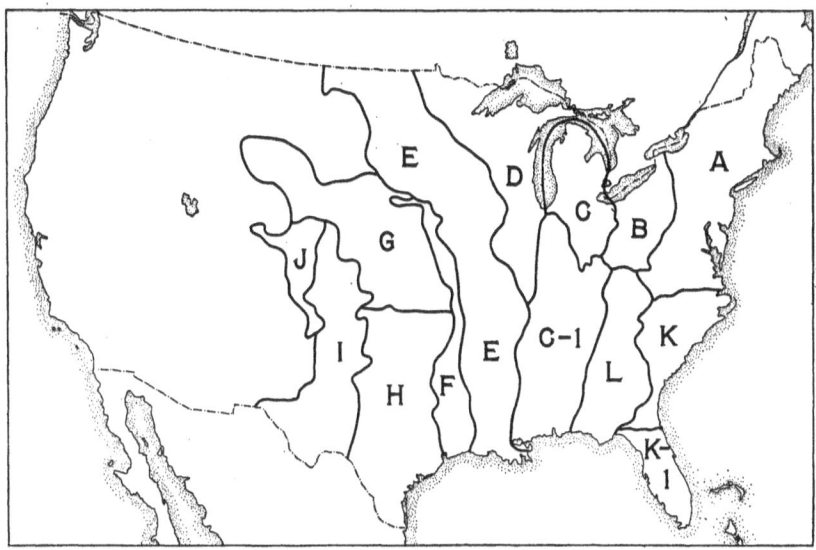

Map 9. Rate zones in Transcontinental Freight Bureau territory applicable on traffic to and from the South Coast.

On September 1, 1888, the tariffs just mentioned were replaced by new schedules setting up the following territories:

1. Missouri River common points; also St. Paul and Minneapolis, Minnesota, and Galveston and Houston, Texas.

2. Mississippi River common points, Dubuque, Iowa, to New Orleans, Louisiana, inclusive.

3. Chicago, Milwaukee, and common points.

4. Detroit, Toledo, and common points, and points east thereof and west of Atlantic Seaboard common points.

5. Atlantic Seaboard common points.⁵

By 1892 the groupings of 1888 had taken the following somewhat expanded form:

⁴ Martin v. Southern Pacific Company, 2 I.C.R. 1, 1888.
⁵ Re Tariffs of Transcontinental Lines, 2 I.C.R. 203, 1888.

1. Missouri River common points.
2. Mississippi River common points.
3. Chicago-Milwaukee common points.
4. Cincinnati-Detroit and common points.
5. Pittsburgh-Buffalo common points.
6. New York, Boston, Philadelphia, and Baltimore, and points common with each.

The published tariffs now gave detailed descriptions of the boundaries of each of the listed territories.[6]

The present method of publishing rates was adopted on January 1, 1909, in order to conform to requirements of the Interstate Commerce Commission; but, according to R. H. Countiss, one-time agent of the Transcontinental Freight Bureau, without material change in rate application. Lettered groups were substituted for common-point designations, but the new lettered groups and the old common-point territories were substantially the same.[7]

In the course of time, following this formal alteration, a number of more important changes occurred. These were, in general, of two sorts. In the first place, there was an extension of the general system. Noteworthy in this process was the creation of new groups L and K in the territory south of the Ohio and east of the Mississippi River. In the West, likewise, groups H and I were set up to cover Texas, Oklahoma, a corner of New Mexico, and parts of western Kansas and eastern Colorado, while group J took care of Denver and the Colorado common points. The other changes consisted in the break-up and readjustment of older zones. In the course of revision, group A, which at one time was limited to two piers in New York City, came to include New England and most of the country east of Pittsburgh and Buffalo and north of the North Carolina–Virginia state line. Group B once covered the New England states, but this latter designation was shifted to indicate a zone including Pittsburgh and Cincinnati. Group C was greatly reduced in scope, yielding space to A and B in the east and to the new group M in the south, while group E pushed north into South and North Dakota and east across the Mississippi River to include the line of the Illinois Central Railroad from New Orleans,

---
[6] Merchants' Union v. Northern Pacific, 4 I.C.R. 183, 1892.
[7] E. R. Johnson and G. G. Huebner, *Railroad Traffic and Rates* (New York: Appleton, 1918).

through Jackson, Mississippi, and Memphis, to Cairo.[8] Subsidiary zones, such as K-1 and C-1, also appeared.

The result of the preceding history has been to create the present system, under which eastern cities are systematically grouped in the process of quoting through transcontinental rates, and all cities in a group are asked to pay the same charge. Boundaries of existing zones are those depicted on page 53.[9]

This system covers rates to and from most of what is known as Transcontinental Freight Bureau territory. It should be observed, however, that carriers do not quote through rates on all commodities to and from all sections of this territory: points in the omitted districts are charged a combination rate based upon the rate to or from

---

[8] Meridian Traffic Bureau v. Abilene Southern, 169 I.C.C. 80, 1930.

[9] The statement in the text is limited to "through rates." Most points of significance in the East enjoy through rates, but there are minor stations in every zone which are on a "combination" basis or are otherwise distinguished. Such situations may be illustrated by a diagram.

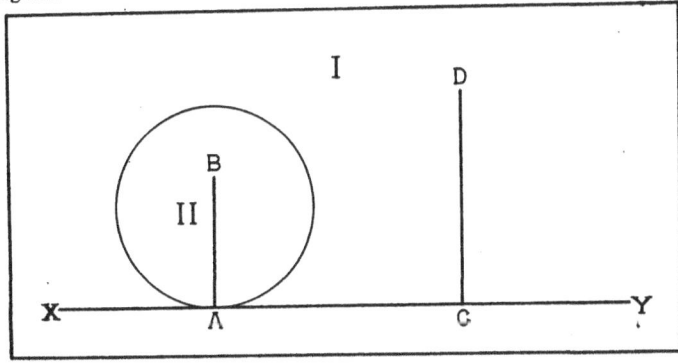

Let the line XY in the diagram indicate a main-line railroad, and lines AB and CD, branch railroads. Let zone I be an area to and from which uniform rates generally apply. Let zone II surround line AB. It may well be, under these conditions, that rates from X to points on AB or DC will be higher than to main-line points within or along the boundaries of zone I, either because no through rates are quoted to branch-line destinations or because rates are quoted upon a higher level than to main-line stations. It may also be that rates from X will be higher to and from points on branch AB but not higher to and from points on branch CD, and this will be likely even if branch AB is independently owned and if branch CD is owned by railroad XY. If, for any reason, rates to branch-line stations are higher than to main-line stations, the effect will be to create a rate island, such as zone II, within the larger group. Islands of this sort are usually small, and they have not been distinguished upon the zone maps shown in the text. They may, of course, have local importance.

some destination in Transcontinental Freight Bureau territory which enjoys through rates. It is always possible that the combination will be on a point at or near the boundary of the nearest group from or to which through rates are available; it is also always possible that the lowest rate will be obtained by combination upon a significant terminal which is farther away.[10]

The exceptions mentioned in the preceding paragraph have some practical importance. We shall presently see, moreover, that there are still other reasons why the standard lettered groups will not serve as an accurate representation of present rate structures between transcontinental territory and the West, although they are the basis of such structures. Let us explain these reasons in general terms, and then examine a series of rate structures which illustrate them.

Actual rate groups depart from the standard pattern for two reasons. In the first place, standard groups are frequently combined. It is common practice, that is to say, for carriers to quote identical rates to several adjacent lettered zones. The identity of the original zones is preserved in these tariffs, and this is convenient; but the boundaries of the zones no longer uniformly mark the locus of a change in the transportation charge. In the second place, standard zones are sometimes entirely neglected for purposes of rate quotation, and other groupings take their place. This is a feature of some commodity tariffs in the area west of the Mississippi River, especially on eastbound business.

The relation of effective zone rates on transcontinental traffic to the basic scheme and the practice of consolidation may be initially shown by reference to the class tariff. Rates and groupings in this tariff apply in both directions.

Table 14 shows the first-class and the Class C rates, by zones, in 1943, on traffic between western termini and transcontinental groups in both directions. First-class rates are used in the illustration for formal reasons, and class C rates because of their representative character in the West. Class C rates, that is, cover "perishables" in California, and these class C rates also more nearly approximate the

[10] For iron and steel articles the Florida peninsula, and for tin articles Georgia, and North and South Carolina as well, have no through rates. This is an example of the conditions mentioned in the text. It is not possible to guess how rates will be made in such circumstances.

transcontinental rates on perishables from California to the Atlantic seaboard than do rates upon any other class. Perishables constitute a large proportion of California eastbound shipments. The table shows the fact of consolidation in that single rates are quoted to groups A, A-2, K, and K-1; to groups B and L; to groups C, C-1, and M; and to groups G, H, and I. The effect of this uniformity is to simplifiy the rate system considerably.

TABLE 14
FIRST-CLASS AND CLASS C RATES BETWEEN CALIFORNIA TERMINALS AND POINTS TAKING GROUP RATES

Group	Rates	
	First class	Class C
	cents per 100 lb.	cents per 100 lb.
A, A-2, K, K-1	611	198
B, L	594	194
C, C-1, M	578	190
D	561	182
E	545	174
F	495	157
G, H, I	462	149
J	403	129

The same practice of consolidation can be graphically described. In map 10 the 198 cent rate applies to the entire Atlantic Coast including groups A, A-2, K, and K-1; the 194 cent rate covers groups B and L; and the 190 cent rate, groups C, C-1, and M, each combination creating a long, continuous band, with equal rates, from the Great Lakes to the Gulf. The reason for such like treatment of points in groups B and L, and, again, of points in groups C, C-1, and M, is doubtless to be found in approximate equality of distance between the designated areas north and south of the Ohio River and the Pacific Coast. The reasons for consolidation of groups G, H, and I under the 149 cent rate are less obvious, but here too the short-line distance from San Francisco to the northern part of the combined group and from Los Angeles to the southern part is, perhaps, a sufficient explanation for the uniform treatment of class shipments which the tariffs provide.

Class tariffs provide a convenient illustration of the use of eastern zones in transcontinental rate making. We must turn to commodity tariffs, however, for the elaboration of carrier rate procedures. This is necessary, first, because most traffic between the East and the West pays a commodity rate, and second, because commodity tariffs display extremes of adaptation which class tariffs do not present. The following pages of this chapter will deal with commodity groups on

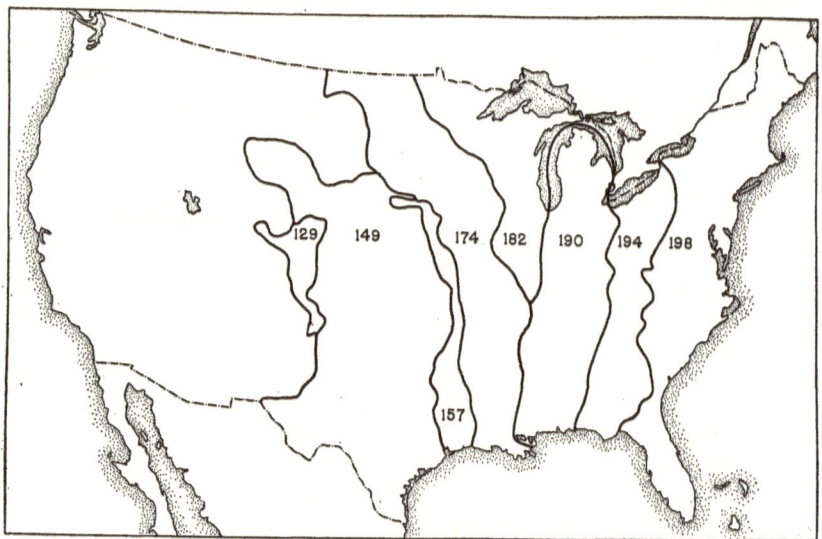

Map 10. Class C rates between South Coast terminals and Transcontinental Freight Bureau groups.

eastbound transcontinental business. The succeeding chapter will consider peculiarities of westbound movements. Maps and analyses of maps will be used in forms with which the reader has begun to be familiar.

On shipments from California to points covered by publications of the Pacific Freight Tariff Bureau there are a few areas of equal rates, but these are relatively unimportant. Most commodity rates in the territory, like class rates, increase with distance, although not in proportion to it.

Succeeding maps show rates from stated points of origin to destinations in Pacific Freight Tariff Bureau territory; each map indicates also charges from South Coast terminals, including the stated point

RATE GROUPS ON EASTBOUND TRAFFIC

of origin, to areas taking group rates in Transcontinental Freight Bureau territory. Rates shown are for transportation only. Charges for refrigeration necessary in the shipment of lettuce[11] and other perishables are additional.

Attentive study of the rates on lettuce shows appreciable regularity in the progress of rates in California where the California state scale prevails and across Arizona and New Mexico. East and north of California, in Nevada and Oregon, however, there are sharp advances in transportation charges, due partly, as in southern Nevada, to enforced circuity in routing.

As a general rule, rail carriers have been authorized to publish rates between points in California and points in the Pacific Northwest which do not serve as maximum rates at intermediate stations, as would otherwise be required by the Fourth Section. Rates from a California point to stations intermediate to Columbia River and Puget Sound points are thus often higher than the rates to the ports. Lettuce and other perishables are exceptions to this generality. They are not subject to water-traffic competition; rail rates on them are therefore on a dry-land basis. The rate to each major population center also applies to many intermediate stations. In the western section, the 60–69½ cent zone includes Portland, Oregon, on the north and the Utah common points on the east. These population

---

[11] Rates on lettuce are the same as or closely related to the rates charged for the transportation of other fresh vegetables.

The following commodities take the same rates as those charged on lettuce:

Cauliflower	Melons	Beans
Celery cabbage	Chinese cabbage	Corn in the husk
Parsley	Peas	Tomatoes
Winter squash	Summer squash	Yams
Celery and celery roots	Cucumbers	Horseradish roots
Sprouts	Peppers	Rhubarb

The following commodities take rates closely related to the lettuce rate, but charges may be different to certain destinations. Shipments may also move on heavier minima; if so, an alternative lower rate will be applicable.

Carrots	Cabbage	Beets
Onions	Parsnips	Potatoes (sweet)
Rutabagas	Turnips	Garlic

The minimum carload rates on lettuce vary somewhat with destination. To Nevada and Utah points on the Los Angeles and Salt Lake Railroad (now Union Pacific) in which the Las Vegas rate is a factor, the minimum is 36,000 pounds. To stations in Arizona and New Mexico the minimum is 24,000 pounds, and to all other destinations it is 20,000 pounds.

centers are at the extreme northern and eastern limits of the districts in which they lie. The 80–89½ cent zone in the north is influenced by the presence of Spokane. The 100–109½ cent zone in the south takes in El Paso and Amarillo; the 110 cent zone, the Colorado common points; and the 130 cent zone, the large Texas blanket. Most of this central western territory, apart from a few important cities, is thinly populated. In the tariffs, the use of special groupings, pecu-

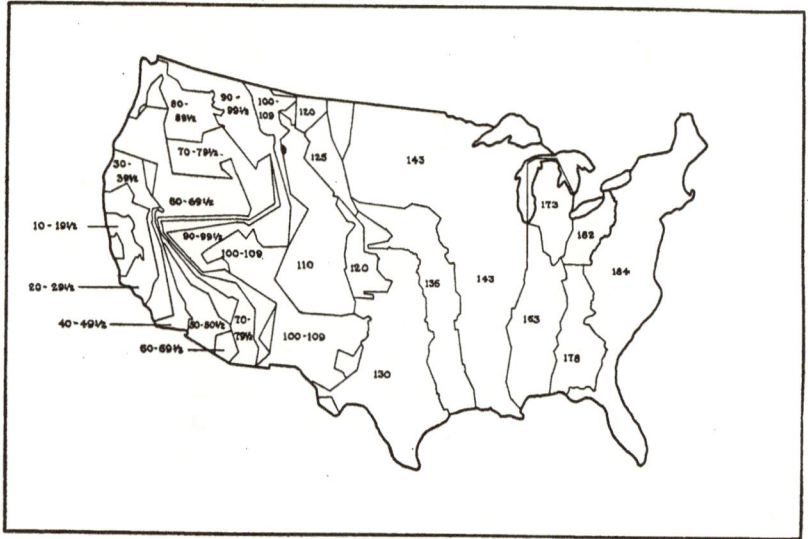

Map 11. Rates on lettuce from Salinas, California.

liar to fruit and vegetable rates, predominates in Transcontinental Freight Bureau territory over reference to the standard transcontinental groups F to J.

Farther east, the broad sweep of the 143 cent zone, including groups D and E of the transcontinental system, has a principal effect of placing Minneapolis, St. Paul, St. Louis, and Chicago upon an equality in rates. The extension of the zone east of the Mississippi also permits the Illinois Central Railroad to participate in transcontinental traffic originating at and destined to more northern centers. We have mentioned this adjustment in discussing class rates.

Beyond the Mississippi, zone boundaries conform to those of the ordinary transcontinental class groups.

RATE GROUPS ON EASTBOUND TRAFFIC

The rate structure for fresh grapes[12] is simpler than that for lettuce. The fresh-grape rate map reveals, like the lettuce map, a succession of sharp increases beyond the California boundary line, followed by broad areas of equal charge. The increases raise the level to 60–69 cents per 100 pounds. The first genuine group is reached at 110 cents; this group, though large, covers a market of only moderate size. Its principal cities include Denver, Colorado Springs, Pueblo, and Santa Fe. The striking feature of the map is the eastern blanket which covers all the transcontinental zones mentioned in the class-rate tariff from E to A, except the peninsula of Florida, and the secondary blanket of 140 cents farther west. The rate of 150 cents applies to most of the markets in which California grapes are sold.

Map 13 depicts zones used in the construction of citrus rates.[13] Most of the groups in Pacific Freight Tariff Bureau territory are

---

[12] The term "fresh grapes" covers a number of varieties, but so far as transportation is concerned all grapes are similar and the same rates apply. Not only is this true, but grape rates are frequently the same as those charged for the carriage of other deciduous fruits and vegetables.

On eastbound movements from Stockton the following distinctions can be made:

1. Within California and Nevada, rates are quoted to apply on fresh fruits and vegetables generally.

2. To Puget Sound destinations, rates are published which apply to grapes alone.

3. To other destinations in Oregon, Washington, Northern Idaho, and Montana, the rate on grapes is that applied to deciduous fruit generally, except that deciduous fruit rates to eastern Montana and the western Dakotas do not cover apples.

4. To all other destinations the deciduous-fruit rate covers all deciduous fruit, including grapes, except apples and pears.

For grapes, the minimum carload weights range from a minimum of 34,000 pounds to a minimum of 20,000 pounds. Minima of 34,000 pounds apply when shipments are consigned to points east of Chicago; minima of 26,000 pounds are required when shipments are consigned to other transcontinental destinations. More specifically, the variations are as follows:

1. To Arizona, New Mexico, and into Oregon as far as Roseburg and Bend, including Stronghold, California, 20,000 pounds.

2. Within California, except to Stronghold, 24,000 pounds.

3. To all points east of a line from Hammond, Indiana, thence along the New York Central Railroad to Cairo and the Illinois Central Railroad to New Orleans, 34,000 pounds.

4. To all other destinations, 26,000 pounds.

Carriers frequently set up graduated minima, associated with graduated carload rates, on shipments to a single destination. The minima indicated in this note are those used to qualify for the lowest rate which it is possible for the shipper to obtain.

[13] Rates on "citrus fruits" apply to citrons, grapefruit, mandarins, oranges, and tangerines. They apply to lemons and limes also, except for shipments to points in Florida

unimportant to the citrus industry. The two largest are those which take, respectively, rates of 40–49½ and 60–69 cents. The first of these covers most of Nevada and part of Utah. This territory is large, but generally sparsely settled. The 60–69 cent zone is supplied at two rates: a 60 cent rate to points beyond Klamath Falls, Oregon, and up to and including Vancouver, Washington, and lower Columbia River towns; and a 69 cent rate applied to the rest of the area. The 60 cent rate is perhaps controlled by actual or potential water competition at Portland and is extended south; the 69 cent rate is that quoted to Puget Sound; this rate is extended east.

In and beyond the 93 cent zone we enter Transcontinental Freight Bureau territory, in which the rates to all places in each zone, subject to exceptions previously explained, are the same. The 93 cent group includes the Colorado common points, Denver and Cheyenne, etc., western Oklahoma, and central, southern, and western Texas. This zone is of unusual extent, possibly because the rate in the South is depressed by the competition of Texas-grown oranges; but farther east the succeeding zones are narrow, and rates rise rapidly to the

---

east of Pensacola. Class rates are used on some of the shorter hauls, but, generally, commodity rates are quoted on these articles.

From Los Angeles, citrus fruits move on class rates up to Casmalia, Allensworth, and Pixley, to points on the Owens Valley Line, and eastward to the state line on the Union Pacific, Southern Pacific, and Santa Fe.

Minimum weights for oranges vary from 20,000 pounds to 39,200 pounds, according to destination. The last-named minimum is required on most transcontinental shipments. The orange minimum is sometimes the same as and sometimes different from the minimum applied to other citrus fruits.

Within the area in which citrus moves on class rates, the minimum weights are 26,700 pounds on all citrus fruits except lemons, and 26,200 pounds on lemons.

To Nevada and to points short of Vancouver, Washington, and the confluence of the Des Chutes River with the Columbia River, lemons and limes take a minimum of 35,300 pounds; grapefruit, of 35,100 pounds; and all other citrus, of 39,200 pounds. This same basis applies to all transcontinental destinations. These same minima are prescribed on shipments to Union Pacific points in Wyoming west of Wamsutter, with the additional modification that tangerines have a minimum of 36,000 pounds. To Arizona and New Mexico, carriers employ the same combination of minima to some destinations as to points in Wyoming east of Wamsutter; to other destinations the minimum is 20,000 pounds for all citrus fruits; while the two systems of minima alternate to still other destinations. No rational pattern is apparent.

To destinations not otherwise described—that is, to Washington, eastern Oregon, Idaho, Montana, Utah, and western Colorado,—a minimum of 27,000 pounds is applied to lemons and one of 33,600 pounds to all other citrus fruits. To Reno, however, the minimum on lemons is 27,100 pounds and that on other citrus fruits is 33,600 pounds. Lower minima, with higher rates, are sometimes available.

131 cent level. It is not unlikely that sharp changes of this sort represent the effect of truck competition or of favorable local railroad rates out of the Texas area. Historically, it appears that the boundary of the main transcontinental zone—now taking a rate of 131 cents— once reached farther west than it does now. Truck shipments east from Texas might easily have broken down the western edge of this large blanket. Inasmuch as it still seemed possible to maintain the

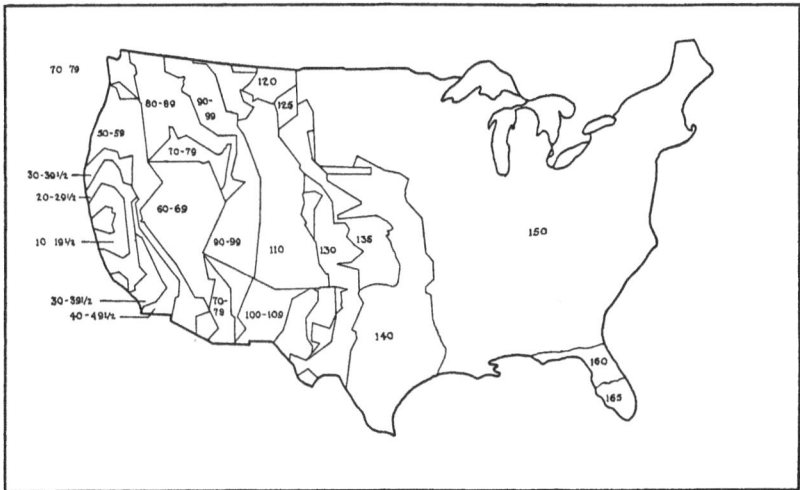

Map 12. Rates on fresh grapes from Stockton.

131 cent rate to destinations close to the Mississippi on the east, there was a spread to be absorbed within a determined distance. This could be done by dividing the critical distance into zones and raising the low Texas to the higher eastern level by a series of narrow steps. If this explanation is correct, the extension of the narrow zones to more northern points may be explained by truck competition again, or by the desire to maintain relationships which had existed before the partial breakdown of the transcontinental blanket had taken place.

That part of the United States east of the transitional area covered by the narrow zones is divided, for the purpose of citrus rate making, into two great districts and a third lesser district covering most of Florida. Of the larger zones, one, with a rate of 131 cents per 100 pounds, includes the Southeastern States except Florida and large portions of the Mississippi and Missouri River basins; and the other, with a rate of 135 cents, includes the Northeast. The variation in charge in this section of the United States does not, therefore, exceed 5 cents over an extreme distance of more than 2,000 miles. These are the zones which lend character to the entire citrus transcontinental rate adjustment. Their obvious effects are, first, to assist California shippers directly in meeting the competition of Florida growers, who

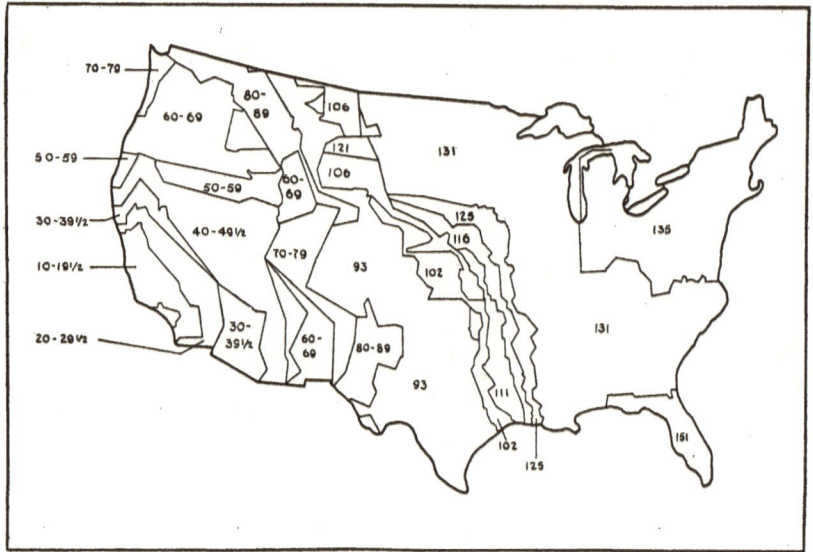

Map 13. Rates on citrus from Los Angeles.

are nearer large eastern markets but whose rates are constructed in another way; second, to make diversion easier of cars consigned from California to eastern markets; and, third, to place interior distributing centers of the United States on a parity with each other so far as freight charges upon oranges are concerned. Most stations in Florida except those on the St. Louis–San Francisco and on the Louisville and Nashville from Flomaton to Pensacola, including these two last-named points, take a rate of 151 cents on most citrus shipments. The exception is that the rate on lemons and limes to Florida points east of Pensacola is 147 cents instead of 151 cents. The 151 cent rate on oranges is, doubtless, little used because the combination of competition of Florida oranges and seasonal fruit quarantine makes shipments from the West difficult during most of the year.

We may now turn from the citrus structure to the rates on sugar.[14]

The striking features of the sugar zoning system include the following:

1. No through rates are published to eastern states, that is, to Georgia, Florida, Alabama, Mississippi, Tennessee, Kentucky, Indi-

---

[14] Rates on sugar, eastbound, apply on sugar, beet or cane. To destinations in California, Arizona, most of New Mexico, western Oregon, Washington, and northern Idaho, rates are quoted on sugar in packages. To all other destinations rates are quoted on sugar in bags.

Sugar moves both under class and commodity tariffs. Large use is made of temporary rates; the application of commodity tariffs is, moreover, frequently adjusted and limited to meet the requirements of particular situations.

Sugar is classified fifth class in the Western Classification. Within California a special intrastate sugar scale is provided, closely related to class rates. For short distances the special rate is the same as fifth class, but, as distance increases, the sugar rates increase more rapidly than the standard class rates, with the result that for distances greater than 25 miles or so the class rates are lower. Since, however, the stipulated minimum in the special scale is 20,000 pounds and that in the class tariff is 40,000 pounds, there remains an incentive to use the special rate for longer distances. Within California, two types of commodity rates also exist, which are published in Sections 1 and 2 of Haynes tariff No. 300, with the proviso that rates published in Section 2 are not applicable where other rates are provided in Section 1. On shipments from Crockett both sections quote identical rates; Section 1 is, however, less complete than Section 2. The minimum carload weight under Section 1 is 80,000 pounds, and that under Section 2 varies from 36,000 to 50,000 pounds. These various types of rates may be used in California in any combination. Care is required in finding the rate or combination of rates which will permit shipment at the lowest cost.

Temporary rates are quoted to most destinations in Arizona, New Mexico, Utah, Colorado, and Wyoming, but not to Idaho. These rates are 3 to 4 cents lower than the permanent rates and have been in effect several years. It has been customary to extend the life of these rates semiannually. Possibly the temporary (lower) rates will eventually be made permanent, in which case the present so-called permanent rates will be cancelled.

Minimum carload weights on transcontinental sugar shipments are 80,000 pounds to destinations in Illinois and to parts of Kansas and Missouri, and 60,000 pounds to other destinations in Transcontinental Freight Bureau territory. On local shipments, including movements to western Oregon, Washington, and southern Idaho, the minima vary from 20,000 to 80,000 pounds.

The following details with respect to sugar movements from Crockett, California, illustrate further the wide and apparently random variation in minima required.

Where sugar moves under class rates under the intrastate class scale, the minimum carload weight is 40,000 pounds. Where sugar moves intrastate under the special intrastate sugar scale on a class-rate basis, the minimum weight is 20,000 pounds. To destinations on the Northwestern Pacific, Rohnerville and south, the minimum is 36,000 pounds. To destinations Loleta and north the minimum weight is 30,000 pounds.

To destinations in California to which sugar moves on commodity rates the minimum weight is 36,000 pounds. There are numerous exceptions; thus to points north of Mount Shasta and Keddie the minimum is 40,000 pounds except to Westwood, Bieber, and White

ana, Ohio, West Virginia, Virginia, the Carolinas, the New England States, Delaware, and the District of Columbia. No through rates are published to New York, New Jersey, Pennsylvania, and Maryland, except to the coastwise piers at New York, Philadelphia, and Baltimore. No through rates are published to the lower peninsula of Michigan or to some stations in southeastern Illinois. The practical result of this is that states east of the Mississippi River are mostly supplied from New Orleans or Atlantic Seaboard refineries, except for such western sugar as makes use of a water haul.

2. Broadly speaking, the arrangement of sugar zones is concentric, but around two distinct focal points.

In the West, the center upon which rates are based is the region of San Francisco—specifically, the refinery at Crockett from which the rates used in the text are calculated. Apparent irregularities in the shape of western zones are due in part to water competition along the Pacific Coast, in part to differences in the rate of progression in different areas, and in part to routing peculiarities which make effective distances from points of origin to points of destination greater than air-line distances between these same stations.

In the East, however, the arrangement of zones tends to be concentric on New Orleans—a major distributing center equivalent to Crockett. Such a plan involves an elaborate combination of routing restrictions and nonintermediate rates. Confused as the system is, the successive zones from New Orleans to the north, with the exception of territory just adjacent to the river, take generally higher and higher rates as charges are calculated to destinations more and more distant from New Orleans and less and less distant from the Canadian border. Rates from Crockett to these various areas are competitive with

---

Horse, when the minimum is 60,000 pounds. To the southern California area, bounded roughly by Ventura, San Fernando, San Bernardino, Redlands, and Santa Ana, the required minimum carload weight is 80,000 pounds. To other destinations in southern California the minimum weight is 40,000 pounds.

The minimum carload weight on consignments to Reno, Nevada, is 70,000 pounds.

To destinations in western Oregon, Washington, and northern Idaho the minimum is 40,000 pounds, except to La Grande and Baker, to which points the minimum weight is 30,000 pounds.

To Illinois and to parts of the 70–79½ cent rate zone the minimum weight is 80,000 pounds.

To all other destinations the required minimum is 60,000 pounds.

rates from New Orleans. The transcontinental rate adjusts itself to the Mississippi Valley rate, even though this requires, for certain shipments, the quotation of prices for the longer hauls which are less than those demanded for shorter movements.[15]

The existence of two foci around which transcontinental sugar rates are built presents difficulties when the circumferences of the

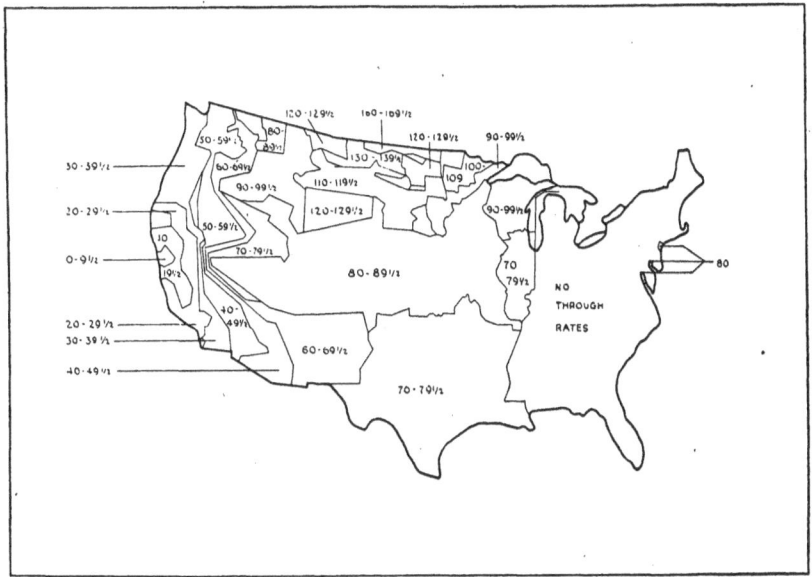

Map 14. Rates on sugar from Crockett, California.

circles intersect. The zone map (map 14) shows that no serious attempt is made to meet this problem in the North. Actually, sugar does not move from Crockett to the Mississippi River crossings by the northern route, because of routing restrictions. It does move through the Central States, however, and here the conflict of California and Louisiana refineries, together with the competition of beet-sugar manufacturers in Colorado, Utah, Wyoming, and western Kansas

---

[15] According to the Interstate Commerce Commission (211 I.C.C. 239, 1935), sugar rates from California to any Middle Western destination are constructed by adding an arbitrary rate to the barge rate from New Orleans, except that specific rates are provided from California to Chicago and to St. Louis. This does not explain the rates to Texas, Oklahoma, Arkansas, and Louisiana, but it does explain the exceptionally low rates to Illinois and adjacent territory and the higher rates to points farther north or to destinations off the river.

leads to the creation of a zone that reaches from the Sierra Nevada on the west to Illinois on the east. Shipments to points in this zone are charged rates which vary between 80 and 89½ cents. Most stations in the zone pay 80 cents. The higher rates apply to points on the northern or southern edges of the district.[16]

Sugar is also shipped from Crockett over the southern route. Such movements may enter the 80 cent zone midway, or they may continue through Texas and Oklahoma to the Mississippi River at rates which do not exceed 79½ cents and may be lower. Presumably, western sugar cannot be sold in eastern Texas or in Louisiana in competition with New Orleans sugar, except by unusual rate absorption, but it may find an easier market farther north. When forwarded from Gulf ports by water to New York, Philadelphia, and Baltimore, the 80 cent rate is applied. The competition from the southern route, together with the competition of Cuban sugar refined in Atlantic or Gulf Coast centers, compels carriers over the central route to quote Fourth Section lower rates to some destinations.[17]

It is evident from the foregoing that the zone system of transcontinental rates applied to sugar has little in common with the standard structure used in connection with other commodities. It is a special arrangement, shaped by competition, and, perhaps, by industry practice, and intended to permit western refiners and western carriers to enter markets from which they would otherwise be barred. Western

---

[16] The 80 cent rate applies to the whole of Iowa, to most of Nebraska except to points north of Niobrara, to the Black Hills, and to Orin and points south in Wyoming. Kemmerer and destinations south thereof in Wyoming pay 80 cents. The same rate is charged to points east of but not including Ogden, Salt Lake City, and Provo in Utah, to main-line points on the Denver and Rio Grande Western such as Grand Junction, Salida, and Walsenburg. Destinations south of the main line, standard or narrow gauge, take higher rates.

Rates higher than 80 cents are charged to other stations in the 80–89½ cent group not indicated above.

[17] The 70–79½ cent group contains nonintermediate rates and is broken up into the following divisions:

1) 72 cents. All of Oklahoma; western Arkansas; northwestern Louisiana, including Shreveport; points in Texas on the lines of the Texas and Pacific and the St. Louis Southwestern railroads.

2) 74 cents. Designated points in central Arkansas.

3) 77 cents. Eastern and southern Arkansas; all of Louisiana, except northwestern Louisiana; all of Texas, except stations on the Texas and Pacific and St. Louis Southwestern railroads.

4) 78 cents. Stations in Kansas and Missouri which do not take the 80 cent rate.

RATE GROUPS ON EASTBOUND TRAFFIC 69

carriers, at the same time, presumably benefit from the business which results.[18]

Map 15 illustrates the rates on eastbound canned goods out of San Francisco.[19]

[18] The analysis in the text understates the complexity of sugar rates. This is partly because the number of zones recognized in the tariffs is much greater than the number shown on the map. In fact, there are more than 135 groups between the Rocky Mountains and the Illinois state line. This multiplication is concealed by the use of ranges in the map, and by the circumstance that identical rates are often applied to several zones.

Moreover, the rate designated as applying to a zone in any case is not always charged to all points within that zone. In most of the country, it is true, groups are defined so that all stations within group boundaries enjoy the group rate, but rates to stations in Michigan, Minnesota, Nebraska, North Dakota, South Dakota, and Wisconsin are quoted to named stations only, although the rates are depicted upon the map as though they applied to areas. Rates to points intermediate between named destinations may be expected to take the higher of the two rates charged to stations between which they lie, but this is not certain to be the case in Transcontinental Freight Bureau territory, where departures from the provisions of Section 4 are frequent and rates are often lower to more distant than to less distant destinations.

[19] Rates on canned goods, eastbound, apply to a list of articles which varies somewhat according to destination. The following articles or groups of articles are always included:

Breads	Sauerkraut (brined)	Broths
Peanut butter	Chowders	Crushed fruit
Fruit in liquid	Jam	Jelly
Clam juice	Fruit Juice	Sauerkraut juice
Macaroni (prepared)	Meats	Condensed or evaporated milk
Mincemeat	Molasses or syrup	Olive or salad oil
Tomato paste	Fruit or vegetable pectin	Pickles, sauces, and
Pimentos	Puddings	salad dressing
Soups	Sausage	Tomato puree
Vinegar	Welsh rarebit	Vegetables

Canned-goods rates apply also to the following articles:

1. To all destinations except nonport destinations in Oregon, Washington, and northern Idaho:

Fish	Drained fruit	Spaghetti and vermicelli
Fruit pulp	Mushrooms	(prepared)

2. To all destinations except ports on the Columbia River and Puget Sound:

Coconuts	Drained fruit	Tomato juice
Vegetable juice	Cooking oil	Pie preparations

The descriptions of articles appearing in the various tariffs are not mutually exclusive; for example, some tariffs list "meat" or "meat mixed with vegetables," a description which would include pork and beans. In other tariffs, pork and beans are listed separately. Some descriptions list olives, while in other descriptions olives fall within the category of "fruits in liquid."

Class rates and "all-freight" rates are used on canned-goods shipments, along with the commodity rates, in California, but transcontinental shipments of canned goods move under commodity tariffs.

The minimum carload weights for canned goods moving eastward from San Francisco

Zones in the canned-goods rate structure show extreme irregularity. The shape of the 20–29½ cent zone in southern California is due to the extension of the water-compelled 22 cent rate to Los Angeles to a considerable adjoining area. Likewise, in the Northwest, low rates to Puget Sound and Columbia River ports influence, because of the possibility of combination rates to intermediate destinations,

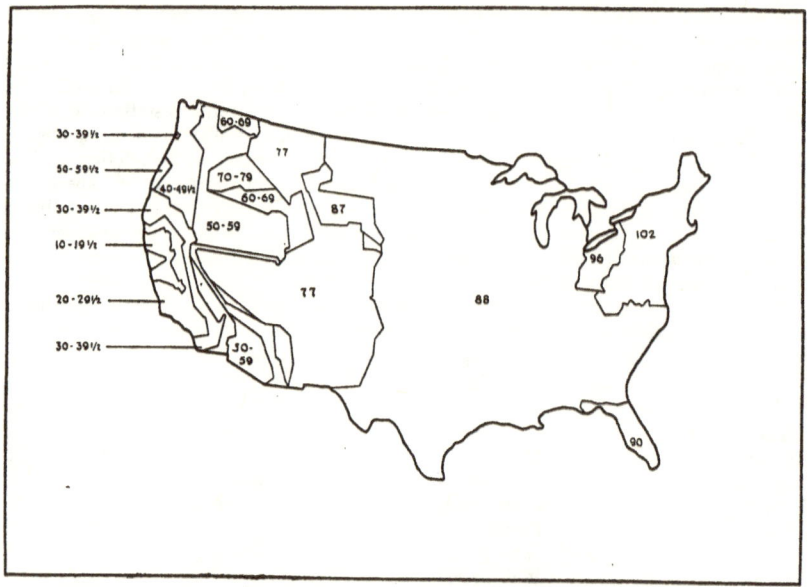

Map 15. Rates on canned goods from San Francisco.

the rate levels farther south. The broad 50–59 cent zone is partly explained by the fact that the Salt Lake rate applies as a maximum across most of Nevada.

Most noteworthy are the 77 cent and the 88 cent groups. The 77 cent zone here includes group J in the transcontinental rate struc-

vary from 30,000 pounds to 60,000 pounds. The general transcontinental minimum is 60,000 pounds.

The California intrastate class minimum is 36,000 pounds, and this figure is used for shipments into Nevada as far as Fernley and Flanigan, and to points such as Fallon and the Tonopah branch, rates to which are made by combination on Fernley. The minimum to points beyond Portland in Oregon and Washington, and to points in Arizona which take less than the group J rate, is also 36,000 pounds. Besides this, a 50,000 pound minimum is required for shipments to Colorado and Mojave Desert points and to some destinations in Oregon short of Portland, and the minimum in certain territory adjacent to San Francisco to which "all-freight" rates apply is 30,000 pounds.

ture, which, for canned goods, is extended to cover most of western Montana and eastern Utah points because these areas are intermediate between San Francisco and other group J destinations. On the map the 77 cent group extends across southern Utah, northern Arizona, and southern Nevada. It should be observed, however, that many stations in this section are not intermediate to group J. Rates to these stations may be combination rates, and the actual charge to destination may be more than 77 cents.

The great 88 cent rate group is more difficult to explain, and no attempt will be made to provide any special justification. It is probable that little traffic normally moves to points in the extreme East at rates of 96 and 102 cents, since most canned goods shipped to this territory move from the Pacific Coast by way of the Panama Canal. One possible reason for higher rates to points east of Indiana and north of the Ohio River is that carriers in Official territory are unwilling to accept a division of the 88 cent blanket charge as sufficient compensation for their share of the transcontinental haul, but prefer rather to rely for revenue upon their back haul from the ports. Southern carriers, nevertheless, do accept their proportion under similar circumstances. Competition between all-rail and water-barge line–rail routes between the Pacific Coast and eastern points is extremely active, and this, by itself, would tend to equalize rail rates to all points in the central and southern Mississippi Valley.

The next map (map 16) shows the rate structure applied to dried fruits and vegetables[20] from Fresno.

The striking fact in the organization of rates on dried fruits and

---

[20] Rates on dried fruits and vegetables apply to dried, evaporated, and powdered fruits, not including candied, crystallized, glacé, or stuffed fruit, but including dried and ground fruit with added sweetening, preservative, flavoring, or coloring. Usually the same rates apply to dried, evaporated, or powdered vegetables, and mixtures of fruits and vegetables are allowed. Dried fruits and vegetables must usually be packed in boxes or cartons. The rate is higher if they are packed in bags.

Minimum carload weights range from 30,000 pounds to 60,000 pounds. The minimum on transcontinental shipments is 60,000 pounds. The variations in prescribed minima may be described as follows:

1. 30,000 pounds. From Fresno:
   a) To points in California to which commodity rates apply.
   b) To points in Arizona and New Mexico up to and including Albuquerque, Belen, and El Paso.
   c) To points in Oregon beyond Medford and Klamath Falls, to northern Idaho and Washington, and to Las Vegas, Nevada.   *(Footnote continued on next page)*

vegetables is that a single rate applies to the entire central and eastern portions of the United States, except for shipments to New York City by way of the Southern Pacific steamship line from Galveston.[21] This is an even greater simplification than appears in canned-goods tariffs.

There are also some peculiarities in the zone structure in Far Western states.

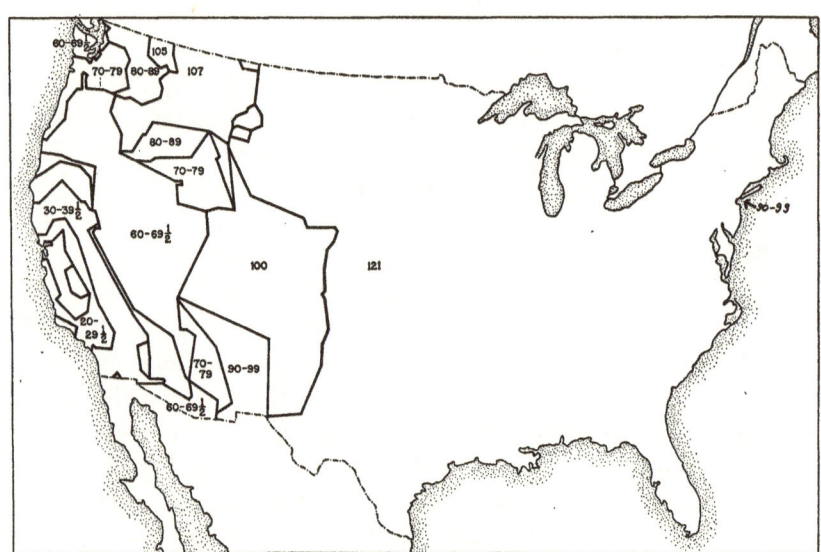

Map 16. Rates on dried fruits and vegetables from Fresno.

In the Pacific Northwest, there are Fourth Section departures at Puget Sound and Columbia River ports, and very high rates, on the other hand, to eastern Oregon points on the Union Pacific. We shall refer to this situation in discussing rate profiles.

In western Nevada, rates increase very rapidly, and as a result Utah common-point rates apply to nearly the whole of Nevada.

In Arizona and New Mexico, contrary to the usual practice, rates

---

2. 36,000 pounds. From Fresno:
    a) To certain destinations in California, Oregon, and Nevada when the movement is on class rates.
3. 60,000 pounds. From Fresno:
    a) To all other destinations. It is generally possible, however, to ship under lower minima at higher costs.

[21] This steamer service was suspended shortly before the war. Present reports indicate that the company does not intend to reënter the trade.

are quite irregular. Much of this irregularity is caused by carrying the Yuma rate eastward to Gila, producing a long narrow tongue in the 30–39 cent zone.

Western dried-fruit and vegetable zones are similar in some respects to zones in the fresh-grape structure. In view of the fact that grapes and dried fruit are separate commodities for marketing purposes, this similarity is surprising. The transcontinental maximum is lower for dried fruits than for fresh grapes, and there are fewer zones. But the points at which rates break are similar for both, and the similarities would be even more marked if the class-rate intervals for grapes were enlarged. East of group J there is less likeness, because the grape zones are broken into the usual pattern for perishables up to the Missouri River, while for dried fruit the blanket begins farther west. It is in Pacific Freight Tariff Bureau territory that the likenesses are most pronounced.[22]

The last map in the series (map 17) shows the rate structure used in shipping wine[23] from Fresno.

Wine rates constitute the simplest of all eastbound commodity structures: a single rate of 99 cents per 100 pounds is charged, irrespective of destination, to all points east of Salt Lake City and the eastern border of Arizona.

In summation, one may say that eastbound commodity tariffs simplify zone arrangements by consolidation of groups for rate-

[22] Within California an almost random alternation of class rates on the intrastate distance scale and railroad published commodity rates produces a considerable distortion of distance as a rate-making factor. The principal effect of this alternation is, however, quite local. Where low commodity rates exist, as to San Francisco, Sacramento, and San Bernardino, their effect is to push the zone borders outward from the point of origin. Beyond the limits of application of such commodity rates, the combination of class and commodity rates produces a rate lower than the through class rate. As distance increases still further, the reduced rate of progression of the through class rate causes it to become less than the above-described combination. The net effect is that certain zones are wider than they would be, and more distant zones are smaller than they would be, under a strict system of distance rate making.

[23] Rates on wine apply to wine (except champagne) in glass, earthenware, or metal cans, boxed or in bulk in barrels. Higher rates usually apply to shipments in tank cars.

The minimum carload weights for wine vary with the length of haul.

1. To destinations to which the rate is less than 99 cents, the minimum is 30,000 pounds.
2. To destinations in Pacific Freight Tariff Bureau territory, to which the rate is 99 cents, the minimum is 50,000 pounds.
3. To destinations in Transcontinental Freight Bureau territory, the minimum is 60,000 pounds, except to Tampa and Jacksonville via boat from New Orleans, when the minimum is 50,000 pounds.

making purposes, but they also complicate them by subdivision. In general, the number of groups is smallest for dry commodities, such as canned goods, dried fruits and vegetables, and wine; while for perishables, such as citrus, fresh grapes, and lettuce, the practice is to attempt a much greater precision in zone adjustment. There are few groups east of the Mississippi River, in any event: 4 for canned

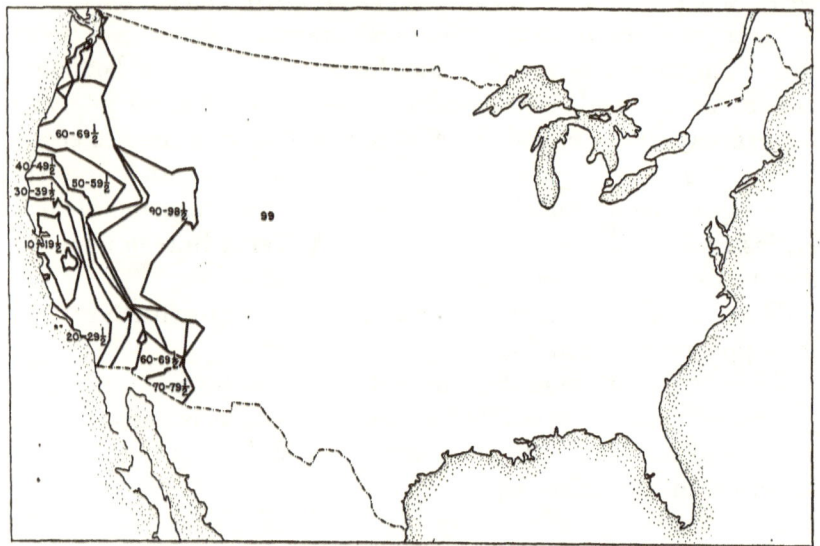

Map 17. Rates on wine from Fresno.

goods, 3 for citrus, 2 for dried fruits and vegetables, 5 for lettuce, and 1 for wine. The difference between perishable and other eastbound commodities is due mostly, with respect to citrus and grapes, to the introduction of special groups west of the river which accomplish an accelerated increase in rates from one rate plateau to another. Only for lettuce is there a relatively fine subdivision of the territory farther east.

The extreme instances of broad groupings in eastbound tariffs include tariffs on dried fruits and vegetables, in which one rate is quoted to all Transcontinental Freight Bureau territory except to New York[24] and to a small section of New Mexico and Colorado; and

---

[24] On shipments only to New York which use the Southern Pacific steamship lines from Galveston.

tariffs on eastbound wine, in which one rate is quoted to all Transcontinental Freight Bureau destinations, wherever located. The extreme instances of specialization occur in eastbound tariffs on citrus, which construct multiple zones west of the Mississippi River and in tariffs on lettuce, in which something very like the class-rate zone distribution is employed, and in those on sugar, for which the adjustments in some areas are very fine. Eastbound grape tariffs provide a simplified zone structure to destinations east of the Mississippi, but, as already pointed out, these tariffs show differentiation in Texas, Oklahoma, New Mexico, and Wyoming.

CHAPTER V

Rate Groups on Westbound Traffic

THE DISCUSSION of westbound rates in the present chapter is limited to movements from Transcontinental Freight Bureau groups of commodities which are imported into California in significant amounts. These commodities are, principally, products of manufacture. Imports from points in Pacific Freight Tariff Bureau territory are omitted, because few manufactured goods are shipped from this area for Coast consumption. Movements on class rates are also omitted, because class tariffs quote the same rates westbound as eastbound, and eastbound rate structures have already been described. The grouping of terminals in South Coast territory in quoting rates on westbound shipments was taken up in chapter iii.

The following articles are selected for examination: dry goods, beverages, steel articles, automobile bodies and parts, clothing, vehicles, canned goods, wine, and tin. Fertilizers are added because of the peculiarities of the rate system applied to this commodity, although the westbound movement of fertilizers is small. This list excludes important categories; it does, however, include an important segment of the total westbound trade. It is to be remembered that each title covers a large number of distinguishable items to which identical rates apply.

We shall consider commodity rate groupings commodity by commodity in the following pages. Rate structures will be illustrated by maps. Profiles will be dispensed with, however, in the discussion here and later, because of the lack of satisfactory tariff files showing local rates in eastern states.

The first of the maps presented depicts the groups used in quoting rates for the westbound carriage of dry goods.[1] Similar groupings

---

[1] Rates on dry goods apply to tablecloths, covers, felts, knit fabrics, bedspreads, doilies, drapes, handkerchiefs, napkins, curtain netting, pads, plush, ribbon, tape, thread, toweling, yard goods, and certain other similar commodities.

The minimum carload weight on dry goods is 24,000 pounds.

appear in the rate structures used for clothing, beverage, steel, and automobile bodies and parts. Rates, as before, are stated in cents per 100 pounds.

Dry-goods rates, like class C rates, are alike from all points along the Atlantic Coast except that no through rates on dry goods are quoted from the peninsula of Florida—practically, this difference is unimportant—and except that lower rates are quoted from steamship

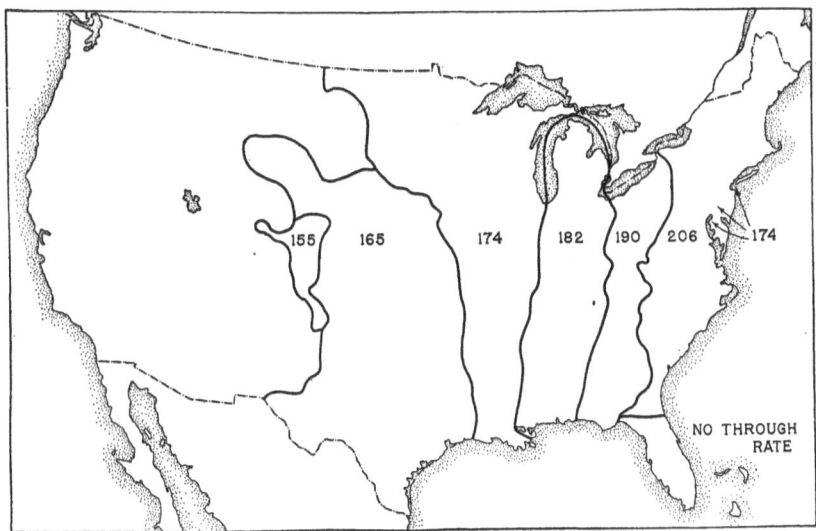

Map 18. Rates on dry goods from Transcontinental Freight Bureau groups to South Coast termini.

piers at New York, Philadelphia, and Baltimore on shipments which move by water to Gulf ports and are thence forwarded by rail. Identical rates are also published from groups B and L, from groups C and C-1, from groups D and E, and from groups F, G, H, and I. This is the class rate pattern for the territory east of the Mississippi River, except for the treatment of Florida; groups west of that river are, however, somewhat simplified. Perhaps the most significant result of the dry-goods tariff is that mills in New England and in South Carolina are placed upon the same level of rates. It is also worth mentioning that the 174 cent rate from New York piers is also the rate charged Minneapolis, St. Paul, Chicago, St. Louis, and New Orleans.

Slightly different from the dry-goods group are those used in quoting rates on beverages.

Group E is distinguished from group D in the beverage tariffs, which means that Chicago pays a higher rate on shipments to South Coast territory than do Minneapolis and St. Paul and St. Louis. The

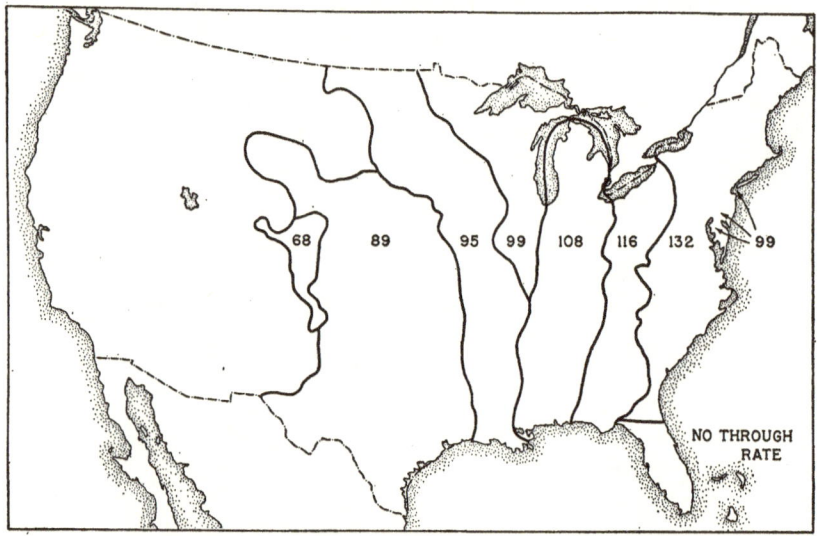

Map 19. Rates on beverages to South Coast termini from Transcontinental Freight Bureau groups.

Chicago rate is also quoted from steamship piers at New York, Philadelphia, and Baltimore, as it is for dry goods.

---

[2] Rates on beverages apply to nonintoxicating cereal beverages; carbonated, flavored, or phosphated beverages (ginger ale, root beer, etc.); malt liquors (ale, beer, stout, etc.); and plain and mineral waters. Malt tonics are included from some points of origin. Shipments must be in packages—not in tank cars—and from points west of the Indiana-Illinois state line, the Wabash and Ohio rivers, and the line of the Illinois Central Railroad the rate on beverages when boxed in tin or glass is lower than the rate when enclosed in other packages. From these latter points of origin, it should be added, the minimum carload weight is higher.

The minimum carload weight for beverages is, generally, 50,000 pounds, except for shipments from group J, when the minimum is 40,000 pounds. There are, however, two exceptions:

1. Beverages boxed in tin or glass may be shipped in carloads of at least 60,000 pounds from designated groups at lower rates than are charged for smaller carload quantities. The rate used in connection with the enlarged minimum is 88 cents from groups C and C-1, and 80 cents from groups D, E, F, G, H, and I.

2. Beverages from specific points of origin (Chicago, St. Paul, La Crosse, Milwaukee, Peoria, Belleville, St. Louis, Kansas City, St. Joseph, Omaha, Galveston, Houston, Denver,

The next map (map 20) shows eastern groupings of the rates on steel[8] from transcontinental groups to South Coast termini.

The most significant adjustment in the transcontinental rate structure, so far as steel is concerned, is the parity of Chicago and Birmingham at the 110 cent level. This parity is not extended to

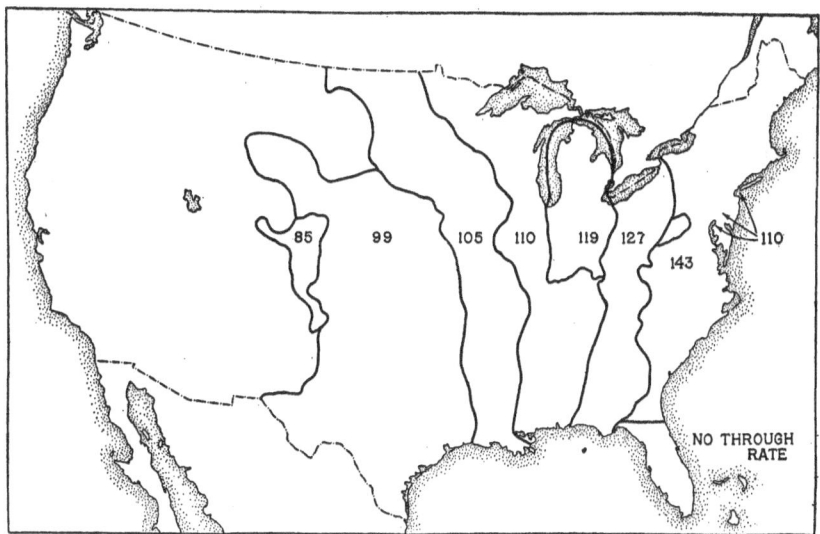

Map 20. Rates on steel and steel articles from Transcontinental Freight Bureau groups to South Coast termini.

Pittsburgh. An additional contrast between the clothing and the steel rates is to be found in the fact that Indianapolis and Detroit in group C take a rate of 119 cents instead of the 110 cent rate applied

---

Golden, Pueblo, and Trinidad) consigned to named destinations in western Arizona may be forwarded at lower minima and also at lower rates than the general rate structure would provide.

[8] Rates on steel articles apply to a very large list of commodities. Illustrative items are structural iron and steel, angles, bars, bolts, nuts, shafting, fencing wire, signposts, boiler ends, building corners, shingles, pipe, bands, and strips. In addition to these and similar products, there are many goods the rates on which conform to the general structure used for steel articles, but with minor variations in eastern groupings. Such items are balls, barrel material, cribbing, molds, castings, ingots, guardrails, rods, rolls, faucets, pipe fittings, rails, and track.

The minimum carload weights on steel articles range from 40,000 to 80,000 pounds. Thus, the minimum on baling ties is 40,000 pounds; that on castings, 50,000 pounds; that on cast iron pipe, 60,000 pounds; and that on ingots, 80,000 pounds. The minimum weights vary, also, with the size of the car ordered.

to points of origin just south of the Ohio River. Most frequently, in these eastern groupings, the rate on the zones just beyond the Mississippi is uniform from the Great Lakes to the Gulf; with respect to steel the Chicago-Birmingham adjustment causes a distortion. Mention should be made of the high rate of 143 cents charged from all Atlantic Seaboard shipping points, except from Florida, from which no through rates are quoted, and from the steamship piers

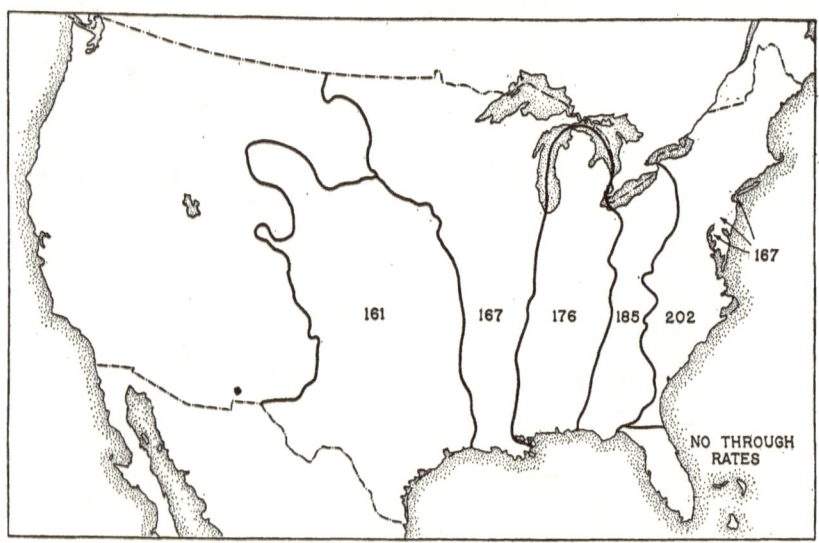

Map 21. Rates on automobile bodies and parts from Transcontinental Freight Bureau groups to South Coast termini.

indicated. The latter are on a parity with Chicago and Birmingham on water-rail movements through Gulf ports. Perhaps it is the rather high rate in group A which produces another variation from the standard pattern of grouping. A small zone with a rate of 129¼ cents lies between groups A and B, providing steel mills in the Johnstown, Pennsylvania, area on the western edge of group A with rates only slightly higher than group B.

Of the westbound commodities here considered, iron and steel show the greatest divergence from the standard pattern. That divergence, with its concomitant specialized arrangements, may indicate that freight rates are of greater importance to iron and steel producers than to the producers of other westward-moving articles.

RATE GROUPS ON WESTBOUND TRAFFIC 81

Rate groups on automobile bodies and parts[4] are shown in map 21. The grouping which characterizes the rates on automobile bodies and parts resembles that on steel, except that Birmingham, in this case, takes the Detroit rather than the Chicago rate. There is a difference, also, in that the Chicago rate is carried farther west and in that group J, which in the steel tariff enjoyed a separate rate of 85 cents, is here absorbed into groups G, H, and I.

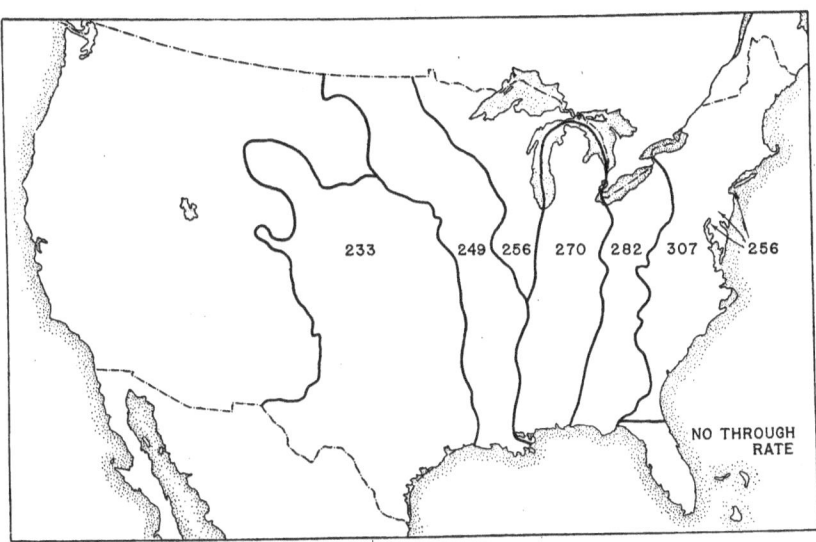

Map 22. Rates on clothing from Transcontinental Freight Bureau groups to South Coast termini.

Map 22 traces the outlines of rate groups in tariffs which quote rates on clothing.[5]

---

[4] Rates on automobile bodies and parts apply to bodies, seats, seat cabs, seat-cab parts, bottoms, battery-clamp spacers, and to carloads in which these articles are mixed with any of a considerable list of enumerated commodities, such as shock absorbers, motors and motor parts, coils, generators and parts, terminals, filters, luggage carriers, horns, bumpers, steering wheels, lamps, windshields, etc. Separate rates are quoted on straight carloads of articles with which mixtures are permitted, but some of these rates, from some points of origin, are higher than those on mixtures which the tariff allows.

The tariff provides carload rates for loadings of 10,000, 12,000, 20,000, and 30,000 pounds. The rates discussed in the text are those for consignments of 30,000 pounds or more. Rates for smaller shipments are higher than those here considered.

[5] Rates on clothing apply to a list which begins with bathrobes and ends with yarn (not including cotton, rayon, or silk yarn) in bales. Among the items mentioned are caps, garments, collars, dresses, gloves, handkerchiefs, hats, jackets, mufflers, night-

The clothing groups resemble the steel and automobile groups in most respects except in the treatment of Chicago territory.

Somewhat simpler than the groupings so far described is that on westbound vehicles.[6]

The obvious difference between the automobile-bodies and the vehicles groupings is that, for the latter, group E territory is consolidated with groups G, H, and I. It is doubtful if this consolidation is

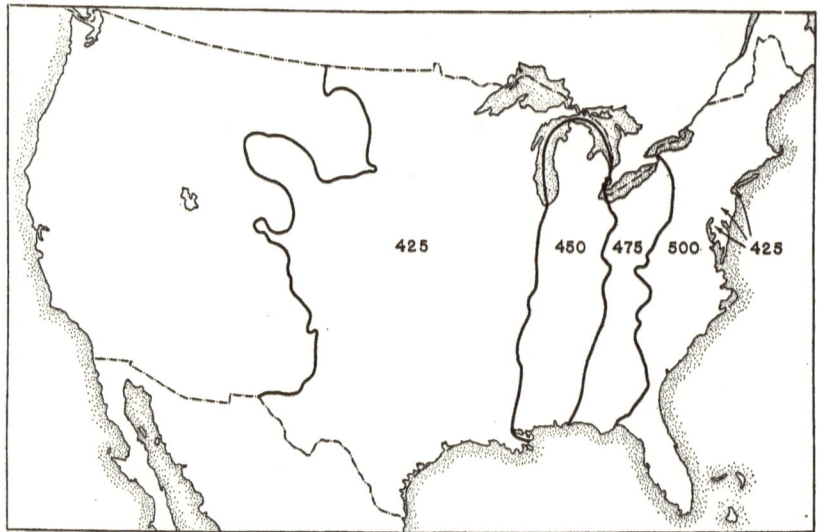

Map 23. Rates on vehicles from Transcontinental Freight Bureau groups to South Coast termini.

of practical importance. A more significant fact, not shown by the map, is that class rates are available for vehicle shipments which

---

gowns, shirts, felt and sheepskin slippers, sweaters, children's suits, underwear, and hosiery. Mixtures of clothing with cotton and rayon piece goods and with cotton and rayon yarn are permitted, with some restrictions. In general, rates are limited to cotton, vegetable fiber, or rayon goods, although some part-wool or all-wool articles such as sweaters and hats are included.

Clothing not listed in the commodity tariff moves on second-class rates, except for furs. This is a much higher basis than that provided by the commodity tariff, as may be seen by contrasting the commodity rates of 307 cents from New York to San Francisco with the class rate of 528 cents between the same two points.

The minimum carload weight on clothing is 20,000 pounds.

[6] Rates on vehicles apply to ambulances, station wagons, passenger automobiles, hearses, and to finished or unfinished parts thereof (but not including cyclometers, headlights, horns, lamps, searchlights, speedometers, or windshields), except from the Florida penin-

undercut the commodity rates from eastern origins on certain movements. This is true, for example, for shipments from group J origins to destinations included in the list of western class termini. The effective rate on such shipments is 403 cents instead of 425 cents. Besides this, class rates are quoted from some, though not from all, eastern groups to some destinations that lie east of the western class termini but are included in the list of termini for westbound com-

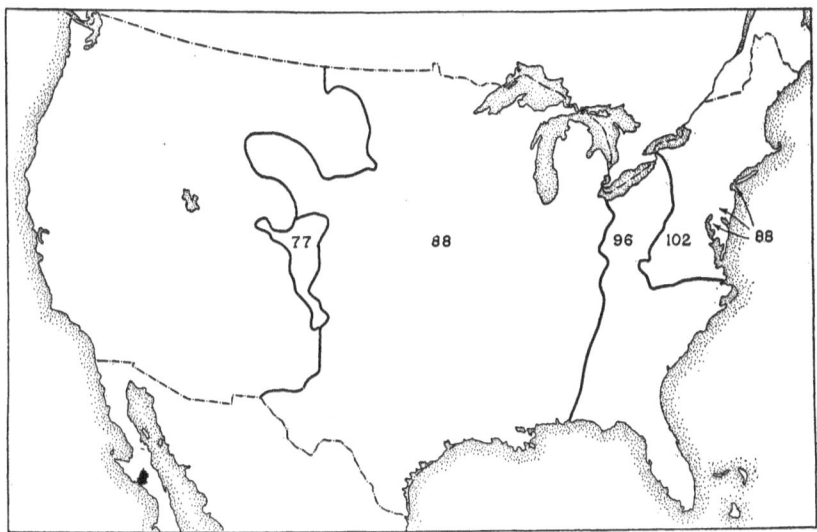

Map 24. Rates on canned goods from Transcontinental Freight Bureau groups to South Coast termini.

modity shipments. This further limits the importance of the 425 cent westbound commodity rate. Rarely, however, are the first-class rates from any point east of Kansas City to a South Coast terminus lower than the commodity rates on vehicles from the appropriate transcontinental group.

---

sula. From the peninsula, rates apply on passenger automobiles only. Mixtures of the specified articles are permitted with tractor trailers, automobile radio receiving sets, firefighting apparatus, tractors, automobile chassis, and snowplows.

Minimum carload weights depend on railroad car lengths. For cars not over 41 feet and 6 inches in length, inside measurement, the minimum weight is 10,000 pounds. For cars over 41 feet and 6 inches in length, but not over 51 feet in length, the minimum is 12,000 pounds. When moving under class rates, the minimum carload weight is 10,000 pounds.

Next to be considered are the eastern groups used in fixing rates on canned goods.[7]

Canned goods illustrate a simplified structure: there are only three significant eastern zones. The largest of these, taking a rate of 88 cents, includes the entire central section of the United States, together with steamship piers at New York, Philadelphia, and Baltimore,[8] on traffic moving to Gulf ports in Texas and Louisiana and thence west

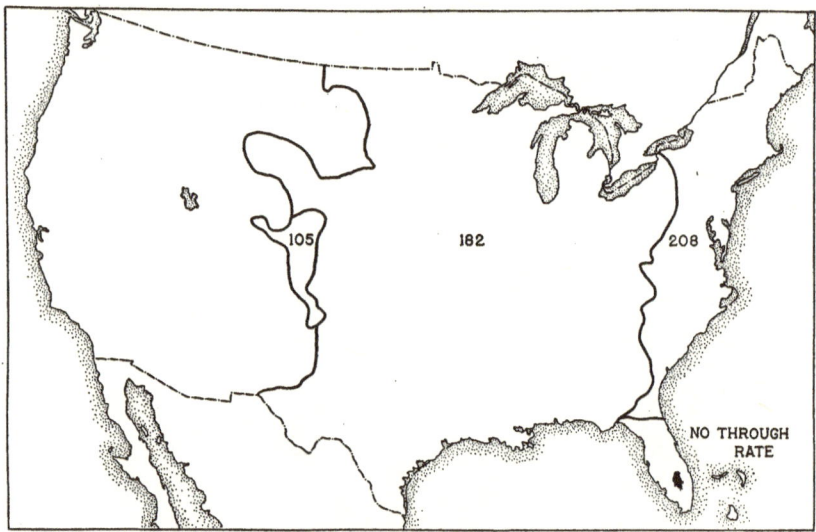

Map 25. Rates on wine from Transcontinental Freight Bureau groups to South Coast termini.

by rail. States in the Southeast pay 96 cents instead of 88 cents, which is the amount also charged from standard groups B and L, while most or all of Virginia, West Virginia, Maryland, Delaware, Pennsylvania, New York, and New England take a rate of 102 cents.

---

[7] The tariff on canned goods westbound covers a variety of substances, including milk, cider, juice, syrup, olive oil, fish, meat, soups, vegetables, pickles, and preserves. Strictly speaking, canned goods need not always be canned. Thus, cider may be shipped in barrels, soups in earthenware containers, macaroni in glass, and mincemeat in pails, and yet the canned-goods rates will apply. Some leeway is also allowed with respect to the outer package—box, crate, carton, or bag—in which cans or other permitted containers are required to be enclosed.

The minimum carload weight for canned-goods shipments is 60,000 pounds. It is, however, possible to ship from all rate groups, except group A, at a 40,000 pounds minimum subject to the payment of a higher rate.

[8] Piers at Miami and Tampa are also included.

Map 25 displays the eastern groups which apply to wine, westbound.[9] This and the two following maps present extreme situations. There are only two groups for westbound wine shipments, besides the small area, including Denver, which takes a rate of 105 cents.

Map 26 covers rates on fertilizers.[10]

There is only one fertilizer group, except that no through rates are quoted from Atlantic Seaboard states. This exclusion of the extreme

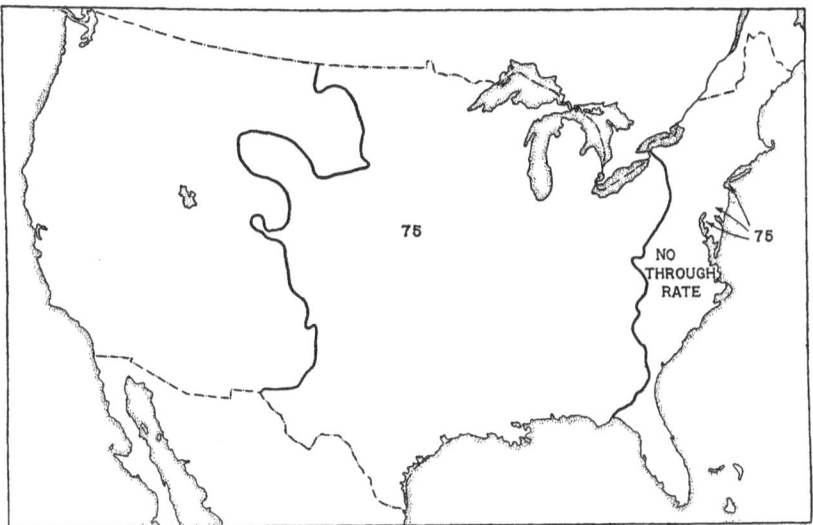

Map 26. Rates on fertilizer from Transcontinental Freight Bureau groups to South Coast termini.

eastern shipping points creates, in effect, a second area, although not a district from which a uniform rate prevails. Little or no fertilizer moves to western termini from eastern points.

---

[9] Rates on wine, westbound, apply to package shipments, excluding champagne. Rates quoted do not apply to wine in tank cars, nor to alcoholic liquors. The latter take a higher commodity rate; consignments of wine in tank cars are charged class rates which range from 372 cents from New York to 248 cents from Denver. Wine moving westward into California is of the higher grades, for which tank cars are not appropriate.

The minimum carload weight for wine shipments is 30,000 pounds.

[10] The term "fertilizers" includes superphosphates and also materials such as sulphate of ammonia, nitrate of soda, cyanimid, tankage, fish meal, muriate of potash, sulphate of potash, dried blood, guano, and manure. Shipments are, usually, in bags or in bulk.

The minimum carload weight in the rate structure described in the text is 80,000 pounds. There is, however, an alternative commodity rate structure at a higher level for shipments with a 60,000 pound minimum, and there is a class carload rate based on a minimum of 40,000 pounds.

The last map in the present series (map 27) is compiled from tariffs on tin articles.[11]

Tin articles take the same rate from all eastern points, except from origins in the Southeast from which no through rates are quoted.

It is clear enough from the preceding pages that rate groups on transcontinental business westbound, as eastbound, range from the very comprehensive to the relatively specialized. In general, the

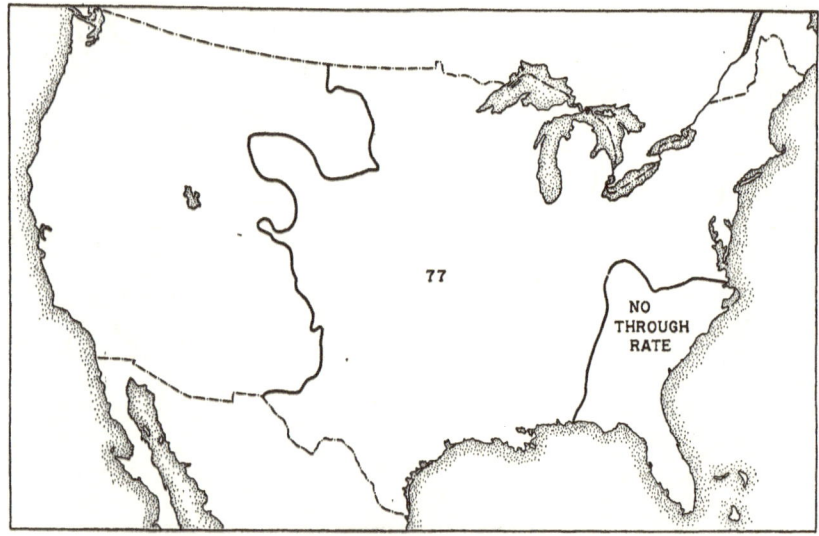

Map 27. Rates on tin articles from Transcontinental Freight Bureau groups to South Coast termini.

number of groups on westbound traffic is smallest for canned goods, wine, fertilizers, and tin; it is largest for dry goods, beverages, steel, automobile bodies and parts, clothing, and vehicles. For tin and fertilizer there is only one through rate to South Coast termini from Transcontinental Freight Bureau territory. For dry goods, beverages, and steel the groupings resemble those in the class tariff. It is true that the maps oversimplify the rate structure on westbound

[11] Rates apply to tin and articles of tin, including tin and terne plate, and to zinc- and copper-coated iron or steel sheets of specified size and thickness. Rates also apply, except from group J, to tin-can stock such as bottoms, caps, faucets, handles, hoops, and spouts. They do not cover tin roofing or rolls.

The minimum carload weight is 80,000 pounds. From all groups except groups A, B, and C, however, carload minima of 50,000 pounds are accepted at a higher rate level. The rates in the text assume a loading of 80,000 pounds.

RATE GROUPS ON WESTBOUND TRAFFIC

traffic because they convey no information with respect to origins in Pacific Freight Bureau territory. The blank spaces in this area which are characteristic of the maps depicting westbound groups do not indicate a peculiarity of the rate structure, but only the fact that points of origin are not represented on the map. But even with this warning, the reader will observe that the practice of grouping or blanketing is followed on westbound traffic as it is on eastbound movements. The pattern is, however, somewhat different. Whereas, on eastbound traffic, groups seem to have been developed rather specifically and separately for each commodity, on westbound traffic the standard pattern of groups is generally used without substantial modification, the only major differences among the various westbound commodity rate structures being differences in the degree to which groups are combined.

CHAPTER VI

Rate Profiles on Eastbound Traffic

THE NEXT subject for discussion is the kind and amount of change that can be observed in the total charge as goods move from western points to destinations in the East.[1]

Most of the goods originating in California are subject, while in the State, to local competition and to regulation. In California itself the controlling element is highway competition, so far as the upper limit of railroad charges is concerned. There is, however, Commission regulation of minimum rates in California, and the railroad schedules approximate, in practice, the minima which the rail carriers are permitted to collect.[2] On this system, rates are related to mileage, with exceptions arising out of the nature of the control which has been mentioned.

From California points of origin, class rates which advance with distance in irregular progression are quoted to eastern points. To clarify and illustrate this statement, there are presented a series of charts setting forth graphically the rates from San Francisco to selected eastern points over stated routes. The class rates chosen for description are those of class C, and the presentation and discussion of these and of succeeding maps illustrating commodity rates will occupy the rest of this chapter.

---

[1] Westbound movements will be neglected in the present chapter, because files of local eastern tariffs are not available.

[2] Within California, the California Railroad Commission has prescribed a uniform system of minimum class rates based on constructive highway mileage. That is, actual miles by highway are adjusted for operation factors such as grade and surface so that constructive mileage is obtained. Class rates related strictly to these constructive distances are then applied. Lower classes are related to first class by fixed percentages. Rates so obtained are applied to all forms of transport which wish to participate in the traffic, regardless of circuity. Rates for shorter hauls frequently exceed rates for longer hauls—a situation which, if unauthorized, would constitute a violation of Section 4. When movement between two points within California passes outside the State, the Fourth Section requirement is observed and the lowest rate constitutes a maximum for intermediate more distant points; an example is the Southern Pacific route from San Francisco to Westwood via Reno, Fernley, and Flanigan.

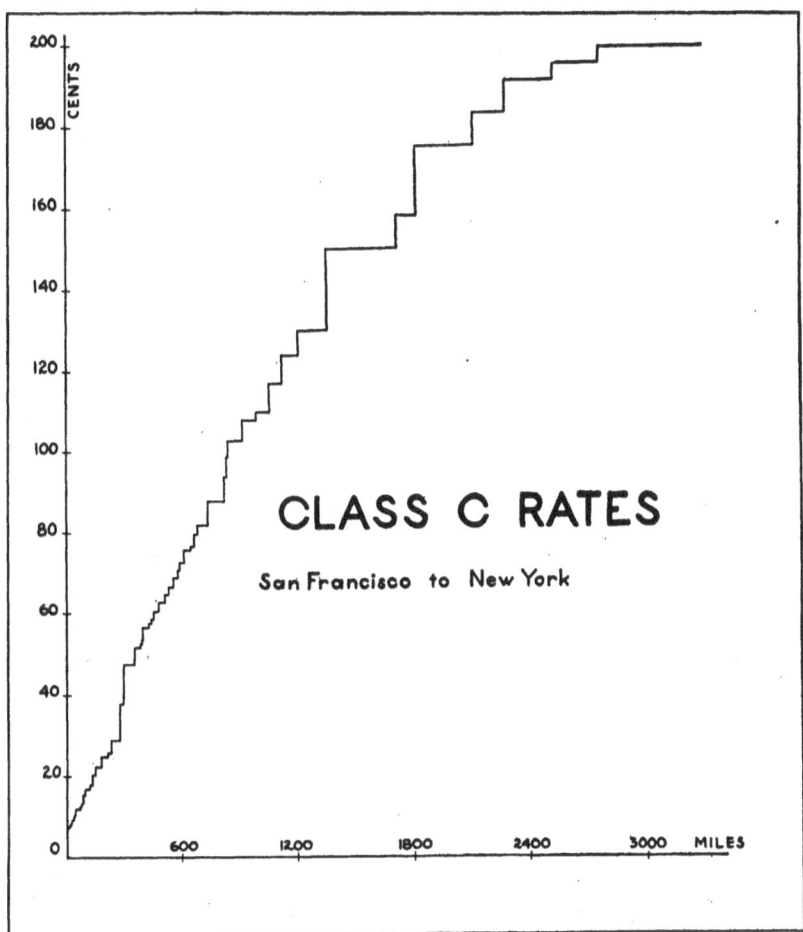

Chart 4. Class C rates, San Francisco to New York via Southern Pacific, Union Pacific, Chicago and Northwestern, Elgin, Joliet and Eastern, and Pennsylvania.

The first chart (chart 4) shows the profile of class C rates on shipments, by way of the central route, from San Francisco to New York City.

The class rate scale reproduced in this chart is that applied upon the central route from San Francisco to New York. Shipments upon this route move over the Southern Pacific from San Francisco to Ogden. Beyond Ogden, shipments are assumed to be handled by the Union Pacific to Council Bluffs and by the Chicago and Northwestern between Council Bluffs and West Chicago. The Elgin, Joliet and Eastern is a belt railroad in the Chicago area. Farther east, the selected route uses the line of the Pennsylvania Railroad from Hobart, where freight is received from the Elgin, Joliet and Eastern, to New York.

On the central route the class scale progresses regularly from San

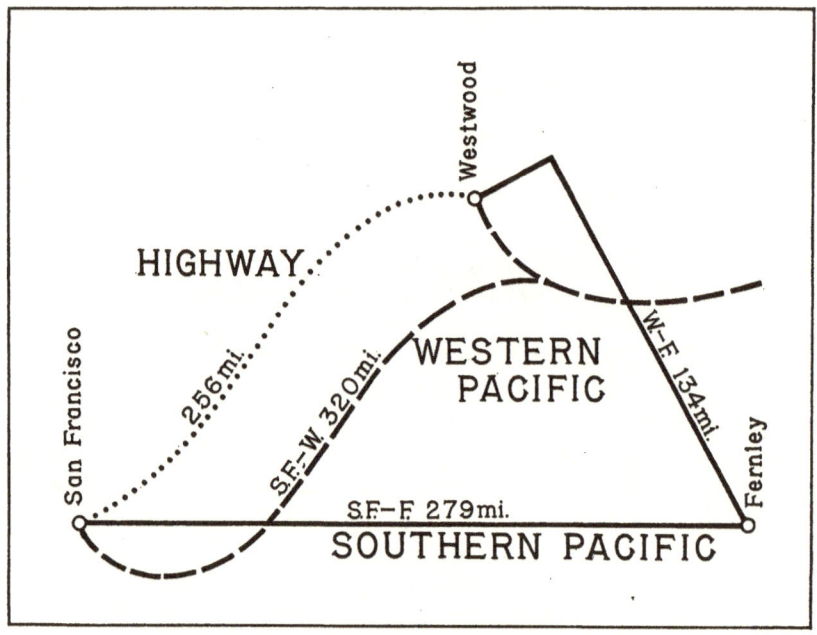

Chart 5. Class C rates from San Francisco to Fernley and to Westwood, California.

Francisco to Fernley in accordance with the California intrastate scale. In the 264 miles from Richmond (15 miles from San Francisco) to Fernley the rate increase is 24½ cents, or 0.093 cents per mile. But from Fernley to Humboldt, Nevada, 101 miles east of Fernley, the rate increases 23 cents or 0.228 cents per mile. This sudden jump is probably the result of a situation outlined in the next chart (chart 5).

Both the Western Pacific and the Southern Pacific operate lines between the San Francisco Bay area and Westwood, California. There is also truck service between the Bay area and Westwood. The highway distance between San Francisco and Westwood is 256 miles, and the truck rate of 28 cents, class C, under the California Commission's minimum highway scale constitutes a maximum which the railroads presumably cannot exceed. The Southern Pacific, therefore, quotes a rate of 28 cents to Westwood, although the Southern Pacific rail distance, 413 miles, would normally justify a higher charge. Inasmuch as shipments which pass over Southern Pacific lines are carried through Fernley, this 28 cent rate is also applied to Fernley. There is no equally effective rail or truck price competition for some distance beyond this last-named station on the Southern Pacific main line; instead, rates to destinations between Fernley and Humboldt rise quickly to a higher level.

Beyond Humboldt, the original rate of progression is resumed. This continues, with slightly larger intervals, as far as Sydney, Nebraska, where the scale begins to develop zones of 200 to almost 400 miles. The final rate, at Latrobe, Pennsylvania, is continued unchanged to the city of New York. The scale as a whole is regular, in Transcontinental Freight Bureau territory, except for a moderate use of zones, with some decreases in the rates per mile, both average and marginal, as distance increases.

The differences between the class C rate profile on the central route and that on the southern route over the Santa Fe are not large enough to justify separate elaboration. Attention may be drawn, however, to the peculiarities of the class C rate from San Francisco, via Puget Sound, to St. Paul. Chart 6 shows the class C profile over the northern route.

The striking feature of the class C scale profile over the northern route is the Fourth Section departure in the Portland area. The controlling factor on rates between San Francisco and Portland is water competition. Railroads meet this competition by quoting low "port-to-port" rates, at three levels: the Columbia River level, which is lowest; the Seattle-Tacoma level, which is higher; and the level to minor Puget Sound ports—Bellingham, Anacortes, Everett, and Olympia,—which is higher still. Intermediate rates may be higher, by permission of the Interstate Commerce Commission, although they may not be more than twice the port-to-port rates. It follows that rates to intermediate destinations are fixed on the lowest of three alterna-

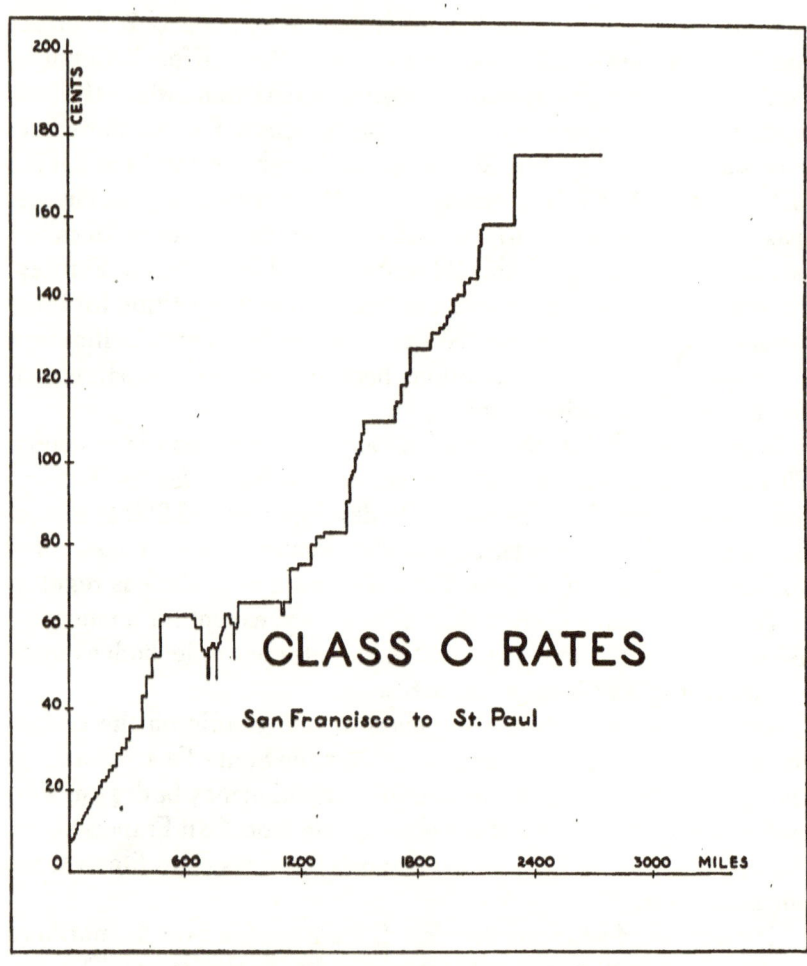

Chart 6. Class C rates, San Francisco to St. Paul via Southern Pacific and Northern Pacific.

tive bases: (1) the rate called for by a progressive mileage scale from San Francisco; (2) the lowest combination of a port-to-port rate and a local class rate, which may include a back haul; and (3) 200 per cent of the port-to-port rate. The class-rate profile shows the extreme irregularity which this complicated system produces at distances from San Francisco which range from 400 to 850 miles.

Both because of the influence of water competition and the competition of short-line railroad routes the class rate schedule beyond Portland is little affected by the Cascade Mountains; beyond Spokane, rates rise rapidly in the Rockies, although there is a blanket of 156 miles around Helena, where the Divide is crossed, owing to competition of the shorter Union Pacific line by way of Pocatello. This accelerated progression is, on the whole, maintained on the subsequent downgrade until, in North Dakota, a rate ceiling is reached which carries the traffic to St. Paul.

We may now turn from the profiles of class rates to profiles illustrative of commodity rates from western points of origin to eastern points. We already know from our study of transcontinental groupings that the differences between class and commodity schedules may be expected to be considerable.

Following the order of the preceding chapter, the first chart (chart 7) will show the rate schedule applied to lettuce.

The shape of the lettuce profile reproduced in the chart is not too different from that of the class C profile. The regular progression in California and the sharp increase when the state line has been passed is evident in both. Again, as in the class rates, but differing here from the practice in many other commodity structures, the ceiling on lettuce is reached only after a haul of almost 3,000 miles, and the amount added for carriage in the eastern part of the country is large. Indeed, the lettuce rate increases 30 cents in the 240 mile stretch between Griffith, Indiana, and Marion, Ohio—approximately 700 miles from New York,—or an increment of 0.125 cents per mile in the latter part of a journey on which the average rate per mile is only 0.055 cents.

Yet, although lettuce profiles lack the characteristic eastern blanket which some other commodity rates display, they do, upon occasion, reveal low uniform charges for distances of some length, followed by a sharp progression. This is shown in the chart for the area west of Ogden (890 miles from point of origin) and in Indiana and in Illinois. Another marked example of a constant rate on lettuce appears on the southern route, not here pictured, where, in Teaxs, a rate of 130 cents, already in force to a point just beyond Sierra Blanca, is continued as far as and including Houston, a distance of approximately 735 miles.

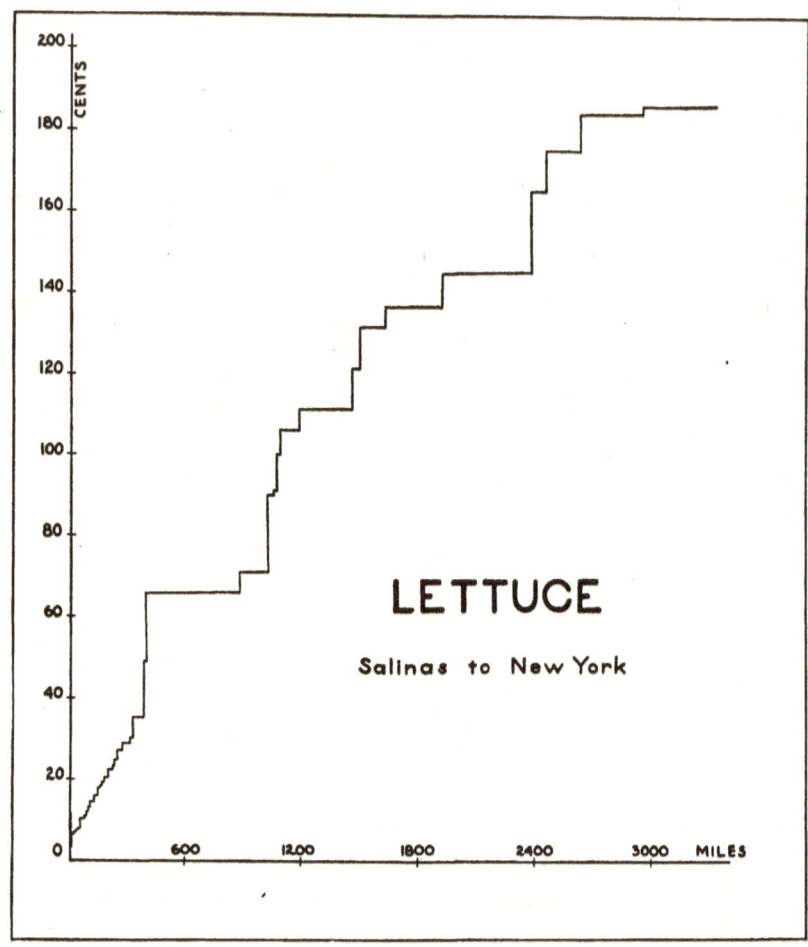

Chart 7. Lettuce rates from Salinas to New York via the Southern Pacific, Union Pacific, Chicago and Northwestern, Elgin, Joliet and Eastern, and Erie.

The next chart (chart 8) describes the rates on fresh grapes.

The profile again shows, in its early stages, the influence of the California intrastate scale. Since this scale reflects highway competition, actual or potential, this means that motor truck charges are limiting for shorter hauls.

For longer distances, it is to be observed that grape rates reach a ceiling of 150 cents per 100 pounds at a distance of 1,800 miles. The equivalent distance when grapes are shipped from Fresno by the southern route over the Atchison, Topeka and Santa Fe is 2,015 miles, but, either way, the rise to the maximum is more rapid for grapes than for lettuce. The chart showing rates over the central route gives a clear illustration of a type of rate making characteristic of

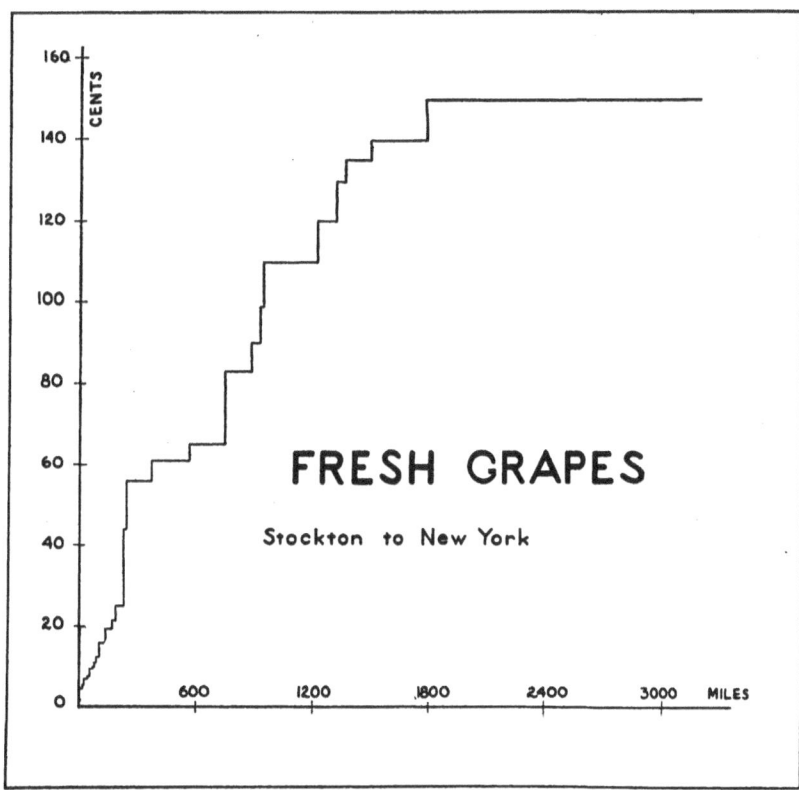

Chart 8. Rates on fresh grapes from Stockton to New York via Southern Pacific, Union Pacific, Chicago and Northwestern, Elgin, Joliet and Eastern, and Erie.

the western area. First, a charge of 25 cents (0.124 cents per mile) takes a consignment from Stockton over the Sierra to Reno, a distance of 202 miles. From this point on, the difference between the Reno rate of 25 cents and the ceiling rate of 150 cents to Denison (1,800 miles from Stockton and 65 miles beyond Council Bluffs) is principally absorbed in three short sections. Between Fernley and Winnemucca (141 miles) the rate increases by 31 cents, or 0.220 cents per mile; between Ogden and Thayer Junction (209 miles) the rate increases by 34 cents, or 0.163 cents per mile; and from Cheyenne, Wyoming, to Grand Island, Nebraska (363 miles), the rate increases by 30 cents, or 0.083 cents per mile. In other words, 95 cents out of a total rise of 125 cents is absorbed in the course of 713 miles of haul in the total distance of 1,598 miles between Reno and Denison. The balance of 30 cents is distributed over a distance of 885 miles at an average increase of 0.034 cents per mile. What this means, of course, is that the central profile presents a series of steep cliffs and relatively level plateaus. The level stretches reflect the pressure of population groups—respectively, the Utah common points, the Colorado common points, and Omaha and Council Bluffs on the Missouri River. Inasmuch as the plateaus are broad, the climb between them must be steep. This steepness does not at all correspond with the physical topography of the country over which the traffic flows.[3]

The profile of citrus rates on the central route is set forth in chart 9.

The ceilings on citrus over the central route are the Chicago rate of 131 cents, first encountered at Cedar Rapids (2,080 miles from Los Angeles), and the New York rate of 135 cents, effective at Deca-

---

[3] It is possible that the apparent suddenness of transition from one rate plateau to another is modified by the use of "combinations." Through rates to a destination upon the eastern edge of a rate plateau, added to the local rail or truck rate from this destination to a point upon the succeeding plateau, may amount to less than the through rate to the point at which the consignment finally comes to rest.

Officials on adjacent railroads may make different adjustments in meeting similar situations; and this may be true of other commodities than grapes. Thus, in western Nevada, the Western Pacific charges a rate of 25 cents on fresh grapes from Stockton to Flanigan. The Southern Pacific collects the same amount to Fernley. The two roads meet and their rates are on a parity at Winnemucca, where the rate is 56 cents. Each has, therefore, an advance of 31 cents to absorb. In distributing the increment, the Western Pacific applies the Winnemucca rate at the first station east of Flanigan, while the Southern Pacific advances its rate more slowly, with an intermediate zone.

Another adjustment has been observed in Texas. The rate on fresh grapes from Stockton to Sierra Blanca, over Southern Pacific lines, is 116 cents. At Sierra Blanca the Texas and New Orleans, a subsidiary of the Southern Pacific, and the Texas and Pacific, a subsidiary of the Missouri Pacific, diverge. Farther east, the rate to Sweetwater on the Texas and Pacific and that to Del Rio on the Texas and New Orleans is alike, 130 cents. This is, in each case, an increment of 14 cents over the rate to Sierra Blanca. The Texas and New Orleans absorbs the increment by advancing its rate by the full 14 cents at the first station east of Sierra Blanca, while the Texas and Pacific continues the Sierra Blanca rate a little way and then increases it through two intermediate zones to the 130 cent level.

The illustrations given seem to reflect arbitrary decisions on the part of persons in authority, indicating diverse policies between railroads.

tur, Indiana (2,479 miles from Los Angeles). The scope of the 131 cent and 135 cent zones is indicated on page 64.

The broad zone at 46 cents on the central route is caused by the Salt Lake City adjustment. Other key rates are those to the Colorado

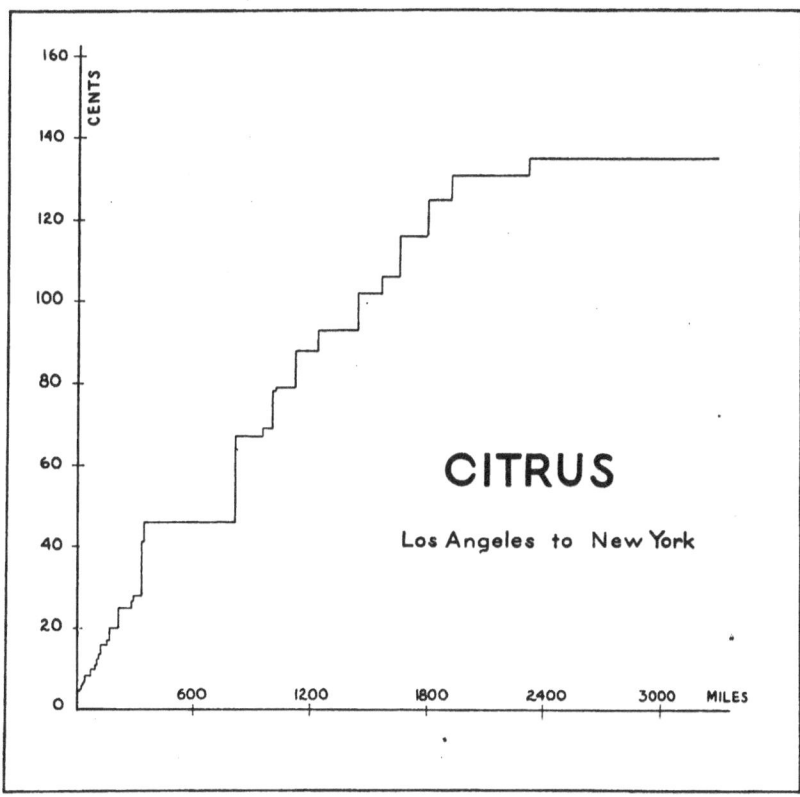

Chart 9. Rates on citrus from Los Angeles to New York via Union Pacific, Chicago and Northwestern, Elgin, Joliet and Eastern, and Erie.

common points (93 cents) and to Omaha (116 cents). The progression of the citrus scale does not vary widely from a straight line between Los Angeles and Cedar Rapids, if one takes account only of the rates to the larger cities upon the route, although there is a tendency, given a determined spread between two major points, to accomplish a disproportionate part of the advance from one point to another during the early part of the distance between the two locations and a smaller proportion during the latter part, thus increasing the total revenue which the carrier is able, or expects to be able, to obtain.

The structure of citrus rates on the St. Paul route emphasizes the

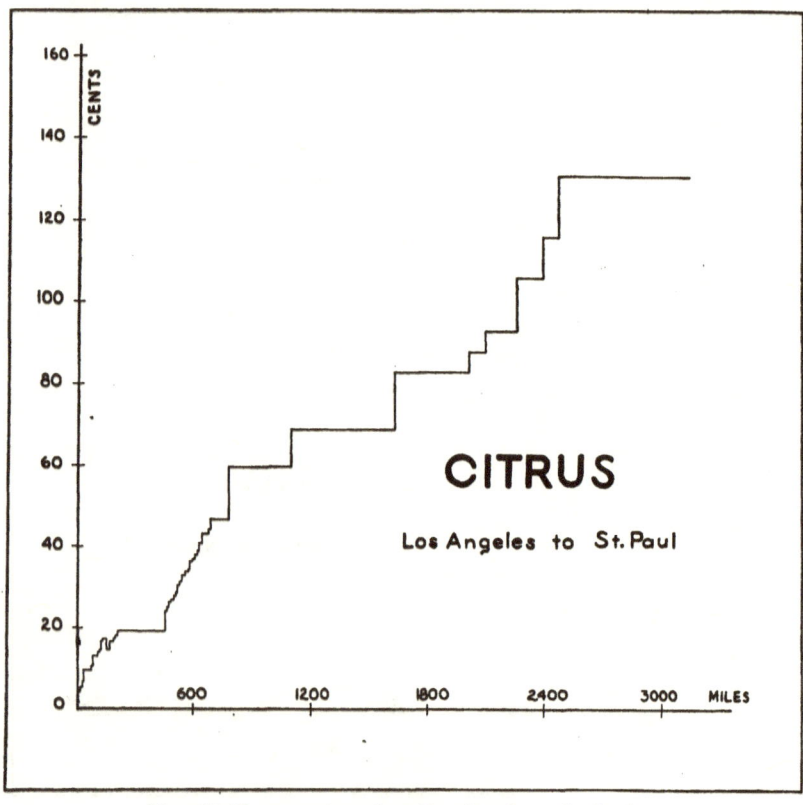

Chart 10. Rates on citrus from Los Angeles to St. Paul via Southern Pacific and Northern Pacific.

importance of key points in commodity rate making, and for this reason a second profile is presented, covering the rates from Los Angeles via Sacramento and Puget Sound to St. Paul.

The first plateau in chart 10, at 19½ cents, terminates at Sacramento, and carries back to Lathrop and Stockton; the 60 cent rate covers Eugene, Portland, and Vancouver; the 69 cent rate applies to stations between and including Centralia, Auburn, Yakima, and

RATE PROFILES ON EASTBOUND TRAFFIC 99

Spokane; and the 83 cent rate includes Butte and Helena. Between Lombard, 54 miles east of Helena and 2,067 miles from Los Angeles, and Glendive the profile rises rapidly, in the course of 411 miles, to the St. Paul level of 131 cents. This is an increase of 48 cents or 0.117 cents per mile in the last stages of a haul of 3,144 miles, or at a greater rate than the increase in charge during the first 216 miles out of Los Angeles.

To express the situation in another way, the railroads charge 135 cents for a haul of 3,304 miles on the central route from Los Angeles to New York and 131 cents for 3,144 miles from Los Angeles to St. Paul. Both rates and distances are approximately the same at these extremes. But on the central route the payment of 83 cents will carry citrus only 1,130 miles from the point of origin; while, on the northern route, 83 cents will pay for 2,067 miles. The reason for this difference is to be found in the competition of the direct Union Pacific route between Los Angeles and Butte. Since the charge to St. Paul is approximately the same as that to New York, rates via the northern route must increase more rapidly than on the central route in the latter part of the rate structure, in order to attain the same final level in the remainder of the distance which is to be overcome.

The next chart (chart 11) is descriptive of the rates on sugar.

The sugar profile reflects, along one continuous route, conditions which were explained in discussing eastern transcontinental groups.

There are four peculiarities in this profile:

1. The rate structure reproduced carries only as far as Chicago. This is because no through rail rates on sugar are quoted from California to Official territory. Eastern consuming points are supplied, for the most part, from Atlantic or Gulf ports. Hawaiian and Philippine sugar, if it moves east at all, travels by water. It is refined at Crockett or San Francisco and is shipped by intercoastal vessel, or it is shipped through the canal in its raw stage and is refined in eastern centers.

2. Rates from Crockett to Chicago are less than to destinations west of the Mississippi River because of water competition, principally from Gulf cities.

3. The blanket rate of 80 cents on sugar begins just east of Ogden, and is maintained across the Continental Divide and across the prai-

ries and plains to the Mississippi River. At the river the rate decreases to 70 cents, and the 70 cent charge applies across Illinois as far as and including Chicago.

4. The rise in rates in the West, from point of origin at Crockett, is rapid. Thus the 80 cent maximum is reached just beyond Ogden, only

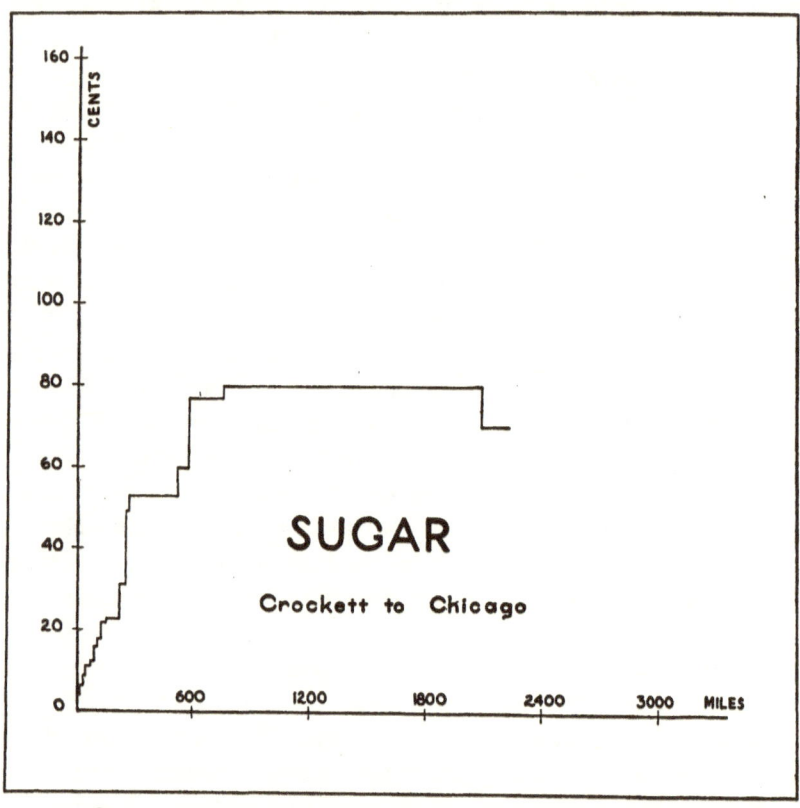

Chart 11. Rates on sugar from Crockett to Chicago via Southern Pacific, Union Pacific, and Chicago and Northwestern.

757 miles from Crockett, although the total distance to Chicago is 2,235 miles; and from the 757 miles one may deduct a subsidiary blanket of 262 miles between Hazen and Elko, Nevada.

In brief, the sugar profile is shaped by competitive pressures, with little or no reference to principles usually considered in constructing a mileage charge.

RATE PROFILES ON EASTBOUND TRAFFIC 101

Chart 12 shows the rates on canned goods, eastbound via Ogden. The profile shows that rates increase in approximate linear progression from San Francisco to Fernley, although they are quoted variously in all-freight, commodity, and class tariffs. East of Fernley

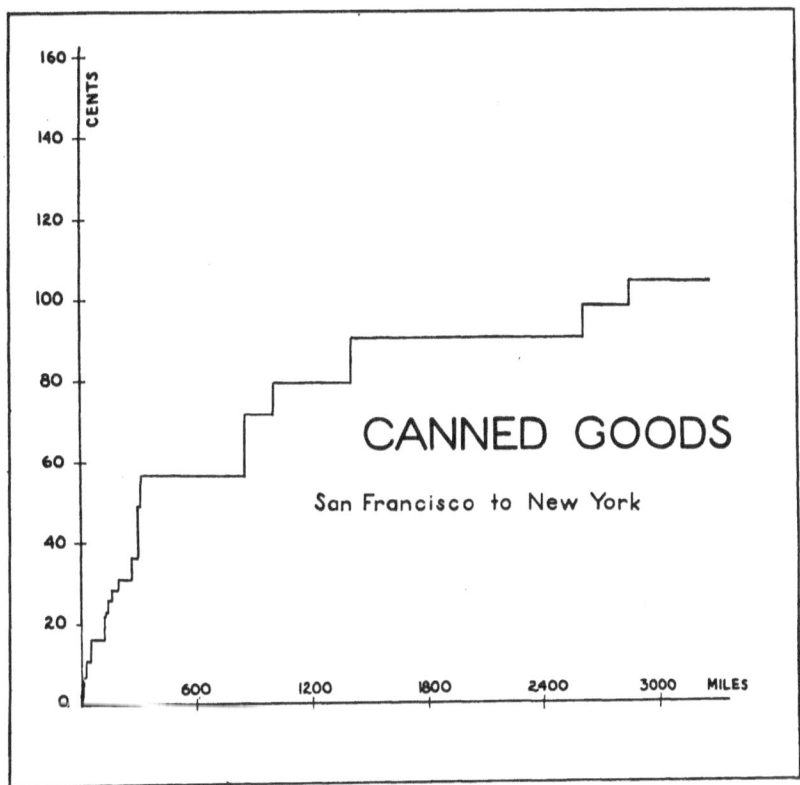

Chart 12. Rates on canned goods from San Francisco to New York via Southern Pacific, Union Pacific, Chicago and Northwestern, Elgin, Joliet and Eastern, and Pennsylvania.

the rate increases steeply to Hazen, 291 miles from San Francisco, and immediately beyond Hazen it rises again to the Utah common-point level of 54 cents. The charge to Lovelock, the first city of any size east of Hazen, is already 54 cents, although the distance from San Francisco is only 347 miles. Thus more than half the rate increases between San Francisco and New York (102 cents) is absorbed in less than the first 400 miles.

The Utah common-point rate carries the freight through Ogden and as far east as Echo. Two large steps then bring the rate to the group J level of 77 cents. Beyond Sidney, Nebraska, at the eastern edge of group J, the rate again increases to 88 cents. This new level is maintained across the great central lowlands up to Bucyrus, Ohio.

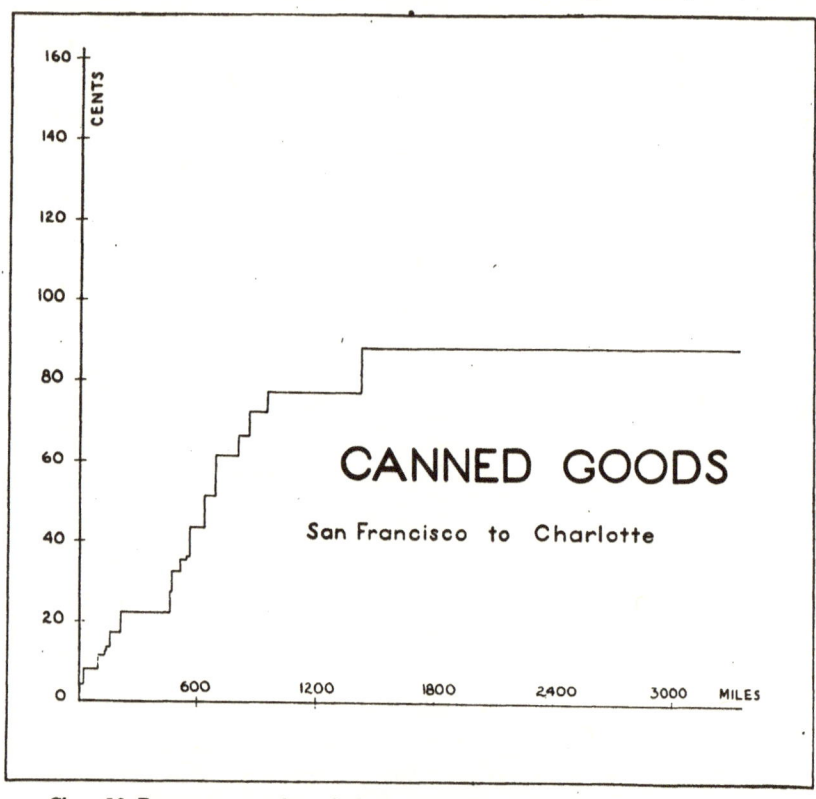

Chart 13. Rates on canned goods from San Francisco to Charlotte, via Atchison, Topeka and Santa Fe, Wabash, Pennsylvania, and Southern.

Two more increases then raise the final charge to the New York quotation of 102 cents. It is probable, as suggested in chapter iv, that this final increment is added because of the unwillingness of carriers in Official territory to accept the small division which would accrue to them if the 88 cent blanket were extended to the northern Atlantic Coast. There is no similar increment on shipments to Southern territory.

We may now add profiles of canned-goods rates over southern and northern routes out of California, in comparison with the picture just given.

Chart 13 shows the canned-goods rate profile from San Francisco to Charlotte, via St. Louis.

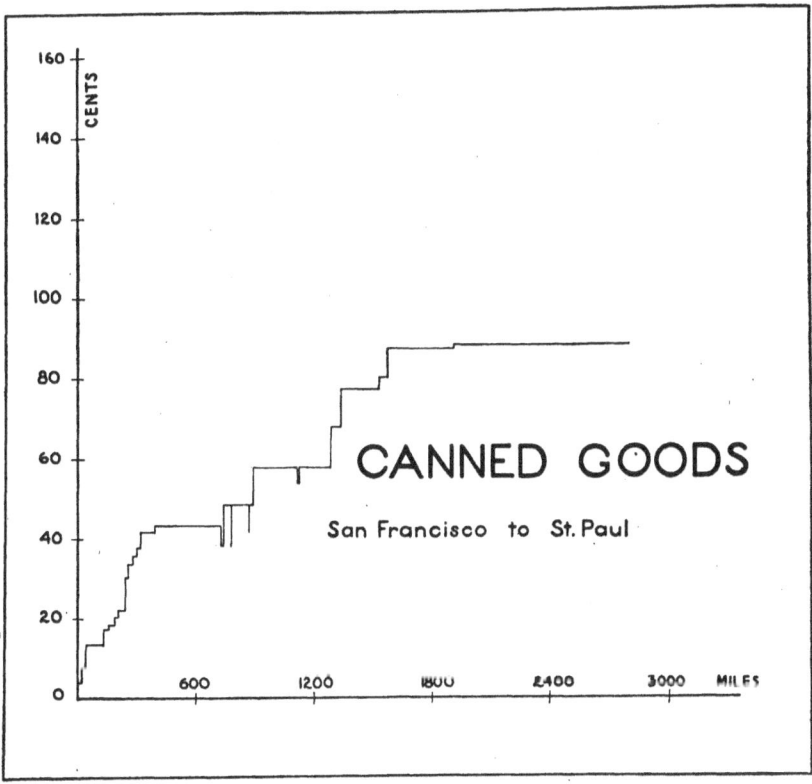

Chart 14. Rates on canned goods from San Francisco to St. Paul via Southern Pacific and Northern Pacific.

The profile by this second route shows two separate linear progressions, at different rates. The first progression is to Fresno, and the second begins beyond Barstow; in between is the Los Angeles blanket of 22 cents. In the first rise from Richmond to Fresno, 191 miles, the rate increases 13¼ cents, or 0.069 cents per mile. In the second increase, which begins just east of Barstow, the rate increases 50 cents in the 492 miles from Barstow to Holbrook, or 0.102 cents per mile. Immediately east of Holbrook the group J level of 77 cents is reached. Although the southern route of the Santa Fe does not pass through stations in group J, the group J rate of 77 cents operates as a maximum west of Dalies because this part of the Santa Fe route is

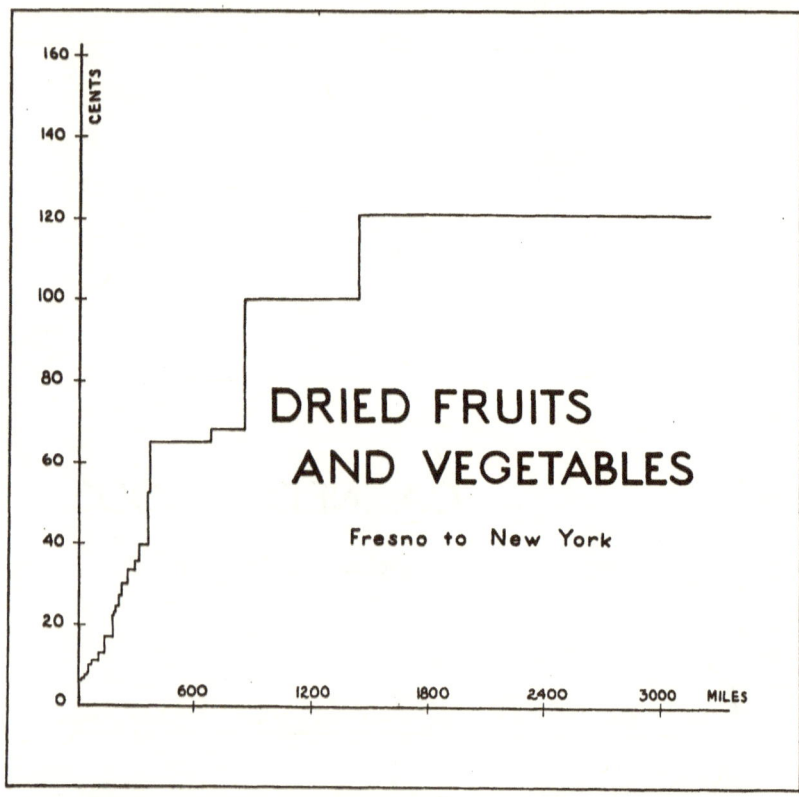

Chart 15. Rates on dried fruits and vegetables from Fresno to New York via Southern Pacific, Union Pacific, Chicago and Northwestern, Elgin, Joliet and Eastern, and Pennsylvania.

directly intermediate to group J. East of Dalies the group J rate still controls the Santa Fe charge as far as Vaughn, but indirectly. At Vaughn the Santa Fe crosses the Southern Pacific. The Southern Pacific rate at Vaughn cannot exceed 77 cents, because Vaughn is intermediate to group J on a route made up of the Southern Pacific via Tucumcari and the Chicago, Rock Island and Pacific railroads, and the Santa Fe must meet its rival's charge if it desires to share the traffic. East of Vaughn, between Vaughn and Clovis, the Santa Fe might raise its rate without diversion of traffic, but it does not do this until the New Mexico–Texas state line is reached. At this point, which is also the point where the territory of the Transcontinental Freight Bureau begins, the rate is raised to 88 cents, and this same rate is thenceforth charged to all subsequent destinations upon the route.

A third chart (chart 14) is explanatory of canned-goods rates from San Francisco to St. Paul.

The chief purpose in presenting chart 14 is to show again how irregularities in rate making may result from water competition. The ceiling rate along the northern as along the central and southern routes is 88 cents, at least so far as most of the Mississippi Valley is concerned. The central route reaches this ceiling in approximately 1,371 miles, the southern route in approximately 1,435 miles, but the northern route only in approximately 1,910 miles. The last-named route has the greater mileage over which to distribute the total charge, but examination of the profile shows that the railroad in this distribution keeps the rate per mile low on that part of the journey which is subject to water competition and raises it rapidly on the remaining part. Thus, on the St. Paul route 41 cents will carry a shipment 861 miles from San Francisco, while on the central route 46½ cents will pay the costs for only the first 291 miles. Rates on the Santa Fe route (see chart 13) advance slowly at first, but even they reach 61 cents at 691 miles, while via Tacoma 57½ cents will carry shipments 1,277 miles. The reader will also note, on the northern route, instances of greater charges for shorter hauls.

Continuing with our series, the next chart (chart 15) illustrates the rate structure applied to dried fruits and vegetables.

The rate structure depicted in chart 15 is comparatively simple. The transcontinental ceiling here is 121 cents per 100 pounds. It is reached, on the central route, just beyond Sidney, Nebraska, at a distance of approximately 1,449 miles from Fresno. The distance to New York, it may be added, is 3,258 miles. Within California the railroad charge increases by small stages, somewhat less regularly than in the typical case. After this, there are only three major increments. The first of these is just beyond Fernley, the second just beyond Ogden, and the third just beyond Sidney. The amount of the concentrated advances and the breadth of the succeeding blanket in each case is remarkable. There are no such exaggerated blankets on the Santa Fe, but the ceiling on this route is reached at about 1,238 miles—an even shorter distance.

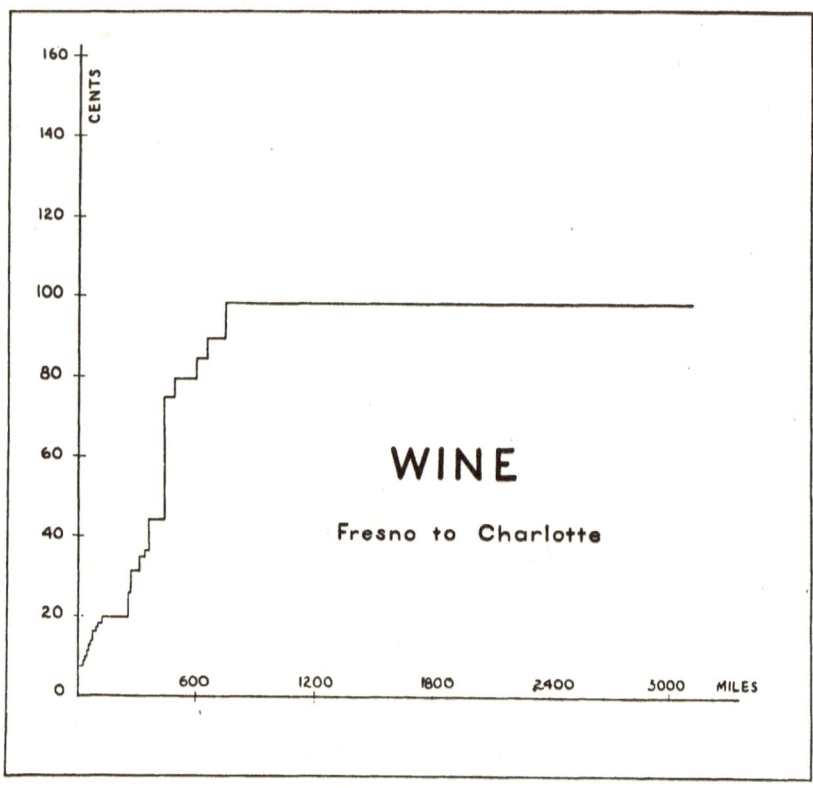

Chart 16. Rates on wine from Fresno to Charlotte via Atchison, Topeka and Santa Fe, Wabash, Pennsylvania, and Southern.

The next profile (chart 16) shows rates on wine from Fresno to Charlotte.

The distance from Fresno to Charlotte is 3,127 miles. The ceiling of 90 cents is reached just beyond Holbrook, Arizona, only 747 miles from the point of departure. On the central route, also, to New York the ceiling is rapidly attained.

The profiles in the present chapter should be examined in connection with the grouping of eastern destinations in chapter iv. The

RATE PROFILES ON EASTBOUND TRAFFIC 107

groupings give the more general view; but the profiles suggest, in more intimate detail, the effects of, and sometimes the reasons for, the delimitation of the boundaries of different zones. Taken together with the chapter on western termini, they provide a picture of a regional rate structure which is of great interest to the people of the West.

CHAPTER VII

Class Rate Levels

WE MAY NOW proceed from the description of transcontinental rate structures to a discussion of the levels at which these structures are maintained. Class rates and commodity rates are to be distinguished in this analysis.

Before we can discuss class rate levels intelligently, some explanation must be provided for what are known as "rate territories." In the present sense, the phrase does not refer to rate zones or groups, such as those which characterize the transcontinental class rate structure, or to areas organized primarily for the purpose of tariff publication. They are formal divisions, constantly referred to in rate proceedings, and convenient in the examination and regulation of railroad rates in the United States.

Class rate territories are useful in rate comparisons, partly because statistics published by the Interstate Commerce Commission are divided into groups which can be reconciled, at least, with the Eastern and Southern territories outlined on the map (map 28) and, by exclusion, with a group comprising the rest of the country. Moreover, the Interstate Commerce Commission has prescribed separate class scales, which can be easily compared, to apply in each of the geographic territories. We shall make use of the territories and of the Commission scales in the discussion which follows. The purpose, of course, will be to obtain some general impression of the relative level of railroad class rates as they may affect the West.

Routine statistics compiled by the Interstate Commerce Commission include figures of average receipts per ton per mile for the Eastern, Southern, and Western districts of the United States, and the Western District in these tables covers Western Trunk Line, Southwestern, and Mountain-Pacific territories substantially as defined above. The commission averages are as shown in the accompanying table (table 15).

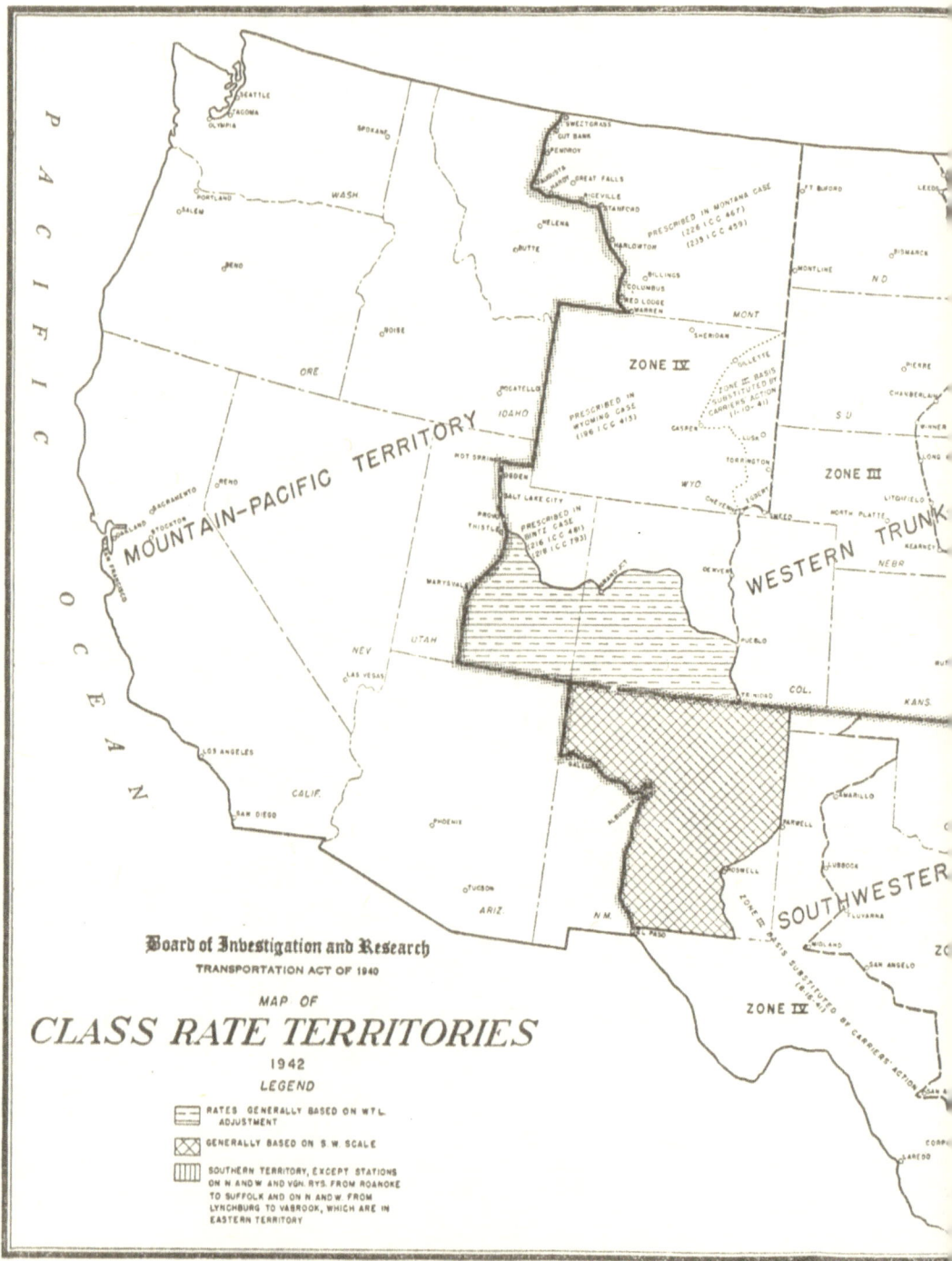

CLASS RATE LEVELS

The general conclusion on the basis of the preceding figures is that average receipts per ton per mile in the Western District are much higher than those in the Southern District and somewhat higher than the average of the United States as a whole. They were, however, lower than the average receipts in the Eastern District for two years. But these statistics are defective for comparative purposes, principally because they do not distinguish freight moving on class rates from that moving on commodity rates, and also because they

TABLE 15
AVERAGE REVENUE PER TON-MILE, CLASS I RAILROADS, BY DISTRICTS

Year ending	All districts	Eastern District	Southern District	Western District
	cents	cents	cents	cents
December 31, 1939........	0.973	1.007	0.839	1.021
December 31, 1940........	.945	0.994	.805	0.982
December 31, 1941........	.935	.989	.819	.946
December 31, 1942........	.932	.948	.848	.961
December 31, 1943........	0.933	0.941	0.853	0.966

SOURCE: United States, Interstate Commerce Commission, *Statistics of Railways in the United States*.

ignore differences in the character of goods handled in the different areas and differences in the average distances over which consignments move.

The Tennessee Valley Authority has examined the level of class rates within Official territory, and, for comparative purposes, the level of rates to Official territory from Canadian, Southern, Western Trunk Line, and Southwestern points of origin. It finds that the average first-class scales so compared bear the percentage relations to first-class rate levels within Official territory shown in table 16.

The rates studied by the Tennessee Valley Authority are interterritorial rates, requiring the use of more than one class rate scale for each percentage except the first. This means that the figures used in computing relative levels are estimates based upon the assumption that distances traveled are, on the average, equally divided between Official territory and the territory in which the movement starts. Comparisons cover hauls which range in length from 200 to 1,500 miles. Transcontinental rates are not represented in the table.

Besides the foregoing, we have data on comparative class rates in different territories which the Board of Investigation and Research, Transportation Act of 1940, has compiled. This Board gath-

TABLE 16
RELATIVE AVERAGE LEVELS OF FIRST-CLASS SCALES
(Rates within Official territory = 100)

Territory	Percentage relation to Official territory
Official only	100
Canadian–Official	110
Southern–Official	135
Western Trunk Line–Official	137
Southwestern–Official	149

SOURCE: Tennessee Valley Authority, *Supplemental Phases of the Interterritorial Freight Rate Problem of the United States*, 76 Cong., 1st Sess., House Doc. 271, 1939, Serial 10338, p. 7.

TABLE 17
PERCENTAGE RELATION OF FIRST-CLASS SCALES, BY TERRITORIES

Eastern	100.0
Southern	138.5
Western Trunk Line, zone I	128.4
Western Trunk Line, zone II	146.0
Western Trunk Line, zone III and Southwestern	160.6
Western Trunk Line, zone IV	184.2
Mountain-Pacific	165.5

SOURCE: Board of Investigation and Research, Transportation Act of 1940, *Report on Interterritorial Freight Rates*, 1943, p. 24. The Board arrives at relationships by totaling rates in each scale at intervals of twenty-five miles and by subsequent comparison of totals. Western Trunk Line, zone IV, has been abolished since the Board's report. The relationships calculated are those on hauls up to 1,000 miles.

ered information and reached conclusions both with respect to rates within and with respect to rates between the major territories outlined on our map 28. Since the Board's investigation is the most elaborate yet published, we may consider it more carefully than our other figures or calculations.

The foundation of the Board's conclusions is to be found in its comparison of scales prescribed by the Interstate Commerce Commission for use in the different rate territories. The Board assumes that rates charged everywhere are the same as rates prescribed. On this basis, it finds that the average relations of class rates to rates charged in Eastern or Official territory are, for other areas, as shown in table 17.

The printed table indicates that the highest levels of first-class rates prescribed by the Interstate Commerce Commission are to be found in zones III and IV of Western Trunk Line territory and in Mountain-Pacific territory. These are intraterritorial rates. In discussing interterritorial rates the Board makes the reasonable generalization that these rates represent a blending of levels in origin and destination territories, although there is a tendency for them to be higher than the proportion of mileage in each territory would justify.[1]

Class rates when so summarized should be relatively high in the West, and the class rates from South Coast territory to the transcontinental groups should also be high because the movement is, characteristically, from and through high rate areas; but no findings are made upon these facts.[2]

The Board publishes, also, with special reference to interterri-

[1] Board of Investigation and Research, Transportation Act of 1940, *Report on Interterritorial Freight Rates*, 1943, p. 241.

[2] It should be remembered that the Mountain-Pacific scale which the Board of Investigation and Research uses for purposes of illustration is not, as are the other scales referred to, prescribed for general application in the area.

Among the more important of the Commission decisions fixing class rates in Mountain-Pacific territory are the following:

1. Portland Chamber of Commerce v. Oregon Railway and Navigation Company (21 I.C.C. 640, 1911). An abbreviated scale was prescribed in this case to apply from Tacoma and Seattle, and from Portland to points in Washington, Oregon, Idaho, and Montana.

2. Arizona Corporation Commission v. Arizona Eastern Railroad Company (113 I.C.C. 52, 1926; 142 I.C.C. 61, 1928). The rates here involved were those between points in Arizona and points in California, New Mexico, and Texas. The Commission prescribed a scale on a substantially higher level and with smaller blocks than those used in the Portland case but with a similar over-all rate of progression.

3. Utah Shippers' Traffic Association v. Atchison, Topeka and Santa Fe Railway Company (172 I.C.C. 306, 1931). In this case the Commission established a class mileage scale for distances up to 1,500 miles between Utah common points on the one hand and, on the other, El Paso and points on the Southern Pacific and Santa Fe in New Mexico and Arizona and in California east of Colton and Daggett. This is generally referred to as the "Mountain-Pacific scale." It was substantially the scale used in the Arizona case, extended and modified by reducing the rate of progression for distances over 800 miles.

The class scales set up in the preceding cases have been applied more or less exactly in a number of other Mountain-Pacific cases, but the entire district is not yet covered. Meanwhile, transcontinental rates have been the subject of repeated discussion, but no mileage scales for this traffic have been laid down.

TABLE 18
INTERTERRITORIAL FIRST-CLASS RATES—COMPARISON OF RATES BETWEEN POINTS IN DESIGNATED TERRITORIES WITH RATES BETWEEN SAN FRANCISCO AND STATED DESTINATIONS
(In cents per 100 pounds)

Territories	Distance	First-class rate
	miles	*cents*
Eastern and Southern:		
Augusta, Ga., to Baltimore	604	165
Augusta, Ga., to New York	789	180
Augusta, Ga., to Rochester, N. Y.	951	209
Eastern and Western Trunk Line:		
Minneapolis to Detroit	601	164
Minneapolis to Cleveland	721	183
Minneapolis to Syracuse	936	209
Minneapolis to Boston	1,267	250
Eastern, Southern, and Southwestern:		
San Antonio to Birmingham	868	246
San Antonio to Atlanta	1,034	272
San Antonio to Chicago	1,179	283
San Antonio to Cleveland	1,384	308
San Antonio to New York	1,896	368
Transcontinental:		
San Francisco to Wells, Nev.	610	189
San Francisco to Ogden	786	238
San Francisco to Castle Rock, Utah	842	270
San Francisco to Church Buttes, Wyo.	920	297
San Francisco to Latham, Wyo.	1,063	341
San Francisco to Laramie, Wyo.	1,213	385
San Francisco to Fulton, Ill.	2,130	545

torial movements, a number of selected rates between points of origin and destination in the United States which lie in different territories. Extracts from this tabulation, with the addition of rates drawn from the transcontinental tariff, are assembled in table 18.

Finally, the Interstate Commerce Commission, in its decision in the class-rate investigation of 1945, compares first-class rates in the different territories as shown in table 19.

The accompanying tables and the information on preceding pages throw some light on the comparative levels of class rates in the Western and other territories of the United States. They do not, however, adequately cover Mountain-Pacific territory, and they do not men-

CLASS RATE LEVELS

TABLE 19
INTRATERRITORIAL FIRST-CLASS RATES—COMPARISON OF RATES IN EASTERN, SOUTHERN, AND WESTERN TRUNK-LINE SCALES
(In cents per 100 pounds)

Distance	Eastern scale	Modified Southern scale	Western Trunk Line scale		
			Zone I	Zone II	Zone III
miles	cents	cents	cents	cents	cents
50	47	57	53	61	65
300	96	134	117	134	147
500	122	173	156	178	196
700	149	206	196	222	244
900	171	235	226	256	282
1,000	182	249	240	273	300

SOURCE: 262 I.C.C. 447, 569, 1945.

TABLE 20
COMPARISON OF FIRST-CLASS RATES IN CALIFORNIA WITH RATES PROVIDED IN OTHER SCALES
(In cents per 100 pounds)

Point of origin: Colorado, California

Destination	Distance	California Intrastate scale[a]	Mountain-Pacific scale	Eastern scale	Southern scale	Western Trunk Line scales		
						Zone I	Zone II	Zone III
	miles	cents	cents	cents	cents	cents	cents	cents
Los Angeles	250	50	124	90	125	109	125	138
Kingsburg	507	79	205	124	176	161	183	201
Marysville	750	112½	271	155	216	205	232	256
Mount Shasta	938	146	318	176	242	233	265	292

[a] California rates, in the text table, are those quoted on carloads, minimum of 20,000 pounds. Smaller shipments take higher rates, as high as double those shown here.

tion the precise subject of transcontinental rates, except as additions have been supplied. Certain statements can, nevertheless, be made with reference to transcontinental charges which are based upon the examination and comparison of local and transcontinental tariffs and of other scales. These statements supplement the statistics just referred to. They are, in succession, as follows:

1. Class rates in California, on intrastate shipments, are relatively low, with whatever movements they are compared. Evidence of this may be found in table 20.

It is obvious from the table that the first-class rates applied to shipments in California are moderate compared with those in other, designated, scales. They are, as a matter of fact, lower than the minimum class rates set up by the Interstate Commerce Commission in 1945.[3]

TABLE 21

COMPARISON OF EFFECTIVE FIRST-CLASS RATES ON THE CENTRAL TRANSCONTINENTAL ROUTE WITH RATES IN SELECTED SCALES

(In cents per 100 pounds)

Destination	Distance	Effective rate	Mountain-Pacific scale	Southern K-2 scale	Eastern scale	Western Trunk Line scales		
						Zone I	Zone II	Zone III
	miles	*cents*	*cents*	*cents*	*cents*	*cents*	*cents*	*cents*
Sacramento, Calif...	92	28½	77	77	61	72	81	88
Truckee, Calif......	211	47½	118	117	84	101	116	128
Lovelock, Nev......	347	113	160	147	103	130	147	163
Winnemucca, Nev..	420	140	176	160	111	141	161	177
Elko, Nev..........	553	174	217	183	130	168	191	211
Ogden, Utah.......	786	238	281	222	160	210	239	263

Point of origin, San Francisco

SOURCE: Board of Investigation and Research, Transportation Act of 1940, *Report on Interterritorial Freight Rates*, 1943, pp. 22–23.

2. Transcontinental class rates between California and eastern points are relatively low in the shorter distances.

Table 21 contrasts effective rates collected on shipments consigned from California to main-line points between San Francisco and Ogden with rates which would be charged under certain other scales cited by the Interstate Commerce Commission and by the Board of Investigation and Research.

The table shows that rates from San Francisco along the central route[4] are lower than those provided in any of the quoted scales, so long as the shipments remain in California; that they are lower than those in any scale except the Eastern scale, as far as Winnemucca;

[3] 262 I.C.C. 447, 704, 1945. The minimum class-rate scale in the Commission's order in this case included the following minimum first-class rates: 240 miles, 98 cents per 100 pounds; 260 miles, 102 cents; 500 miles, 140 cents; 740 miles, 176 cents; 925 miles, 203 cents.

[4] The term "central route" refers to the route from San Francisco via Ogden over the Southern Pacific. The rate used requires a minimum of 20,000 pounds to California and Nevada destinations.

and that they approximate the rates of Western Trunk Line scale II to Ogden, a point on the eastern edge of the Mountain-Pacific group. The comparison is here based on one route only, but rates from San Francisco over the central route are not low in comparison with rates along the southern and northern routes.

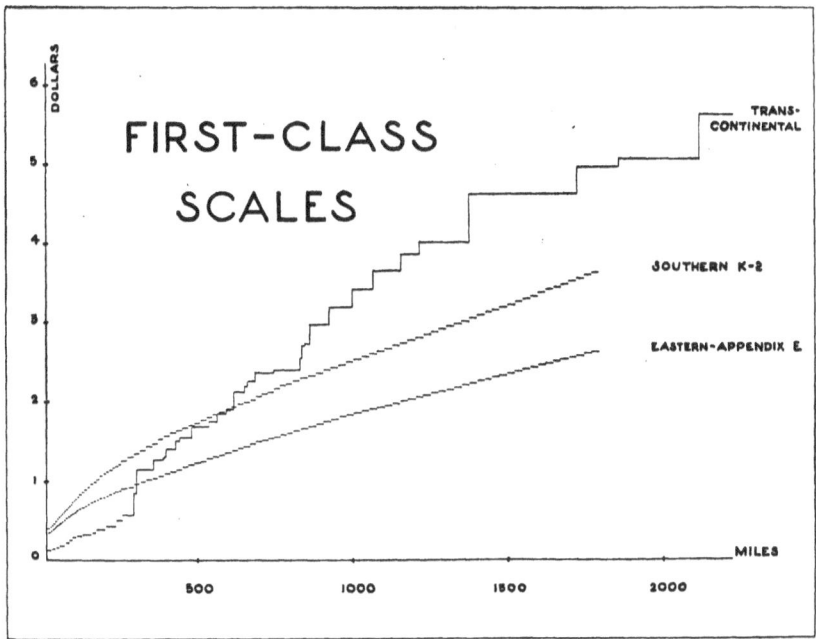

Chart 17. First-Class scales, Transcontinental, Southern, and Eastern, 1942.

3. Transcontinental class rates from California are relatively high on the middle-distance and long-distance hauls, especially after 750 or 800 miles. This fact can be conveniently shown in two charts.

The first of these (chart 17) compares the transcontinental first-class rates with rates according to the Southern and Eastern scales.[5] It shows that the transcontinental rate is low at the beginning, but that it is higher than the Southern scale for distances above 610 miles and higher than the Eastern rates for indicated distances above 291 miles.

[5] Changes ordered in the class-rate investigation of 1945 are not included.

The second chart (chart 18) compares the transcontinental rate, first-class, with rates under the various Western Trunk Line scales before the adjustment in 1945.

The conclusions to be drawn from the second chart are similar to those expressed in the first. High as the Western Trunk Line scales

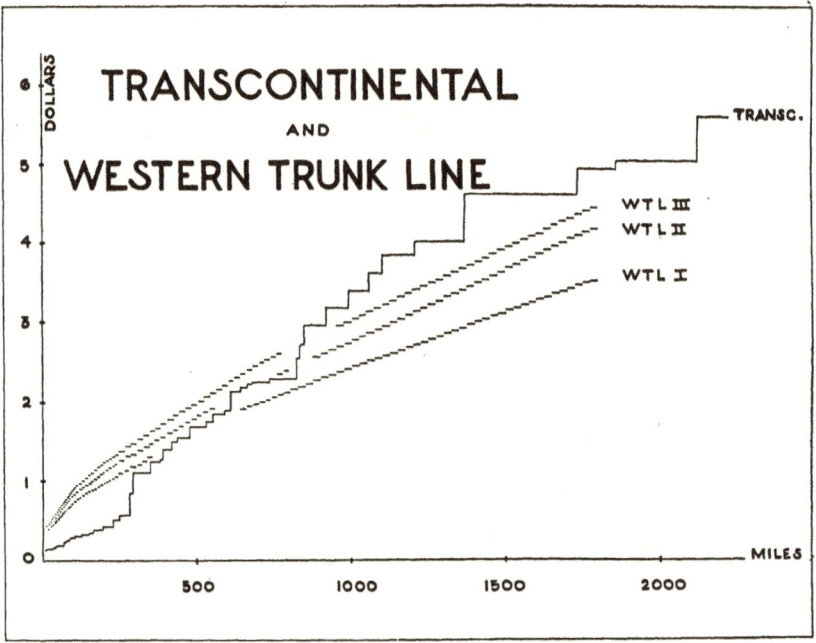

Chart 18. Transcontinental and Western Trunk Line scales, 1942.

are, the transcontinental scale climbs above them at distances ranging between 410 and 840 miles. For short distances, however, transcontinental rates are relatively low, and on very long hauls they again become lower than Western Trunk Line scales II and III because the progression of the transcontinental charge at extreme distances is very slow.

CHAPTER VIII

Commodity Rate Levels

COMMODITY rate levels for shipments between South Coast termini and eastern points are more difficult to discuss than are class rate levels, because of the greater number of tariffs and the independence of the different scales. Commodity rate structures, moreover, more than class rate structures, assume eccentric relationships. It is probably impossible, for these reasons, to reach conclusions which are not subject to important exceptions with respect to the relative level of commodity rates in different areas. The observations in this chapter are offered therefore, with reserve, although they are based upon samplings which are believed to be significant, and some of them refer to official reports.

Distance considered, most commodity rates upon exports of California specialties are moderate, and over the longer distances they are often low compared with rates per mile on movements of the same commodities elsewhere in the country, or with percentages of first class which the Interstate Commerce Commission has, in the past, suggested as reasonable for those commodities.

Table 22 sets forth the rates, in cents per hundred pounds per mile, charged on eastward movements of certain of these California specialties.

On the central route from California through Ogden, 1,250 miles carries into Wyoming; 2,000 miles, into eastern Iowa; and 3,000 miles, into New York and Pennsylvania. In the last two areas, representing the Mississippi Valley and the Atlantic Coast, western producers and carriers meet market, water, and truck competition to which they must adjust themselves.

The principal carrier competition for canned goods shipped from California is that between railroads and intercoastal carriers. Prior to 1927 the rates from Pacific Coast territory to transcontinental groups A to N was 105 cents per 100 pounds on a minimum of

60,000 pounds, except to Colorado common points, to which the charge was 98 cents, and 128 cents on a minimum of 40,000 pounds. The 105 cent rate was blanketed back to a line drawn roughly through eastern Montana, western Wyoming, and central Utah and Arizona. These rates did not apply to canned fish, for which the tariff provided 80 cents on a minimum of 77,000 pounds and 95 cents on a minimum of 70,000 pounds.

TABLE 22

RATES PER MILE ON TRANSCONTINENTAL SHIPMENTS, EASTBOUND
(In cents per 100 pounds)

Commodity	Route[a]	Rate per mile		
		1,250 miles	2,000 miles	3,000 miles
		cents	cents	cents
Canned goods	1	0.055	0.044	0.034
Citrus	2	.074	.066	.045
Fresh grapes	3	.096	.075	.050
Lettuce	4	.088	.072	.061
Dried fruit	5	.080	.061	.040
Wine	6	.079	.050	0.033
Sugar	7	0.064	0.040	.....

[a] Numbers in the route column signify the following:
1. San Francisco to New York via Southern Pacific, Union Pacific, Chicago and Northwestern, Elgin, Joliet and Eastern, Pennsylvania.
2. Los Angeles to New York via Union Pacific, Chicago and Northwestern, Elgin, Joliet and Eastern, Erie.
3. Stockton to New York via Southern Pacific, Union Pacific, Chicago and Northwestern, Elgin, Joliet and Eastern, Erie.
4. Salinas to New York via Southern Pacific, Union Pacific, Chicago and Northwestern, Elgin, Joliet and Eastern, Erie.
5. Fresno to New York via Southern Pacific, Union Pacific, Chicago and Northwestern, Elgin, Joliet and Eastern, Pennsylvania.
6. Fresno to New York via Southern Pacific, Union Pacific, Chicago and Northwestern, Elgin, Joliet and Eastern, Pennsylvania.
7. Crockett to Chicago via Southern Pacific, Union Pacific, Chicago and Northwestern.

In 1927, rail carriers proposed to reduce the 105 cent charge to 90 cents on shipments from Pacific Coast points to groups B to J, inclusive, group N, and to portions of group M. This was in order to check an increasing diversion of traffic to the water lines.[1]

The intercoastal water rate at this time was 45 cents, and it was asserted that shipments moving through the Panama Canal to the Atlantic seaboard were competing with all-rail shipments at destinations within 275 miles of Chicago. Water carriers objected to the cut, on the ground that 90 cents was less than a reasonable maximum for the transportation of Pacific Coast canned goods to eastern defined

[1] It was not intended to change the 128 cent rate on the minimum of 40,000 pounds.

COMMODITY RATE LEVELS 119

territories. The Interstate Commerce Commission ruled that 90 cents was, in fact, too little, but that 98 cents might be allowed. As a result, the railroads let the old rates stand.

Four years later, in 1932, rail carriers again appeared before the Commission. This time they asked permission to reduce the 105 cent rate, on a minimum of 60,000 pounds, to 90 cents per 100 pounds, and the 128 cent rate, on a minimum of 40,000 pounds, to 105 cents. The destinations indicated were transcontinental groups B to J inclusive. Rates on canned fish were to be left unchanged. Canned goods at this time were reaching Chicago by ship, barge, and rail via New Orleans at a cost of 87 cents from San Francisco, and combined water-rail rates via Atlantic ports were lower than transcontinental all-rail charges to destinations as far from the East Coast as Pittsburgh. The Interstate Commerce Commission still entertained doubts in the matter, but it now reasoned that the carriers could cover their out-of-pocket costs on a rate of 90 cents, that shippers were interested in the proposed reduction, and that the railroads should be allowed to go ahead. Commissioner Eastman dissented, on the ground that the new rates from the Pacific Coast to the considered destinations would be relatively much lower than rates from Atlantic and Gulf ports.[2] This is the recent history of transcontinental charges on canned goods.

The present rate from San Francisco to Chicago is 88 cents on a minimum of 60,000 pounds. This is slightly lower than the rate which the Commission condemned as too low in 1927 and reluctantly permitted in 1932. Reference to the eastbound groups outlined in chapter iv will show rates of 96 cents and 102 cents to points in Ohio and in the Northeast, or to groups B and A of the transcontinental tariff. So far as group B is concerned, this represents a slight increase over the rates of 1932; for most destinations in the West the current tariff constitutes a slight decrease.

There is not much doubt that transcontinental rates per mile on canned goods are low. It is not so certain that the canned-goods schedule from intermediate territory is lower than elsewhere, but, at least, the Interstate Commerce Commission examiner who exam-

---
[2] 188 I.C.C. 687, 1932. All rail rates on canned goods from North Atlantic ports were then, generally, 30 per cent of first class.

ined certain of these schedules in 1944 proposed only a temporary correction. With respect to rates in the Utah area, the examiner reached two conclusions. The first was that canned-goods rates from points in Utah were absolutely reasonable. This was because rates from Utah origins to destinations in transcontinental groups A, B, and C were 28½ per cent of first-class rates, whereas the Commission had frequently approved rates equivalent to 35 per cent of first class as reasonable. The second conclusion was that canned-goods rates out of Utah were, temporarily, comparatively unreasonable. The examiner's recommendation was that, until effective water competition should be resumed, rates from the Utah points of origin concerned in the case before him should be less than rates from the Pacific Coast by 11 cents to destinations in group A and by 10 cents to destinations in groups B and C.[3]

Rates on dried fruits and vegetables are also affected by carrier competition. Much of this traffic, as of canned goods, is carried by water to Gulf and Atlantic ports and thence transported by rail, barge, or motor truck to interior destinations.[4]

Competition between the direct rail lines and the combined facilities of the other agencies explains both the low rail rate on dried fruits and vegetables and the broad blanket in this rate structure described in chapter iv. The actual rate of 121 cents to New York is higher than the 88 cents charged on canned goods, and the divisions accruing to eastern carriers are presumably also greater, but the rate is still low, compared with the percentages of 32.5 and 27.5 of first class, which the Interstate Commerce Commission has referred to as reasonable from time to time in various other sections of the country.[5]

The rates on citrus are limited both by carrier and by producer competition. In a leading case in 1928, the Interstate Commerce Commission concluded that the rates on oranges from Florida to destinations in the North, West, and in Southern territory might properly be 40 per cent of the first-class rates.[6]

---

[3] Proposed report in No. 28665, E. R. Blackington and Son Cannery Co. v. Alton R.R., *Traffic World*, August 26, 1944. See also 253 I.C.C. 433, 1942.

[4] 216 I.C.C. 411, 1936; 237 I.C.C. 175, 1940.

[5] The percentages of 32.5 and 27.5 per cent of first class calculated on shipments from Fresno to New York would yield 199 and 168 cents, respectively.

[6] 144 I.C.C. 603, 1928.

This was a reduction which improved the position of the Florida producers in their competition with growers in California, as the California rates were not, at this time, altered. Subsequently, moreover, the development of truck-water transport between Florida and northeastern markets compelled the eastern carriers to lower their charges by additional amounts to a level which had not previously been anticipated.[7]

By 1938 the rate on oranges from Orlando, Florida, to New York had become 64.5 cents for a haul of 1,153 miles, as compared with a rate of 99 cents from Arcadia to New York in 1928 for a distance of 1,259 miles. These and other changes approved in 1938 constituted an over-all cut of approximately 37 per cent.[8]

Transcontinental rates on citrus are to be viewed in the light of this eastern competitive situation. In 1928 the transcontinental charge for the transportation of oranges was 159 cents from Los Angeles to New York (3,129 miles) and 155 cents to Chicago (2,231 miles). The present rates are 135 cents to New York and 131 cents to Chicago, or 0.043 and 0.059 cents per mile, respectively, on the distances given. The rates from Orlando to the same destinations are 62.55 cents and 84 cents, or 0.056 and 0.070 cents per mile.[9] Forty per cent of the first-class rates from Los Angeles—the basis approved by the Interstate Commerce Commission in 1928—would be 244 cents from Los Angeles to New York and 224 cents to Chicago. The Commission observed in 1928 that the history of the California rates up to that time indicated the desire of the transcontinental carriers to enable the California growers to market their crops in the large eastern seaboard cities in competition with fruit from Florida and from foreign countries, rather than attempt to hold the rates at a level of maximum reasonableness for the transportation service performed.[10] This policy appears still to influence the level of the transcontinental charge.

Sugar rates, even more than citrus rates, are competitive to destinations in the Mississippi Valley.[11]

---

[7] 211 I.C.C. 535, 1935.
[8] 226 I.C.C. 315, 1938.
[9] On distances supplied by carrier.
[10] 144 I.C.C. 603, 1928.
[11] The Interstate Commerce Commission remarked in 1937 that practically all existing rates on sugar within the United States were determined mainly by carrier competition. (220 I.C.C. 623, 642, 1937.) This was an overstatement, but it probably expresses the facts.

In 1933, in comprehensive proceedings, the Interstate Commerce Commission approved rates of 39 cents from New Orleans to Chicago (921 miles) on a 60,000 pound minimum and 34 cents on an 80,000 pound minimum to enable the north-and-south railroads to meet the competition of Mississippi River barge lines. At the same time, the Commission allowed a rate of 42 cents from New York to Chicago, which was 27.5 per cent of first class, and a 65 cent rate from California to Chicago on a minimum of 80,000 pounds. This last rate was a reduction from the 86 cents previously charged. On business from California, relief from requirements of Section 4 was granted, permitting carriers to charge less for longer than for shorter hauls. One member of the Commission protested that the California-to-Chicago rate was too low.[12]

In 1935, on showing that the percentage of eastbound sugar moving from California by rail was declining as compared with that handled by the ships, the Interstate Commerce Commission authorized a rate of 60 cents on an 80,000 minimum and 65 cents on a minimum of 60,000 pounds from San Francisco, Crockett, Oakland, Stockton, and Los Angeles to Chicago, with higher rates to intermediate points.[13] There was some question of whether or not these rates were compensatory, and the evidence was discussed in the Commission's report.

The present charge from San Francisco to Chicago is 70 cents on a minimum carload of 80,000 pounds, which represents a slight increase above the 1935 levels.

The rates quoted are to competitive territory, and they are evidently low by comparison both with transcontinental rates on other commodities and with the Commission's findings of reasonableness in other areas. The Interstate Commerce Commission has fixed sugar rates in different parts of the United States, at various times, at levels corresponding to from 20 per cent to 30 per cent of the first-class rates. The lowest Chicago rates on this basis would be 112 cents, and the highest 168 cents, or more than twice the amount that the carriers collect.

---

in Eastern and in Southern territories. The records of the Commission are full of rate proceedings in which carrier and market competition in these areas have been explained.

[12] *Sugar Cases of 1933*, 195 I.C.C., 127, 1933.

[13] *Sugar from California to Chicago*, 211 I.C.C. 239, 1935.

COMMODITY RATE LEVELS 123

It should be added, however, that rates to interior destinations are relatively, and often absolutely, much higher than rates from California to Illinois. The reader is referred on this point to map 14 in chapter iv (p. 67). To cite but one example, the present rate from San Francisco to Ogden is 77 cents, which is approximately 30 per cent of the first-class rate of 238 cents, or the highest standard which the Commission has approved.[14]

In wine shipments, the competition is both between eastern and western producers in Middle Western markets and between rail and steamship lines on transcontinental hauls. The extensive character of the eastern rate blanket for wine shipments was mentioned in chapter iv. On the problem of the level of the rate, we have two recent decisions of the Interstate Commerce Commission.

In the first of these cases, complainant sought a reduction in the tank-car rate eastbound. The charges on shipments of eastbound wine were then 115 cents on wine in glass, earthenware, or metal cans, boxed, minimum 30,000 pounds; 90 cents on wine in bulk, in barrels, minimum 50,000 pounds; and 105 cents on wine in tank cars, to each of which charges were added 3 cents of emergency charges. The Commission refused to lower the tank-car rate to the level of barrel charge.[15]

The complainant in the second case was a producer in Brooklyn, New York, who desired lower westbound rates on shipments to the Pacific Coast. The commodity westbound rate, then as now, was 208 cents. The present eastbound rates of 99 cents (minimum 50,000 pounds), 116 cents (minimum 40,000 pounds), 124 cents (minimum 30,000 pounds), and 116 cents (tank-car rate) were in effect. The petitioner sought a parity in eastbound and westbound rates. The Commission did not issue the requested order. It was the view of the Commission that the eastbound rail rates on wine were depressed below a reasonable maximum basis because of the keen com-

[14] The present rates to Ogden have Commission approval. In 1937, Division 3 of the Commission refused to reduce rates on sugar from San Francisco to Elko, Nevada, to the level of 30 per cent of the first-class rate, or 59 cents. (222 I.C.C. 701, 1937). The Division held that the existing rate of 61½ cents had not been shown to be unreasonable. The following year, however, the Commission reversed Division 3, declaring that 59 cents to Elko and 76½ cents to Salt Lake City and to Ogden (757 miles) was the most that should be charged. (227 I.C.C. 162, 1938.) The effect of this was to approve a 77 cent rate to Ogden.
[15] Black v. Alton, 222 I.C.C., 647, 1937.

petition between rail and water carriers for the substantial tonnage which moved eastbound.[16]

The preceding pages summarize transcontinental eastbound rates on canned goods, dried fruits and vegetables, citrus, sugar, and wine—all commodities on which carrier and producer competition is severe. Conditions with respect to the remaining items on our list are somewhat different, although the rates charged for their transportation need not, for this reason, be regarded as high.

Lettuce is one of these remaining items. It is inserted in the list of commodities which move eastbound in order to illustrate rates on fresh vegetables. Reference to table 23 will show that the average rates per mile charged on lettuce shipments to distances of 1,250, 2,000, and 3,000 miles are higher than the average rates applied to other eastbound movements which we have so far considered.

Not enough information is available in records used for this study to permit a confident characterization of the lettuce rate. Rates on lettuce have, however, been considered by the Interstate Commerce Commission, notably in the Southeastern[17] and in the Southwestern Vegetable[18] Cases. Far Western vegetable rates were also discussed in Pacific Coast Vegetable Growers v. Southern Pacific.[19] In both of the major cases the Commission concluded that vegetable rates could properly be set up as percentages of the first-class rate. The approved ratios varied with different types of products, but for lettuce the Commission set a maximum of 45 per cent of the first-class rate in both the Southeast and the Southwest. Table 23 compares the Southeastern lettuce rate, so calculated, with 45 per cent of first-class rates over the central route published in the transcontinental tariff, and with transcontinental rates on lettuce which are actually charged.

Rates on lettuce from California are lower than maximum rates—

[16] The Commission remarked: "The rate of $2.08, minimum 30,000 pounds, from New York City to Los Angeles, 2,964 miles, all-rail, yields $624 per car, 21 cents per car-mile, and 14 mills per ton-mile. These earnings are not excessive. In the opposite direction, the joint all-rail rate of $1.24, minimum 30,000 pounds, produces $372 per car, 12.6 cents per car-mile, and 8.4 mills per ton-mile. Similarly, the eastbound joint all-rail rates of 99 cents, minimum 50,000 pounds, and $1.16, minimum 40,000 pounds, result in revenues of $495 and $464 per car, 16.7 and 15.7 cents per car-mile, and 6.7 and 7.8 mills per ton-mile, respectively." (245 I.C.C. 441, 444, 1941.)

[17] 200 I.C.C. 273, 1934.
[18] 200 I.C.C. 355, 1934.
[19] 185 I.C.C. 689, 1932.

i.e., 45 per cent of first class—approved for the Southeast and the Southwest for equivalent distances. Moreover, in 1932, rates on lettuce from California and Arizona of 175 cents to New York and 146 cents to Chicago were found reasonable over the objections of the

TABLE 23

Maximum Lettuce Rates on Basis Approved by the Interstate Commerce Commission, Compared with Effective Rates

(In cents per 100 pounds)

Distance	Forty-five per cent of first-class rates under Southeastern scale	Forty-five per cent of first-class rates from Salinas over central route	Effective rate on lettuce from Salinas over central route
miles	*cents*	*cents*	*cents*
100	35.6	28.8	12.0
250	56.3	46.8	26.5
500	77.9	90.0	65.0
750	97.2	121.5	65.0
1,000	112.1	151.7	70.0
1,250	127.8	180.9	110.0
1,500	143.6	207.9	120.0
1,750	159.8	207.9	135.0
2,000	175.5	245.3	143.0
2,250	190.8	252.5	143.0
2,500	205.7	260.1	173.0

Pacific Coast Vegetable Growers and Shippers Transportation Committee.[20] The present rates are 184 and 143 cents.[21]

Grapes are included in the tariff list of fresh deciduous fruits. In 1927 the rates on fresh deciduous fruits, including grapes, was 173 cents on shipments from California to transcontinental groups A to M inclusive, except to group J, and 162 cents to group J. The minimum was 26,000 pounds. Shippers requested a rate of 144 cents. The Interstate Commerce Commission discussed the complaint at length and ordered rates of 160 cents and 150 cents to be substituted for the charges of 173 and 162 cents. Reference was made, in the

[20] 185 I.C.C. 689, 1932.

[21] Special problems other than those related to the reasonableness of rates are the treatment of competitors in Idaho, Colorado, Oregon, Texas, and other states, estimated and minimum weights, containers, refrigeration, and running time. The relations of Phoenix and the Imperial Valley to central California in the marketing of lettuce have been indicated. On a commodity such as lettuce the quality of the service rendered is, of course, of more than usual importance.

decision, to the "Hoch-Smith" resolution.[22] On appeal to the courts, the Commission order was reversed on the ground that the Hoch-Smith resolution had not introduced, as the Commission had supposed, any new factor in the fixing and adjustment of rates.[23] In 1932, on rehearing and further elaborate consideration of the applications referred to in the preceding paragraph, the Commission held that the 173 cent rate was reasonable. All reference to the Hoch-Smith resolution was now excluded from the case.[24]

In 1936, carriers voluntarily reduced the 173 cent charge to 155 cents with a minimum of 27,500 pounds to Eastern territory, and a minimum of 26,000 pounds to Chicago and points west. They also agreed to publish an alternative rate of 143 cents with a minimum of 34,000 pounds. Subsequently, in 1938, as a result of authorized general rate increases, the 143 cent rate became 155 cents and the 155 cent rate became 163 cents. These are the present rates out of California, except that to groups F and I a rate of 140 cents is now applied with a minimum of 26,000 pounds.

It seems clear enough, in the light of comment and analysis by the Interstate Commerce Commission, that eastbound rates on the major products which California ships to eastern states are, generally, low. In some cases it has even been questioned if these rates covered the carriers' out-of-pocket costs.

Let us now turn to a discussion of rates other than those on the exports of California. These rates are, characteristically, either westbound rates on manufactured goods shipped to the Pacific Coast or outbound rates on the same articles from California cities. Charges like these have not been before the Interstate Commerce Commission to the same degree as rates on eastbound movements, because the categories are more numerous and, individually, less important, and because shippers are less well organized. The absolute and, in some relations, the relative levels of the rates must, nevertheless, be examined.

The discussion which follows will consider westbound and western local rates from several points of view and will reach conclusions which will be as reliable as the small number of the situations studied and the uncertainties inherent in any comparisons will permit. Essen-

---

[22] 129 I.C.C. 25, 1927.   [23] 281 U.S. 658, 1930.   [24] 185 I.C.C. 299, 1932.

tially, the process will involve sampling, comparison, and suggestion, rather than dogmatic conclusions.

We may begin the discussion of westbound rates with a brief statement of rates per mile on westbound movements similar to that presented on page 118 for transcontinental shipments eastbound.

TABLE 24

RATES PER MILE ON TRANSCONTINENTAL SHIPMENTS, WESTBOUND

(In cents per 100 pounds)

Destination, San Francisco. Route, Pennsylvania–Elgin, Joliet and Eastern–Chicago and Northwestern–Union Pacific–Southern Pacific.

Commodity	Rate per mile		
	1,250 miles	2,000 miles	3,000 miles
	cents	cents	cents
Beverages	0.054	0.048	0.044
Automobile bodies and parts	.129	.084	.067
Canned goods	.062	.044	.034
Clothing	.187	.125	.102
Dry goods	.124	.087	.069
Fertilizers	.060	.038	No through rate
Steel	.068	.053	.048
Tin	.062	.039	.026
Vehicles, passenger	.340	.213	.167
Wine	0.084	0.091	0.069

Table 24 gives the rates charged for shipment of certain articles which move westward in considerable volume from Transcontinental Freight Bureau points of origin to destinations upon the South Coast.

Commodity rates per mile on westbound shipments of clothing and vehicles are higher at all the distances indicated than are commodity rates on Pacific Coast exports. The westbound rates per mile on wine and automobile bodies and parts are generally higher than those on eastbound agricultural movements. Westbound rates on beverages, canned goods, steel, and tin are relatively low. These facts are to be noticed; they doubtless mean little, however, because of the differences in the character of the movements for which the rates are charged. At least they indicate that, while some westbound rates are high, others, for one reason or another, are depressed to levels comparable with those of some eastbound rates.

The elements of a westbound rate structure in which the Pacific Coast is really interested are as follows.

From the point of view of the consumer it is desirable that westbound rates should be low. *Ceteris paribus,* low transportation rates may be correlated with low retail prices.

From the point of view of the western producer and distributor, three things are important:

In the first place, the distributor seeks low rates for short hauls out of coastal trading centers. Such rates protect him, in a measure, against direct less-than-carload shipments by eastern producers to scattered local markets, and they enable him, in any case, to distribute products, wherever produced, at an attractive delivered price.

Second, the western producer and distributor desire the advantage of what we may call low "middle-distance rates" because these rates expand his markets. In this, sparse population of the intermountain area makes eastward rates less significant than those to the Pacific Northwest.

Third, western interests demand a generally favorable relationship between westbound transcontinental rates from the Mississippi Valley and the Atlantic Coast and eastbound rates from Pacific termini. This they interpret as meaning equality of rates on manufactured products in both directions. As a minimum, western manufacturers expect eastbound rates per mile over long distances as over middle distances which are as low as rates charged per mile for carriage of similar articles westbound. For some traffic, moreover, they also desire rates to eastern points or areas which do not exceed the rates paid by eastern producers in shipping to those points or areas, whatever the relative distances may be. It is not clear, indeed, that equality in rates per mile would be of much service to the western manufacturer. It is probable, on the contrary, that if the Pacific Coast market is insufficiently broad to absorb the entire output of a manufacturer, the freight absorption which would be necessary in selling the balance of his production across the continent to other markets, most of which lie east of the Missouri River, is likely to be so large as to render profitable operation impossible. But this may not always be so. In the first approximation, at least, rates per mile on manufactured products which are higher eastbound than westbound do give the

TABLE 25
Short-Haul Rates from Atlanta, Dallas, Chicago, and Minneapolis
(In cents per 100 pounds)

Class or commodity	Atlanta to Charlotte, N. C. (259 mi.)	Dallas to Houston, Texas (250 mi.)	Chicago to Belle Plaine, Iowa (254 mi.)	Chicago to Dumas, Mo. (252 mi.)	Chicago to Toledo, Ohio (234 mi.)	Minneapolis to Venlo, N. D. (257 mi.)
	cents	cents	cents	cents	cents	cents
First class	125	135	110	99	87	130
Automobile bodies and parts	88	61	39	58	32	46
Beverages	23	25	22	22	24	26½
Canned goods	42	21	30	28	26	36
Clothing	88	115	39	69	74	91
Dry goods	88	70	39	50	87	60
Fertilizers	14	22	18	17	18	23
Steel articles	31	40	26	32	26	42
Tin cans	50	57	45	45	35	59
Vehicles, passenger	125	40	53	58	87	65
Wine	55	74	39	40	38	52

TABLE 26
Short-Haul Rates from San Francisco and Los Angeles
(In cents per 100 pounds)

Class or commodity	Intrastate			Interstate	
	San Francisco to Tulare (250 mi.)	San Francisco to Redding (236 mi.)	Los Angeles to Needles (308 mi.)	San Francisco to Fernley (279 mi.)	Los Angeles to Yuma (251 mi.)
	cents	cents	cents	cents	cents
First class[a]	47½	50	56	108	96
Automobile bodies and parts	31	32½	36½	36½	34
Beverages	20	22	33	33½	25
Canned goods	22	18	33	33½	25
Clothing	55	74	82	97	86
Dry goods	55	74	88	45	61
Fertilizers	15	16	18	22½	20
Steel articles	17	22	31	33½	15
Tin cans	37	40	43	43	38
Vehicles, passenger	96	100	108	74	61
Wine	15	35	39	39	39

[a] Minimum carload weight 20,000 pounds.

appearance of discouraging local manufacture. Absolute equality in eastbound and westbound rates would in any case be more satisfactory than equality in rates per mile, but also more difficult to obtain.

The rate relations mentioned will be dealt with in succeeding pages. It should be borne in mind that the particular commodities chosen for comparison in this discussion are those which move westward to California in volume. The rates on such westward-moving commodities, rather than those on traditional California specialties, may be the rates pertinent to the future economic development of the area.

Let us first consider in determining present facts the problem of short-haul distributing rates out of San Francisco and Los Angeles. The term "short haul" for the purpose of discussion here refers to transportation over a distance of approximately 250 miles. Comparisons which contrast rates out of San Francisco and Los Angeles for movements of about this length with charges for similar hauls from selected eastern cities appear in the following tables. Distances shown in the tables are by routes over which a reasonable share of traffic may be expected to move. These are not necessarily the shortest routes.

Table 25 presents the rates in cents per 100 pounds upon sample articles shipped from Atlanta, Dallas, Chicago, and Minneapolis, for distances of approximately 250 miles, which we have called short hauls.

Comparable rates on articles shipped from San Francisco and Los Angeles are as shown in table 26.

If the charges given in tables 25 and 26 are reduced to rates per mile, and if selected eastern and western interstate rates are compared with average short-haul intrastate rates per mile from San Francisco to Tulare and Redding and from Los Angeles to Needles, results are as shown in table 27, which suggests three conclusions:

1. By and large, California intrastate rates for hauls approximating 250 miles are lower than those for the selected movements in other sections of the country. This is not true for every commodity, but it is true, so far as the evidence on which the table is based is concerned, for most commodities in all sections and for all sections taken as a whole.

COMMODITY RATE LEVELS 131

2. The sections with which comparisons of California rates are made are related to these rates in the following order:

Origin and destination	Percentage of California intrastate rates per mile
Dallas to Houston	157
Atlanta to Charlotte	156
Minneapolis to Venlo	146
Chicago to Toledo	125
Chicago to Dumas	123
Chicago to Belle Plaine	111

3. Rates from San Francisco and Los Angeles to points just across the boundary in adjacent states are substantially higher than intrastate short-haul rates in California, but lower than other rates illustrated by the table except distributing rates out of the city of Chicago to points in Iowa. The relation of these rates to California intrastate rates is as follows:

Origin and destination	Percentage of California intrastate rates per mile
Los Angeles to Yuma	121
San Francisco to Fernley	119

TABLE 27
COMPARISON OF RATES ON SHORT HAULS
(Average of rates per mile from San Francisco to Tulare and to Redding, and from Los Angeles to Needles = 100)

Class or commodity	Atlanta to Charlotte	Dallas to Houston	Chicago to Belle Plaine	Chicago to Dumas	Chicago to Toledo	Minneapolis to Venlo	San Francisco to Fernley	Los Angeles to Yuma
First class	250	280	224	204	193	262	201	198
Automobile bodies and parts	270	194	122	183	109	142	104	107
Beverages	95	106	93	93	110	110	128	106
Canned goods	176	91	128	121	121	152	130	109
Clothing	128	173	58	103	119	133	131	129
Dry goods	125	103	56	73	136	85	59	89
Fertilizers	92	142	115	108	124	144	131	129
Steel articles	136	182	116	144	126	185	136	68
Tin cans	128	151	117	119	99	152	93	193
Vehicles, passenger	126	42	55	60	97	66	69	63
Wine	189	264	138	142	145	180	125	138
Arithmetic mean	156	157	111	123	125	146	119	121

132 TRANSCONTINENTAL RAILROAD RATES

Following the discussion of short-haul rates, we may consider rates for middle distances—from approximately 750 to approximately 1,000 miles.

On middle-distance hauls from California ports to ports of the Pacific Northwest, rates are relatively low.[25] The same relation does not, however, hold with respect to rates from California in other directions.

TABLE 28

MIDDLE-DISTANCE RATES FROM CHICAGO TO NAMED DESTINATIONS
(In cents per 100 pounds)

Class or commodity	Atlanta, Ga. (793 mi.)	Dallas, Texas (1,007 mi.)	Utica, N. Y. (724 mi.)	Venlo, N. D. (705 mi.)	Cheyenne, Wyo. (995 mi.)	Amarillo, Texas (1,010 mi.)	Minneapolis, Minn. (460 mi.)
	cents	cents	cents	cents	cents	cents	cents
First class	210	261	142	205	274	267	139
Automobile bodies and parts	147	91	53	72	96	93	49
Beverages	38	43	39	43	77	53	24
Canned goods	70	68	43	57	57	73	32
Clothing	147	183	121	130	128	187	97
Dry goods	147	136½	142	94	128	134	39
Fertilizers	31	43	32	36	48	44	24
Steel articles	64	85	45	67	89	87	33
Tin cans	84	136	71	92	149	125	39
Vehicles, passenger	210	184	142	141	192	216	86
Wine	116	104	62	82	110	107	39

Table 28 presents a series of middle-distance commodity rates, plus first-class rates, from Chicago to destinations in the East, South, Southwest, West, and Northwest. Chicago is, possibly, the most important railroad center in the United States, and rates on movements from this center outbound may serve as a standard by which the level of transcontinental rates over moderate distances can be measured.

The distances covered in table 28 range, as earlier indicated, from approximately 700 to approximately 1,000 miles, with one shorter haul included—that from Chicago to Minneapolis, 460 miles.

In comparison with these rates, table 29 shows rates from San Francisco, eastbound, over the Ogden route, and south and east over the Santa Fe.

[25] The general nature of these nonintermediate port-to-port rates has been indicated in earlier chapters. Because of the widespread authorization of nonintermediate rates, the pattern of rate progression is much less regular northward than eastward.

If we reduce middle-distance rates to rates per mile, as we did with short-haul charges, and compare the average per mile of rates from San Francisco to Promontory Point and Point of Rocks on the main line of the Southern Pacific and to Audley and Houck on the main line of the Santa Fe—stations distant, roughly, 750 to 1,000 miles from San Francisco—with the average rates per mile on ship-

TABLE 29

MIDDLE-DISTANCE RATES FROM SAN FRANCISCO TO NAMED DESTINATIONS
(In cents per 100 pounds)

Class or commodity	Promontory Point, Utah (762 mi.)	Point of Rocks, Wyo. (1,002 mi.)	Audley, Ariz. (758 mi.)	Houck, Ariz. (1,002 mi.)
First class	238	341	211	261
Automobile bodies and parts	110	143	97½	103½
Beverages	52	99	60	68
Canned goods	54	77	61	72
Clothing	203	248	187	232
Dry goods	138	155	140	155
Fertilizers	40	79	48	63
Steel articles	60	127	61	85
Tin articles	106	155	87	117
Vehicles, passenger	125	464	145	249
Wine	83	99	85	99

ments from Chicago to the destinations given, we have the results shown in table 30, on the following page.

It is evident from the foregoing that rates from San Francisco eastbound for distances ranging from approximately 750 to approximately 1,000 miles along the lines of the Southern Pacific and the Santa Fe are generally higher on the whole list of commodities taken than on the samples used as illustrative of eastern rates. The excess of the charges out of California on middle-distance hauls is in striking contrast with conditions on the short hauls, where the California scale is lower. This excess, it may be added, is more pronounced at 1,000 miles than at 750 miles, although it exists in either grouping.

On the whole, the high rates on middle distances for the movement of indicated articles out of California, as compared with rates out of Chicago in various directions, are probably due to three conditions.

In the first place, this movement, for the distances given, has not yet assumed large importance on the Pacific Coast. Hauls of middle length from California reach sections of the country which are lightly populated. These do not and cannot be expected to furnish markets of great consequence. Another circumstance is that the selected hauls

TABLE 30

COMPARISON OF RATES ON MIDDLE-DISTANCE HAULS

(Average of rates per mile from San Francisco to Promontory Point, Point of Rocks, Audley, and Houck = 100)

Class or commodity	Chicago to Atlanta	Chicago to Dallas	Chicago to Utica	Chicago to Venlo	Chicago to Cheyenne	Chicago to Amarillo	Chicago to Minneapolis
First class	89	87	66	98	92	89	101
Automobile bodies and parts	143	70	57	79	74	71	83
Beverages	61	54	68	77	97	66	66
Canned goods	117	91	79	108	76	96	93
Clothing	75	74	68	74	52	75	85
Dry goods	111	81	117	80	77	80	51
Fertilizers	60	66	68	79	74	68	80
Steel articles	86	89	66	101	95	91	77
Tin cans	80	102	74	98	114	94	64
Vehicles, passenger	95	66	70	72	69	77	67
Wine	140	99	83	112	107	102	82
Arithmetic mean	96	80	74	89	84	83	77

out of Chicago all terminate at some rather large city, whereas in the West the terminal points are generally unimportant. A third explanation is technical. Eastbound rates from California are zoned over sizable distances. It follows that the same rate which is charged to a point 750 or 1,000 miles from San Francisco may also be charged for transportation to points considerably beyond. This possible extension may be allowed for, in setting the price to nearer points.

In addition to all this, high rates for middle distances are an expression of carrier policy in the sense that western railroads increase rates rapidly out of California from an initially low level to ceilings which they do not afterward exceed. Railroads in the Middle West do not, apparently, follow this policy to the same degree. These statements explain but do not alter conclusions based on comparison of middle-distance rates.

Table 31 compares eastbound and westbound rates on long-distance transcontinental movements of those commodities with which we are now familiar.

It appears from the table that rates on automobile fenders, beverages, clothing, fertilizers, steel articles, tin articles, and passenger vehicles are all higher eastbound than westbound. First-class rates

TABLE 31
Transcontinental Rates, Eastbound and Westbound,
between Chicago and San Francisco
(In cents per 100 pounds)

Class or commodity	Eastbound	Westbound
	cents	cents
First class....................................	561	561
Automobile bodies and parts (fenders)...............	178	167
Beverages....................................	99	99
Canned goods.................................	88	88
Clothing (cotton shirts, overalls)...................	275	256
Dry goods....................................	174	174
Fertilizers....................................	99	75
Steel articles..................................	127	110
Tin articles...................................	165	77
Vehicles, passenger.............................	495	425
Wine..	99	182

and rates on beverages, canned goods, and dry goods are the same in both directions, and the rates on wine in packages is lower on eastbound than on westbound movements. The differences are considerable where they exist. Thus the rates on steel articles are 127 cents eastbound and 110 westbound, and those on clothing are 275 cents and 256. The contrast between the eastbound rate of 99 cents on wine (minimum, 50,000 pounds) and the westbound rate of 182 cents (minimum, 30,000 pounds) is extreme, and it remains large even if the eastbound rate of 124 cents (minimum, 30,000 pounds) is used for purposes of comparison.

It may be doubted, however, if the differences between Chicago–San Francisco and San Francisco–Chicago rates, where they exist, have much significance. In the first place, the articles chosen for illustration move to the West in large volume, and westbound rates on these commodities may be expected, therefore, to be relatively low. A different choice of commodities might give different results. Secondly, few Pacific Coast producers are likely to ship or to be interested in shipping the articles mentioned from San Francisco or Los Angeles to Chicago or New York.

The location of the area in which the westbound rate out of Chicago becomes equivalent to the eastbound rate out of San Francisco or Los Angeles is, however, important, because this area constitutes what may be called a "rate shed," the position of which determines the market limits of eastern and western shippers to the extent that railroad rates control.

It is possible to arrive at some conclusion with respect to the areas in which rates from San Francisco and Los Angeles meet westbound rates from Chicago. This will be sufficient to fix the rate shed, so far as the tariffs studied supply the necessary detail.

Total distances between Chicago and San Francisco are 2,264 miles by way of Ogden and 2,513 over the Atchison, Topeka and Santa Fe Railway.[26] The halfway points on these routes are, therefore, 1,132 and 1,256 miles from points of origin. The question is whether the actual meeting points of transcontinental east- and westbound rates are at these locations or whether they are farther east or farther west. The answer, as one might expect, depends somewhat on the commodity selected for illustration.

Considering first the central route via Ogden, the critical area so far as rates on canned goods, clothing, and wine are concerned is in the general neighborhood of Cheyenne.

Study of table 32 shows that eastbound and westbound rates meet once (canned goods) at Cheyenne and three times between Borie and Cheyenne or between Maxwell and Cheyenne.

Along this central route, the meeting points of eastbound and westbound first-class rates, and of rates on automobile bodies and parts, beverages, fertilizers, steel, tin containers, and vehicles, lie between Black Butte and Promontory Point. The meeting point of rates on beverages is between Promontory Point and Point of Rocks. This can be determined from table 33. The two groups of meeting points on the central route may be estimated to be, respectively, about 1,264 and 900 miles from San Francisco.

---

[26] Santa Fe figures are supplied by the carrier. They are slightly less than the distances published in the Official Guide.

Let us now turn to the Santa Fe route via Albuquerque. On this line, Houck and Lupton, both in Arizona, are respectively 1,002 and 1,013 miles from San Francisco. The distance from San Francisco to Lucy, New Mexico, is 1,248 miles, and that to Pedernal, New

TABLE 32

TRANSCONTINENTAL RATES VIA OGDEN FROM SAN FRANCISCO AND CHICAGO
(In cents per 100 pounds)

Commodity	Destination							
	Black Butte, Wyo.		Borie, Wyo.		Cheyenne, Wyo.		Maxwell, Neb.	
	From S. F.	From Chicago	From S. F.	From Chicago	From S. F.	From Chicago	From S. F.	From Chicago
	cents	cents	cents	cents	cents	cents	cents	cents
Canned goods	77	88	77	88	77	77	88	64
Clothing	248	256	248	256	248	128	248	128
Wine	99	182	99	153	99	110	99	91
Dry goods	155	168	155	168	155	128	165	128

TABLE 33

TRANSCONTINENTAL RATES VIA OGDEN FROM SAN FRANCISCO AND CHICAGO
(In cents per 100 pounds)

Class or commodity	San Francisco to Promontory Point	Chicago to Ogden	San Francisco to Point of Rocks	Chicago to Black Butte
	cents	cents	cents	cents
First class	238	399	341	340
Automobile bodies and parts	110	167	143	119
Beverages	52	80	99	80
Fertilizers	40	70	79	60
Steel	60	95	127	95
Tin containers	106	149	155	149
Vehicles	125	260	464	260

Mexico, is 1,261 miles. The distance from San Francisco to Canyon, Texas, is 1,506 miles, and that to Lester, Texas, is 1,501 miles. Houck and Lupton, Lucy and Pedernal, and Canyon and Lester are, therefore, equivalent so far as distances are concerned.

Table 34 sets forth railroad eastbound rates from San Francisco and westbound rates from Chicago on the commodities listed.

The general conclusion with respect to the Santa Fe route is that eastbound and westbound rates meet between Lupton and Houck, on the one hand, and Lucy and Pedernal, on the other, for first-class shipments and movements of automobile bodies and parts, beverages, clothing, fertilizers, and vehicles. The halfway point between these pairs of stations is, approximately, 1,127 miles from San Francisco. The meeting point of eastbound and westbound rates on canned goods is at Pedernal, 1,261 miles from San Francisco; that of rates on tin

TABLE 34

Transcontinental Rates via Santa Fe Lines from San Francisco and Chicago
(In cents per 100 pounds)

Class or commodity	San Francisco to Houck	Chicago to Lupton	San Francisco to Lucy	Chicago to Pedernal	San Francisco to Lester	Chicago to Canyon
	cents	cents	cents	cents	cents	cents
First class............	261	457	350	317	399	282
Automobile bodies and parts...............	133½	167	143	111	161	99
Beverages............	68	80	68	63	78	56
Canned goods.........	72	88	77	88	88	78
Clothing.............	232	256	240	222	248	197
Cotton piece goods.....	155	174	155	159	165	141
Fertilizers............	63	75	79	53	79	46
Iron and steel.........	85	110	109	103	127	92
Tin containers........	104	149	140	149	157	130
Vehicles, passenger.....	249	425	275	269	399	220
Wine.................	99	182	99	127	99	113

containers, between Lucy and Canyon; and that of rates on wine, between Capron and Amarillo, approximately 1,640 miles from San Francisco. With three exceptions, therefore, the meeting point is about 1,100 miles from San Francicso, or a little farther from San Francisco than on the central route. The meeting points of rates on canned goods, tin containers, and wine are slightly farther east.

In the course of the present study, rate relationships to the Pacific Northwest have not been treated in the same detailed fashion as those to intermountain points immediately east of California. Limited sampling indicates, however, that the point of rate equality from shipments converging on the Northwest from San Francisco and Chicago lies east of the coastal states. The exact location of the point will differ with each commodity, but it can generally be expected to lie somewhere in the sparsely settled intermountain area.

Let us now state general conclusions with respect to western rate levels which the evidence in this chapter seems to support. These conclusions are as follows.

1. Local rates, for distances of approximately 250 miles, are definitely lower in California than in other parts of the country, so far as our samples are representative. Rates are also low on hauls for similar distances which begin in California and terminate in adjacent states, although these rates are not equally depressed.

2. Middle-distance rates on the transcontinental routes, for distances of from 750 to 1,000 miles, on a selected list of manufactured goods, are higher out of San Francisco and Los Angeles than are rates for similar movements out of Chicago.

3. Eastbound rates from San Francisco to Chicago on manufactures are, on a number of items, higher than the corresponding rates from Chicago to San Francisco. The conclusion is based upon examination of rates on commodities typically moving from east to west. This difference is not, probably, significant.

4. The area of rate equivalence between eastbound and westbound transcontinental rates lies, on the central route, for the categories of manufactures examined, at a point west of the geographical center of the line. This is due to higher eastbound ceilings or to more rapid rate acceleration during the western part of the transcontinental haul, or to both influences. On the southern route the area of equivalence is close to the geographical center. Commodities shipped eastward over the Atchison, Topeka and Santa Fe from San Francisco begin their journey with a substantial mileage in California. This tends to hold down the eastbound rate and to push the meeting point of eastbound and westbound charges somewhat farther to the east.

5. Rates per mile on transcontinental shipments of California exports are generally low. This is partly because of carrier competition, and partly it is the result of an adjustment designed to assist western shippers in penetrating eastern markets. The depression in eastbound rates is most marked for canned goods, sugar, wine, citrus, and dried fruit; it is least noticeable for fresh fruit (grapes) and fresh vegetables (lettuce).

These conclusions are different from the findings with respect to class rates, especially in the matter of charges upon the longer hauls.

CHAPTER IX

Summary and Conclusion

WE MAY now conclude this descriptive study with something in the way of summary and comment on the material presented in preceding chapters. The conclusion will concern itself with matters of technique and with a partial appraisal of the transcontinental rate structure as a whole. The effect of the transcontinental rate system upon the western economy will not be discussed, nor will earlier descriptions be repeated in detail.

The organization of origin points on local traffic in, to, and from California has been considered in the chapter on class rates and in the sections which deal with shipments of citrus, grapes, lettuce, and other eastbound movements. It will be remembered that rates are quoted from one point only on short hauls and that, as distance increases, the same rate is applied from several origin points, creating zones of moderate size, the boundaries of which vary with the point of origin at which the process begins. In local traffic, each tariff has its own system of grouping, and a great deal of irregularity exists. Although, as explained, the tendency is for origin zones to become larger as the distance between point of origin and point of destination becomes greater, this observation must be taken as only roughly true. An exact statement would, perhaps, be limited to the conclusion that origin groups are small or nonexistent for California intrastate traffic; that they are larger for traffic moving to points in Mountain-Pacific territory east of the boundary of California; and that they become still larger for traffic between California and Transcontinental Freight Bureau territories. This arrangement has nothing particularly distinctive or different from practice in many other places, so far as local business is concerned. It is on long-distance traffic that the system is developed to an unusual degree.

A second feature of transcontinental tariffs which previous chapters have now, perhaps, enabled us to appreciate, is the use which

SUMMARY AND CONCLUSION 141

these tariffs make of eastern groupings. These so-called "transcontinental groups" are interesting as an example of rate technique, and they are significant because of their effects.

As we have pointed out earlier, in the territory west of Colorado common points there are few rate groups containing more than one important town. This may be the result of historical accident, or it may reflect the absence of competing cities and the fact that rail lines are not so situated as to require grouping to handle business in this district without charging more for shorter than for longer hauls. In Utah, near and including Salt Lake City, there is a group, and there are considerable areas of equal rates in the shipment of particular commodities such as sugar, but zoning in the Far West does not attain the importance of a major device. Farther east, however, the use of zones is a characteristic of transcontinental rates.

We have discussed, in chapter iv, the history of transcontinental zones. It would be lending too much importance to history, however, to account for the eastern-zones technique solely upon historical grounds. The system has, in fact, conveniences which may be enumerated.

1. There is, to begin with, the advantage of simplified quotation, and there is, at the same time, carrier recognition of the fact that the unit on which rates are quoted may properly include more miles on long hauls than is appropriate on shorter hauls. Both of these considerations would justify some grouping in trancontinental traffic. If groups were used merely as a convenience in rate making, however, the zones should be concentric on the point of origin or destination. Our maps in chapter iv show some rough concentricity in rates on shorter hauls from California origins to destinations in Pacific Freight Tariff Bureau territory, although generally without zoning. Farther east, however, where there are zones, the areas of equal charge tend to straighten out, especially east of the Mississippi River. Zone boundaries on westbound shipments to California are also straightened in this eastern district, probably owing to competition between cities and to the ease of truck-line and water-borne communication.

2. From the point of view of the carrier, the zone system has the merit of permitting competing parallel railroads to meet each other's

competition at a uniform rate over an enlarged territory without authorization under Section 4 of the Interstate Commerce Act. This is particularly true of long zones running from north to south. Transcontinental railroads are, in a broad way, parallel with each other on routes from east to west. The system of grouping allows lines on southern latitudes and lines on northern latitudes to compete in districts which they could not otherwise all supply. *Ceteris paribus*, circuitous routing reduces revenue per ton mile, but this is readily accepted.

3. North-and-south railroads benefit, also, by the flexibility of routing which a zone system makes possible. Indeed, it would be difficult for such railroads to participate in transcontinental business unless group rates were put in force. Students of rate geography have noticed that the boundaries of groups often follow the lines of railroads which run transversely to the direction of the main current of traffic. Where this is true, and sometimes elsewhere also, the participation of the cross roads is increased.[1]

---

[1] The statements that the eastern boundaries of transcontinental groups are drawn along the lines of transverse railroads, and that large cities are usually found on the eastern rather than on the western edge of transcontinental zones, can be supported by illustrations; but there are exceptions also.

The following may be mentioned as illustrations.

Group F in the transcontinental tariff offers an example of the coincidence of a zone boundary and a transverse railroad line.

The fact is spread upon the record that the present eastern boundaries of groups E and D were determined by the desire of the Illinois Central Railroad to compete for transcontinental traffic. Prior to 1927, the boundary of these zones, as far north as Cairo, was the Mississippi River, including east-bank crossings. The Illinois Central, however, hauled transcontinental freight to and from New Orleans, Memphis, and St. Louis. These cities were in groups D and E, but the Illinois Central served them over its main line running through group M. In doing so, the Illinois Central necessarily charged less for longer than for shorter hauls. To avoid this, on September 15, 1927, groups D and E were extended eastward to include all points on the main line of the Illinois Central from New Orleans through Jackson and Memphis to Cairo. (169 I.C.C. 80, 1930.) This change permitted the Illinois Central to handle traffic to and from the West without violating Section 4.

The eastern boundary of the 140 cent group in the tariff on fresh-grape shipments follows the line of the Chicago and Northwestern to Council Bluffs; the Chicago, Burlington and Quincy to Kansas City; the Missouri Pacific to Carthage; the St. Louis and San Francisco to Fort Smith; and the Kansas City Southern to Port Arthur, applying to all the cities mentioned a single rate.

Certain transverse lines can be identified in the citrus tariff which determine rate boundaries through considerable distances. For example, the eastern border of the 93 cent zone beginning at Denison, Texas, follows the Southern Pacific to Corsicana and the Burlington–Rock Island railroads to Galveston. The eastern border of the 111 cent zone supplies another illustration, inasmuch as this boundary follows the line of the

SUMMARY AND CONCLUSION 143

4. The same pressure which develops from the competition of parallel railroads results from the competition of rail with water and highway transport. Traffic from the Pacific Coast reaches Gulf and Atlantic Coast cities by water at low rates, and is distributed therefrom by barge, truck, and rail. The wide reach of many eastern transcontinental groups is explained by a competition in the East and Middle West which, without grouping, would tempt rail carriers to charge, if possible, lower rates for longer than for shorter hauls, to meet the competition of other agencies. The canned-goods rate structure supplies an illustration.

5. Market competition, or, more exactly, producer competition, may produce the same effect as the competition of carriers. Thus, in the citrus rate structure, the level and shape of certain of the transcontinental zones appears to be controlled by competition of Texas growers. This pressure is important west of the Mississippi and, possibly, also farther east.

6. On eastbound shipments, groups afford a convenience to the western producer in selecting markets for his goods. The ability of the western grower to meet competition at any given point is a function of the level of the rate to that point; but the distribution of shipments, especially with the practice of diversion, is easier when rates to all points in a considerable area are the same. Routing restrictions may hamper circuitous movements, but they do not prevent them.[2]

Kansas City Southern from Fort Smith to Lake Charles. However, zone lines on the citrus map do not generally follow railroad routes for long distances.

Diligent search aided by a little imagination would increase the number of examples of transverse railroad mileage in association with transcontinental zone boundaries, but it is doubtful if the evidence is sufficient to establish a general rule. Frequently, group borders follow branch lines from station to station or strike out across country in a way which seems unrelated to railroad location.

With respect to the position of cities in eastern groups, the following cities lie at or close to the east edge of their respective zones: Minneapolis, St. Paul, St. Louis, Memphis, Jackson, New Orleans, Chicago, Detroit, Cincinnati, Chattanooga, Montgomery, Buffalo, Pittsburgh, and the Atlantic Seaboard cities as a whole. Denver, Fort Worth, Little Rock, Des Moines, Indianapolis, Cleveland, and Atlanta are central in the zones in which they lie. On the whole, the evidence supports the rule suggested in the text; there are, however, many influences at work.

[2] Tariffs generally permit circuitous movements in territory west of the Mississippi and the line of the Illinois Central; the practice becomes more difficult in districts progressively farther east, until it becomes substantially impossible, along the Atlantic Coast, for a carload to reach southern territory by way of New York or to reach New York by way of southern territory.

7. On westbound movements, finally, the grouping of origin points increases the range of the western buyer's choice. Probably a still more important fact is that it places eastern producers on an equality or on a measured inequality in competing for the western market. This, historically, was the reason for the first construction of eastern zones, and it still remains an important influence in their delineation and perpetuation. It is not an accident that large cities are found on the eastern edge of transcontinental zones; this is, rather, evidence of the influence which producing and distributing centers have on zone construction. It is true, however, that zones also cover districts where producers are few or highly concentrated or where no transcontinental movement is expected. Carriers may then use broad zones because division will serve no useful purpose. The fertilizer group, westbound, is of this kind, and some extensions of other zones can likewise be explained.

The facts mentioned in the preceding paragraphs are those usually referred to in explaining and in justifying transcontinental zoning practice. There seems no doubt that the system has many conveniences. It is, however, open to some objections. These include the following.

1. Transcontinental zones, and especially large zones, encourage circuitous routing. This is argued, indeed, as one of their advantages; and it is an advantage from the point of view of carriers which are "off-line" or otherwise at a disadvantage in direct competition. The result, however, may be, and often is, to increase the national burden of transportation cost.

2. Transcontinental zones offset advantages of location. The problem here is complicated, except on the assumption that there are "natural advantages" in an absolute sense, among which nearness to market ranks high. But, on any assumption, it is unlikely that the transcontinental zone system as we have it today accurately promotes the distribution of industry which a community would consciously prefer.

3. This is particularly true when the shapes and boundaries of existing zones are attentively considered. Like other elements in the rate structure, present zone practice reflects, in detail, a mixture of historical tradition, distance calculation, competitive pressure, and

SUMMARY AND CONCLUSION

arbitrary decision applied to the building of a rate structure which it is often impossible to understand.[3]

The Interstate Commerce Commission has remarked that it would not approve groupings as extensive as those carried in transcontinental tariffs, if these groups had not been long in effect.[4]

Apart from the Commission's position, it is obvious that some large-scale blanketing can scarcely be avoided as long as competitive carriers and the long-and-short-haul clause of the Interstate Commerce Act persist.

It is clear that if there are alternative routes between any two stations, it is only by coincidence that the routes will be of identical length. If there is to be competition, circuitous lines between named

[3] A special example of how the use of rail mileage plus the enforcement of Section 4 of the Interstate Commerce Act may cause the distortion of a zone is the following:

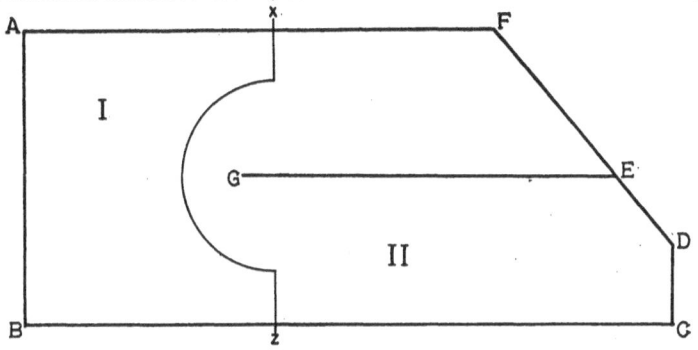

Let G in the diagram be a point on line EG, accessible from the west only by the roundabout routes AFEG or BCDEG. The rate from A or B to G can hardly be less than the rate to intermediate points on these circuitous hauls, because this would produce a discrimination forbidden by Section 4 of the Act to Regulate Commerce. As a result, point G may be assigned, for rate-making purposes, to the zone numbered II on the diagram, rather than to the zone numbered I, although, as the crow sometimes flies, it is nearer A or B than are points E or D, or even than points X or Z. The consequent distortion of the boundary separating zones I and II is shown on the diagram by the irregular line from X to Z.

[4] According to Sharfman (*The Interstate Commerce Commission*, Vol. III B, p. 686), this favorable attitude has been due to the following considerations:

1. Some grouping is required in the interest of simplicity and economy.

2. Any change in rates is disruptive, but "a change from precise equality is more obviously disruptive of the rate structure, and perhaps more likely to call for sweeping commercial and industrial readjustments, than where, on complaint, certain rates are altered in a totality that consists of a scheme of interrelated differentials."

3. Consumers' interests are promoted by access to wide territory of supply.

4. The Commission's decisions carry some implications that a precise equality of rates is essentially fair.

termini must (1) charge higher rates for shorter than for longer hauls, (2) blanket terminal and intermediate rates over considerable areas, or (3) apply to intermediate stations rates which reflect all along their route the competitive pressure at the terminus. The last alternative will, in many cases, require carriers to charge lower rates than those which they could defend, independently, as reasonable; and it will not meet the needs of carriers which desire to compete at a series of points that are successively more distant from point of origin upon their lines and successively less distant upon the lines of a competitor.

Practically, the choice will be made between blanketing and charging higher rates for shorter hauls. If neither policy is possible, an alternative may be mileage rates. There will then be always one "short-line" carrier, charging lower rates than any other—a condition under which competition cannot persist and the financial integrity of many existing carriers cannot, perhaps, be maintained.

While the same basic groups are used for both eastbound and westbound traffic, there are indications that the arrangement of groups has been more carefully specialized and fitted to a particular commodity on eastbound than on westbound movements. Presumably, this reflects differing evaluations by shippers of the significance of the transport rate to them. California producers must ship a substantial part of their total output to transcontinental destinations. Most eastern manufacturers can be expected to find only a small part of their market on the Pacific Coast. The former, then, have an incentive to press the carriers for special adjustments; the latter are likely to be content with the general pattern.

The third aspect of transcontinental tariffs which has been developed in the present study is the rate of progression of transcontinental scales; and on this subject, too, some remarks are appropriate.

We may begin by reference to the concept of distance in railroad rate making.

Under a strict mileage system, lines connecting points taking equal rates from any selected point of origin should, if conditions are everywhere uniform, be concentric to the point of origin of the traffic, and the resultant isodapanes should succeed each other at equal spatial intervals for each uniform increment of charge.

Map 29 is drawn to show points of equal air distance from San Francisco, the lines following each other at intervals of 100 miles. It also shows what the relationship of rates would be in a tariff built rigidly upon air distances.

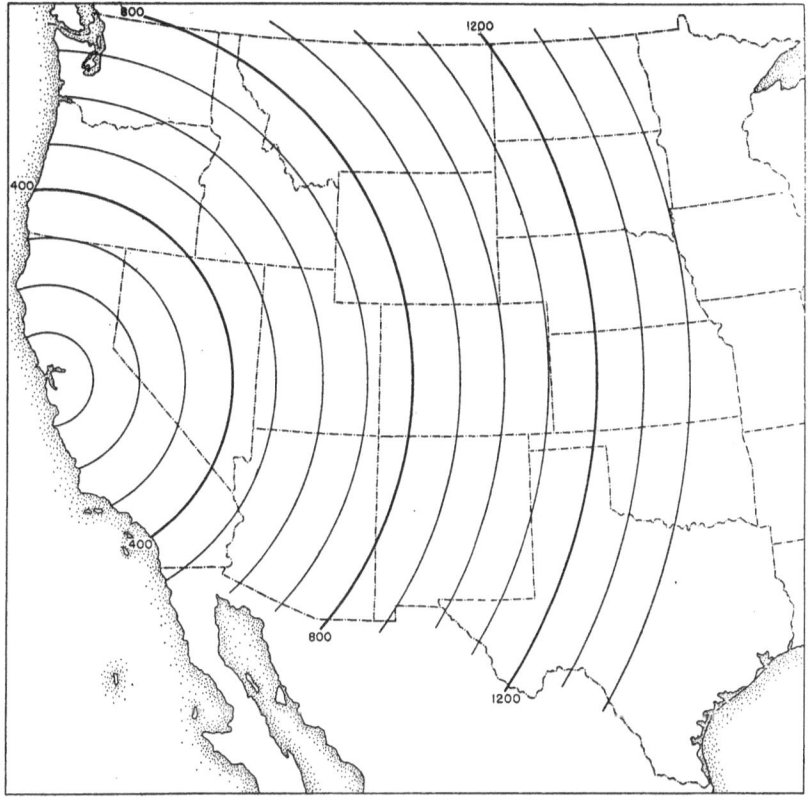

Map 29. Air distances from San Francisco, by intervals of 100 miles.

Rates could be easily calculated if they were quoted in conformity to distance in the manner suggested by the map. The system would not, however, be realistic, because the air distances used would not reflect the mileage over which shipments move, or the cost or effort required for their transportation. This would be true even of shipments by air carriers, but it is still more obviously true of rail or highway consignments, which move by routes influenced by peculiarities of terrain. Map 30, therefore, which shows distances from a selected point of origin on rail routes over which it is physically possible to move shipments, is necessary to correct the first.[5]

Examination of map 30 will show that points equally distant from place of origin by air may be unequally distant over land routes.

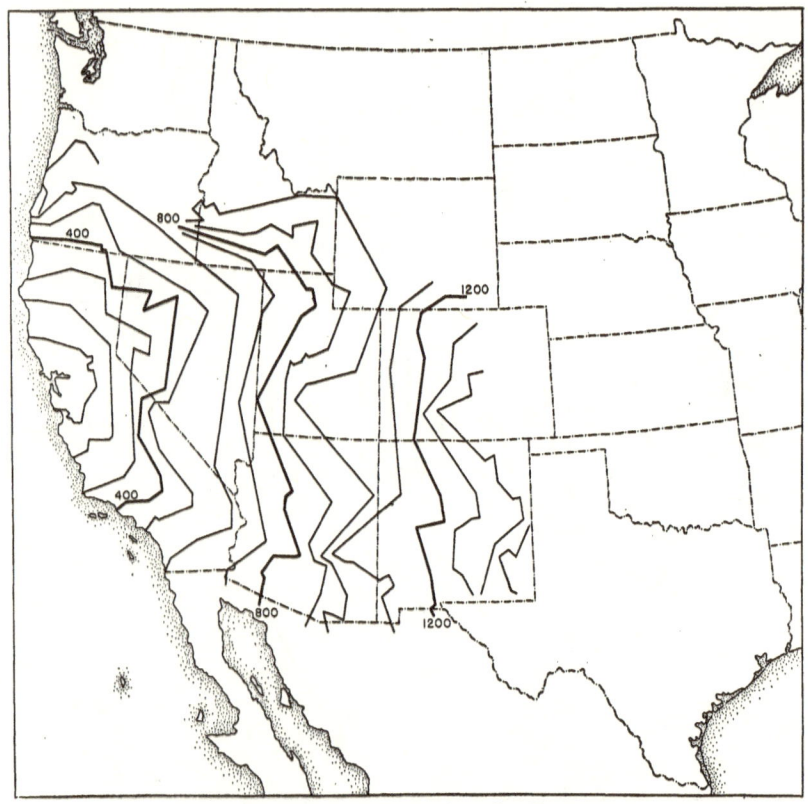

Map 30. Rail-route distances from San Francisco, at intervals of 100 miles.

When the land route is direct, a shipment can reach a point comparatively far from the point of origin as the crow flies; when the land route is crooked or indirect, one mile of straight-line displacement may require several miles of travel.[6]

---

[5] The Interstate Commerce Commission, in fixing mileage rates, requires the use of the shortest routes over which traffic can be moved without transfer of lading. This definition is used here.

[6] Among the possible reasons for the irregularities shown in map 30 are the following:
1. *Irregularities of terrain.* Some physical barriers may be insurmountable by direct

SUMMARY AND CONCLUSION 149

In the Far West, circuity is accentuated by the fact that mountain barriers intervene which are traversable only at widely separated points, and by the relative scarcity of rail routes. Hence in this area traffic from an origin as in California, when consigned to a destination directly east, may have to travel many miles north or south to the nearest practicable mountain pass; and, after this, it may have to proceed south or north an equivalent distance beyond the mountains in order to arrive at the place of business of the consignee.

Because carriers are operated as individual entities, and hold traffic to their own rails even when it is not the shortest possible route, a map showing distances measured over the routes along which traffic actually moves would be still more irregular.

Map 31, already reproduced on page 51 as map 8, sketches the rate structure governing shipments from San Francisco to destinations in Pacific Freight Tariff Bureau territory. It is presented for convenient comparison with the two maps previously discussed.

The obvious conclusion from map 31 is that rates from San Francisco to Pacific Freight Tariff Bureau destinations do not increase in proportion to air distances. It will be evident on examination, also, that they do not vary with rail-route mileages in any close degree, although this fact is not so obvious. Thus doubling the route distance sometimes triples rather than doubles the rate. On the whole, the rate system appears to be even more complicated than the rail-route mileage system, although the route system is not simple, and much more irregular than would be any structure controlled by air mileage. These comparisons throw some light on the character of Far Western rates. The essential facts can, however, be

---

attack. The land route is then forced to a detour. Or, they may be surmountable, but only by such a prolongation of the land route as will reduce the rate of grade.

2. *Incompleteness of route coverage.* Direct routes are generally established between important centers, but minor stations are served by branch lines radiating from the main stems which connect the major points. Freight which moves to a minor station by way of a branch-line junction accomplishes a detour. The air distance may sometimes be less from the point of origin to the minor station than is the land route distance from the point of origin to the branch-line junction. And what is true of branch-line points may be equally true of destinations on cross-road connecting lines which diverge from a common point of origin. The short route, in this event, will consist of a combination of a haul on the cross road with a haul on one or the other of the main lines which the cross road connects. This short route will always be longer than the distance from the point of origin to the junction of cross road and main line, and it will also be longer than the air-line distance from the point of origin to the terminating point.

better expressed in rate profiles, to the consideration of which we may now turn.

Under a strict mileage system the line of rates on a profile will rise in regular proportion to increases in distance traveled. Minor

Map 31. Class C rates from San Francisco to destinations in Pacific Freight Tariff Bureau territory.

modifications in such a mileage system may occur (1) when rates are quoted by mileage groups and not by units of a single mile, and (2) when the width of these mileage zones becomes greater as the distance from the point of origin increases. Most so-called mileage tariffs contain these modifications. The first simplifies the method of quoting rates, and usually does so without changing the general contour which the mileage profile presents. The second may also

SUMMARY AND CONCLUSION 151

preserve the original contour of a mileage graph. When, however, the increment of the rate from zone to zone is not proportionately augmented, the increase in length of a succeeding over a preceding zone will reduce the average rate charged per mile as the shipment moves farther and farther from the point of origin. This will substitute for a line of uniform straight progression a series of lines of different slopes tending toward the horizontal on an appropriately drawn graph.

Major modifications in mileage rate making occur when the succession of increments in rates and variations in breadth of zones becomes irregular and the changes cease to relate themselves to distance but are explainable only in other terms, such as competition or the desire to extract maximum revenue from a territory with known characteristics.

The place of transcontinental rate systems among the categories mentioned can be ascertained by comparison. It can also be shown graphically. For this last purpose, chart 19 compares the profile of first-class rates prescribed by the Interstate Commerce Commission for use in certain portions of Mountain-Pacific territory with (a) the profile of first-class rates from San Francisco to New York over the central route, and (b) with the profile of rates on canned goods[7] from San Francisco to New York.

The tariff prescribed by the Interstate Commerce Commission in the Mountain-Pacific cases is an example of a modified mileage rate. It quotes rates by groups, and these groups or zones become longer as length of haul increases. Up to distances of 100 miles, rates are quoted for mileage groups of 5 miles; from 101 to 240 miles, the unit is 10 miles; from 241 to 1,000 miles, the unit is 20 miles; and for longer distances, the unit is 25 miles. The increment of charge for additional distances hauled declines per mile as distance increases.

The transcontinental class tariff, like the Mountain-Pacific scale, quotes rates which tally exactly with each of a series of succeeding stations in a group or zone. The transcontinental rate zones are, however, generally broader than those prescribed in the Interstate Commerce Commission scale, and they are much less regular. Be-

---
[7] Actual rates on canned goods have been multiplied by three before graphing, so as to bring the profiles more nearly in line with the profiles of first-class rates.

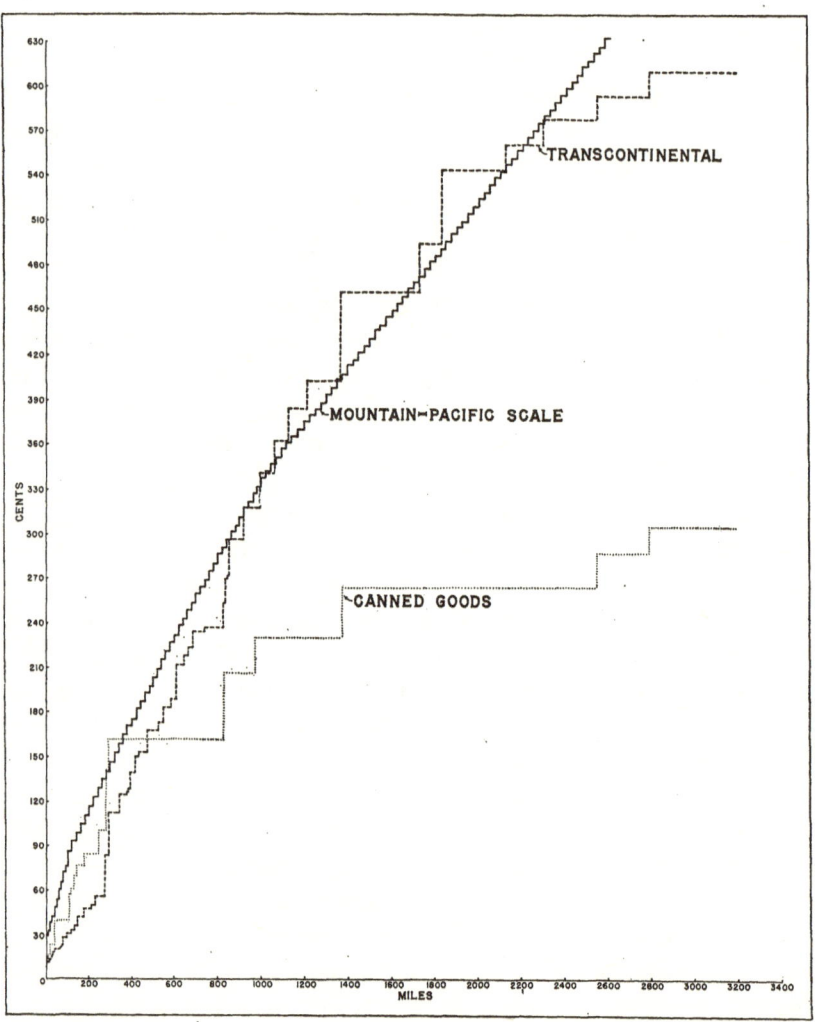

Chart 19. Profiles of (1) first-class rates under the Mountain-Pacific scale, 1943; (2) first-class rates from San Francisco to New York, via Ogden; and (3) commodity rates on canned goods from San Francisco to New York.

ginning with small units, the class tariff sets up zones of 20 or even 40 miles. In the distances between 600 and 1,200 miles, zones of 60 or more miles are common, and beyond 1,200 miles the zones lengthen to 200 miles or more, culminating in a zone of 400 miles between Latrobe, Pennsylvania, and New York. The zones are

SUMMARY AND CONCLUSION

irregularly spaced, and the increases in rates from zone to zone are varied.

The canned-goods tariff presents the following representative characteristics of transcontinental commodity rate making:

1. The level of rates is low, much lower than the level of class rates or even than the level of rates on perishables.

2. The zones are very broad.

3. The increases in rates between points of origin and of destination are markedly concentrated in certain segments of the haul. In the canned-goods tariff the advance in rates from nothing at San Francisco to 102 cents at New York is accomplished in three major steps: a rise of 54 cents in the first 292 miles; a second rise of 34 cents in the 546 miles from Echo, Utah, to a point a few miles east of Sydney, Nebraska; and finally, an advance of 14 cents in the last 641 miles between Bucyrus and New York. The entire distance from San Francisco to New York is 3,184 miles, and the sum of the portions of the line in which rates increase as distance grows greater is only 46 per cent of the whole route.

4. The relation between the breadth of rate zones and the increments of charge between zones is such that the average rate per mile declines as distances grow longer.

5. The canned-goods rates approach their maxima more rapidly in the later stages than do the transcontinental or the Mountain-Pacific class scales.

Table 35 shows the cumulative percentage of the total rate attained at each stage along the haul for these three scales.

In the Mountain-Pacific scale the halfway mark is reached at a distance of approximately 1,100 miles, and the three-quarters mark at approximately 2,000 miles. On the transcontinental route the halfway mark for first-class rates is less than 1,000 miles from point of origin and the three-quarters mark is reached at about 1,500 miles. In the canned-goods schedule the rate at 750 miles is already half of the maximum charged for the entire haul, and the rate at 1,500 miles is 88 per cent of the ceiling price. These facts are an expression of rate policy which the profile has already revealed.

The characteristics of transcontinental profiles which have just been pointed out suggest certain further observations.

We have referred to the lack of correspondence between distance and price charged in the transcontinental schedules. But comparison of profiles with railroad contours given in chapter i will also show that these profiles do not reflect, with any precision, irregularities in terrain. This is true of class and, still more, of commodity rates. Rates rise rapidly, of course, as traffic proceeds eastward from Cali-

TABLE 35
CUMULATIVE PERCENTAGES OF TOTAL RATE AT INDICATED DISTANCES

Distance from point of origin	Mountain-Pacific scale (first class)	Transcontinental class tariff (first class)	Canned-goods tariff
miles	*per cent*	*per cent*	*per cent*
250	18	9	33
500	28	28	53
750	38	39	53
1,000	47	56	75
1,250	54	66	75
1,500	60	76	86
1,750	67	81	86
2,000	74	89	86
2,250	80	92	86
2,500	87	95	86
2,750	93	97	94
3,000	100	100	100

fornia, and it is common knowledge that elevations above sea level become greater and grades multiply; but the more closely profiles are scrutinized, the less the correspondence between rates and physical obstacles seems to be. Detail can be supplied to the degree desired. Large increases in rates occur, sometimes, when grades are rising, but they are found also when grades are descending. On the central route the scale ignores the advent of the Sierra and recognizes the presence of the Rockies only after trains have completed half the total climb. For some commodities the largest single jump on this route takes place at a point beyond Sydney, Nebraska, when the mountains have been entirely passed. On the Santa Fe route, the Tehachapi Mountains do not hasten acceleration of the class rate, and the big increase which occurs beyond Needles comes before and not during the conquest of the Continental Divide. Finally, on the route to St. Paul via Puget Sound, rate progression is steeper as locomotives descend the eastern slopes of the Cascades than when trains are climbing the western slopes, although the difficulties presented by the Rockies do seem to be acknowledged by a more rapid increase in charge.

It does not, of course, follow from the foregoing that the general level of rates is unaffected by the difficulties which physical obstacles place in the way of transport in the western area. It may well be that transcontinental scales are higher than they otherwise would be if these difficulties did not exist; it is not true, however, that rates are high in districts where the strain on transport is particularly great.[8]

Another fact is that transcontinental profiles combine, with some general symmetry in form, a great deal of irregularity in detail. The neglect of local conditions which may be expected to affect operating costs is not extended to other influences, particularly of a political or business kind.

By "political" in the previous paragraph is principally meant the effect of state boundaries upon rates or, more accurately, the effect of passing from one political jurisdiction to another. It is noteworthy that the California-Nevada and the California-Arizona state lines present real obstacles in the sense that rates rise when or soon after they are crossed. Obviously, it is not the state line itself which explains the rise, but the relative severity of regulation in the areas on either side.

By "business" the authors have in mind circumstances connected with the acquisition of traffic. The effect of this upon tariff profiles is interesting. Let us suppose, as is actually the case, that competition is effective at some points upon a carrier's transcontinental line but not at others, or that organized shipper pressure, or the possibilities of industry development, set the maximum rates possible at some

---

[8] The Interstate Commerce Commission observed, in the Class Rate Investigation of 1945: "It has long been recognized that it is unwise from the standpoint of both shippers and carriers to attempt to reflect in any rate schedule or rate structure all the minute and unsubstantial variations in the cost of service that occur on different divisions or segments of the same railroad or between individual railroads or groups of railroads. The tendency has been, rather, to deal with average costs in such manner as to avoid needless rate variations and to permit the freest possible movement of traffic." (262 I.C.C. 447, 693, 1945.) The variations in cost of service occasioned by the Sierra and the Rocky Mountains are not, however, minute and unsubstantial.

156 TRANSCONTINENTAL RAILROAD RATES

locations while the rates at other places are indeterminate. The problem may then be stated as follows: Given determined rates at selected points, the one rate being higher than the other, how is the difference between these two levels to be absorbed? There are five possible answers, as follows:

1. The difference in charge between that applied to the point

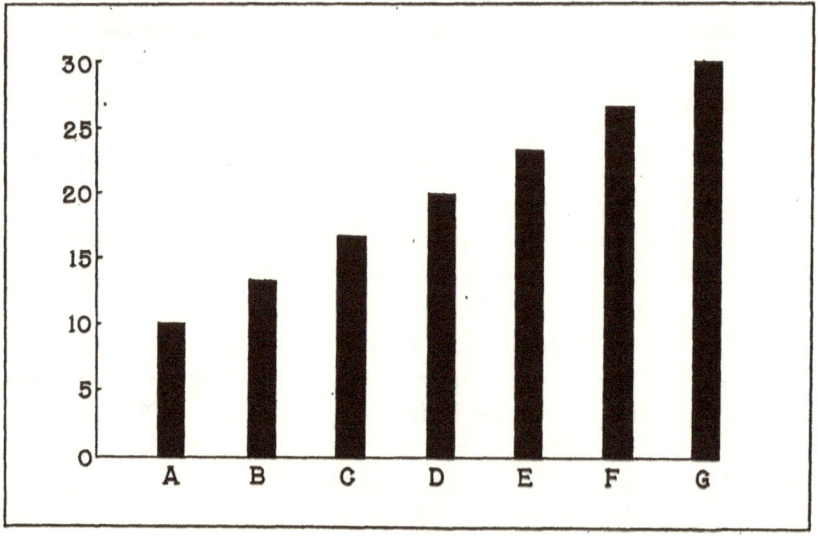

Alternative I

taking the lower rate and that taking the higher rate may be absorbed in regular steps, each of which steps is proportional to the distance traversed.

Let A and G in the diagram (alternative I) represent two points at which the rates from a relatively remote origin are fixed by competition, regulation, or by some other influence. Let the fixed rate at A be assumed to be 10 cents and the fixed rate at G, 30 cents. The policy described in the preceding paragraph will be illustrated by the diagram.

2. The original rate may be continued through all intermediate stations until the point of highest charge is reached, and there increased by the full permissible amount. The graphical representation of this practice will be as in the second diagram (alternative II).

SUMMARY AND CONCLUSION

3. The rate at the point of lowest charge may be increased at the next succeeding station to a level equal to the rate at the point of highest charge. The result will be as shown in the third diagram (alternative III).

4. The whole increase may take place at an intermediate point apparently chosen at random.

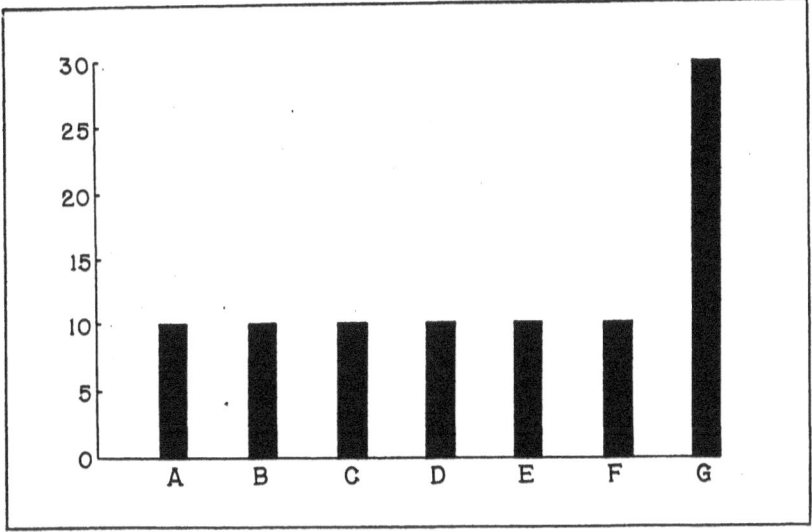

Alternative II

5. The increase may be in varying random amounts and may take place at stations apparently chosen at random.

Which of the alternatives will be adopted will depend upon conditions in the intermediate area, upon regulative control, or perhaps simply upon the idiosyncrasies of railroad officials who make the rates. It is probable that alternative III will yield the highest revenue and that alternative II will produce the lowest revenue, although actual results will depend upon the degree of elasticity in the demand for transportation service. The influence of regulation would favor alternative I. On the other hand, alternative I somewhat, and alternative III to a much greater degree, will tempt the shipper to unload at A and to forward his goods to succeeding points by truck or by any other available means of transport. Alternative II will also offer this possibility, but the only likely point of transfer will now be at F, for at all other points the railroad will clearly offer the lowest total charge. On the whole, alternative I will be easiest to defend against criticism, if the adjustment adopted is attacked. The transcontinental class tariff presents a modified form of alternative III, a fact which accounts for some of the characteristics of its profile which would

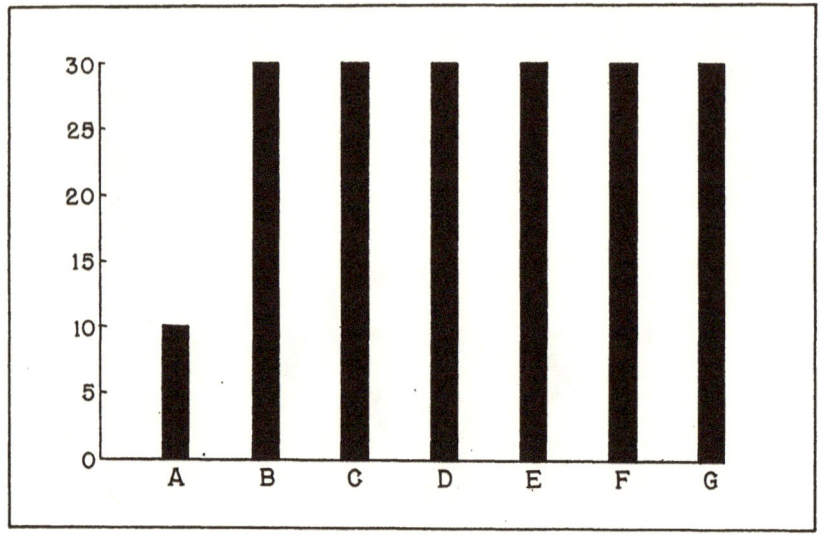

Alternative III

otherwise be unexplained. It should be added that commodity profiles examined in the present study suggest a tendency to accept this solution generally in the western area, but the policy of the railroads is not uniform, and local variations occur which, as has been said, can be explained only by reference to differences in opinion between particular railroad men.

The final conclusions from the study of transcontinental rate making with which this monograph has been concerned may now be stated, but with restraint so far as value judgments are involved. This is because we cannot assert that a rate system is better or worse than some alternative until we decide what industrial objective the Pacific Coast should seek and until we are ready to estimate the repercussions of transport costs upon production and upon sales. Much

SUMMARY AND CONCLUSION 159

thinking has still to be done on these matters. Rate structures are ultimately good or bad according as they produce good or bad results; and we are not yet sure what results are to be sought in the western area or how transportation will work to realize them.

Conceding the necessity of restraint, we may venture, however, the following last remarks.

In the first place, we may repeat again the comment that the present rate system is highly complicated in detail. This is, fundamentally, because of the desire of carriers which are confronted by different geographical and institutional handicaps to meet each other's competition at a maximum number of points. The urge to compete leads to arbitrary equalizations which when expressed in tariffs require expertness to decipher and which must lead often to mistakes.

Actually, the mechanical procedure by which rates are made available to the shipping public makes it difficult for the shipper who cannot afford a large specialized traffic department to be certain that he is in fact obtaining the lowest possible rate. The possibilities of combinations of class and commodity rates, or of local class or commodity rates the sums of which are less than the through rates, make it impossible, in any given case, to be certain of the lowest rate without substantial investigation. While the law is silent on the exact degree of clarity required in the published tariffs, it does use the word "plainly" more than once.[9] It can reasonably be held that present publishing practices do not "plainly" state the rates, and that so far as they do not the Interstate Commerce Commission, which has authority to determine the method and form of publication, is responsible. A useful subject toward which the Commission might direct its attention is that of promoting simplification in the presenta-

[9] Section 6 (1) of the Interstate Commerce Act reads, in part: "The schedule printed as aforesaid by any such common carrier shall plainly state the places between which property and passengers will be carried, and shall contain the classification of freight in force, and shall also state separately all terminal charges, storage charges, icing charges, and all other charges which the Commission may require, all privileges or facilities granted or allowed and any rules or regulations which in any wise change, affect, or determine any part or the aggregate of such aforesaid rates, fares, and charges, or the value of the service rendered to the passenger, shipper, or consignee. Such schedules shall be plainly printed in large type, and copies for the use of the public shall be kept posted in two public and conspicuous places in every depot, station, or office of such carrier where passengers or freight, respectively, are received for transportation, in such form that they shall be accessible to the public and can be conveniently inspected."

tion of railroad rates to the end that not only carrier employees and large shippers, but also small and casual shippers, will be able to discover easily the appropriate rate to be charged.

A second conclusion is that, contrary to common assumptions, transcontinental rates are, on the whole, favorable to western shippers on local hauls, on traffic up and down the Pacific Coast, and on exports over long distances to the eastern states. This is the business on which low rates are needed most. A further question of the degree to which the relatively high rates to the middle or mountain areas are harmful to Coast interests has been considered in chapter viii.

Rates on westbound movements over long distances are not obviously favorable to the western user of imported goods, whether as processor of materials or as direct consumer, and detailed examination of tariffs suggests that westbound rates are not as well adapted to consumer interests in California as eastbound rates are suited to consumers in the East. A definitive statement in this matter is, however, difficult to make.

A third remark is that the profiles of the transcontinental rate structure are irregular. This has already been explained. The irregularity is in part an inevitable consequence of zone rate making, and it will be defended or attacked according as one accepts or rejects the arguments which may be presented to justify the use of zones. But it is also the outcome of policies which have been described; and in the intermediate distances, especially, there is reason to believe that a simpler and more formal adjustment might yield the carriers a reasonable return and at the same time cause less dissatisfaction among those who must pay the rates.

The fourth and most striking peculiarity of transcontinental rate making is to be found in the eastern groupings which railroads have long recognized. The conclusion of the text is that these zones enlarge the area of competition between individual western carriers and that they equalize, to some degree, the shipping costs of western, eastern, and southern producers on movements to interior markets. It is also true that the zones enable some carriers, with relatively indirect routes, to share in traffic which may be necessary for their survival. This suggests that a policy of zoning is sound under present carrier organization and from the point of view, at least, of western agriculture. Final judgment must be reserved until the full possibilities of western industry and agriculture and the most desirable relations between the Pacific Coast and other areas have been more attentively examined.

A last and general observation is that the existence of the transcontinental rate structure distorts geographical and topographical relationships in the Far West in ways which geographers seldom stop to appreciate. Distance is a known concept, and elevation is a fact which is assumed to be apparent. But when distance and elevation are measured in terms of shipping costs, as they must be when the effect upon industry is to be described, we confront a geography which is molded not only by physical conditions, but also by the relations of carriers to each other, by the interest of management in maximum movements and maximum gross and net returns, by historical incident, and by the personalities of individuals who have made and who make decisions which the carriers observe. There are mountains in the West, but there are plains, too, in areas which we think of as mountains, and there are ascents in western Kansas and Nebraska which the surveyor's instruments do not reveal. It should be obvious that a new kind of topography is required to estimate the effect of this changed landscape upon the people who dwell therein. These inhabitants will do well to ponder upon its implications from the regional and from the national point of view.

Index

Aggregate of intermediates: tariff clauses relating to, 33–34; on class traffic originating at San Francisco, 36–37; between points in South Coast territory and transcontinental groups, 38–39; straightens zonal borders, 52; on sugar, 65 n.; on dried fruits and vegetables, 73 n.; general effects of, 159

All-freight rates, 30–32

Automobile bodies and parts: grouping of points of destination, westbound, 48; of points of origin, 81; articles taking automobile and parts rates, 81 n.; minimum carload weights on, 81 n.; relative rate levels on various hauls, 127–138

Beverages: grouping of points of destination, westbound, 48; of points of origin, 78; articles taking beverage rates, 79 n.; minimum carload weights, 78 n.; relative rate levels on various hauls, 127–138; see Wine

Board of Investigation and Research: study of relationship between classes, 25 n.; of volume of class traffic, 30; comparison of intra- and interterritorial rates, 110–112

California Railroad Commission: minimum class rates prescribed by, 88 n.; rate scales of, 113

Canned goods: destination of westbound shipments of, 40; grouping of points of origin, eastbound, 41–43; of points of destination, westbound, 47; of points of destination, eastbound, 68–71; of points of origin, westbound, 83–84; articles taking canned-goods rates, eastbound, 69 n.; articles taking canned-goods rates, westbound, 84 n.; profile of rates on, 101–105, 152–153; recent history of rates on, 117–120; relative rate levels on various hauls, 127–138

Citrus: destination of eastbound shipments of, 40; grouping of points of origin, 41–43; of points of destination, 61–65; profile of rates on, 96–99; recent history of rates on, 120–121

Class rates: definition of, 23; comparison with commodity rates, 28–29; proportion of traffic moving on, 30; grouping of western points of origin and destination, 36–39; of eastern points, 50–58; undercut commodity rates on vehicles, 83; in California, 88; profiles of, 89–93; from San Francisco to Fernley and Westwood, 90–91; comparative levels of, 108–116; prescribed by the Interstate Commerce Commission in Mountain-Pacific territory, 111 n., 151–152; first-class scales of, 115–116, 151–152. *See also* Comparison of rates

Class-rate territories, map facing p. 108

Classification: rates to and from California governed by Western classification and exceptions, 24; number and distribution of carload ratings in, 24–25; relationships between classes, 25–28; consolidation of mixed carloads in, 30

Clothing: grouping of points of destination, westbound, 47; of points of origin, 81–82; articles taking clothing rates, 81–82 n.; minimum carload weights, 82 n.; relative rate levels on various hauls, 127–138

Combination rates. *See* Aggregate of intermediates

Commodity descriptions, difficulty in interpreting, 33

Commodity movements, destinations of representative articles originating in Mountain-Pacific territory, 40

Commodity rates: comparison with class rates, 28–30; grouping of points of origin, eastbound, 41–46; of points of destination, westbound, 47–49; of points of destination, eastbound, 58–75; of points of origin, westbound, 76–87; on shipments eastbound from California, 117–127. *See also* Comparison of rates

Comparison of rates: class rates in different rate territories and districts, 109–113; on selected movements, 112–114; comparison of first-class scales, 115–116; average rates per mile on westbound shipments of selected commodi-

[163]

INDEX

Comparison of rates—*Continued*
ties, 127; comparison of short-haul rates from San Francisco and Los Angeles with short-haul eastern rates, 129–131, 160; of middle-distance rates from San Francisco with middle-distance eastern rates, 132–134; of eastbound and westbound transcontinental commodity rates, 135–136; areas of equivalence (rate sheds) between eastbound and westbound transcontinental rates, 136–137; general conclusions on, 138–139

Competition: influenced the original selection of western termini, 35; between producers of lettuce in California and Arizona, 44–45; between producers of citrus in California and Florida, 63–65, 121; between San Francisco and New Orleans in shipments of sugar, 66–68, 121–122; between rail and water carriers in California, 90–91; between rail carriers, 99; between rail and water carriers, 99, 105, 117, 118, 120

Containers, rates on, 30
Contours. *See* Elevation
Curvature, effect on costs, 13

Density of traffic: on transcontinental railway lines, 15–19; comparison with eastern railroads, 19; effect on costs, 19–20

Distances: by air routes, 3–4; by rail, 4–5; by water, 5–7; method of measurement of, 3–4 n.; points of equal air distance from San Francisco, 147; of equal rail-route distance, 148

Dried fruits and vegetables: destinations of eastbound shipments, 40; grouping of points of origin, 41–43; of points of destination, 71–73; profile of rates on, 105–106; affected by carrier competition, 120

Dry goods: grouping of points of destination, westbound, 47; of points of origin, 76–77; articles taking dry-goods rates, 76 n.; minimum carload weights, 76 n.; relative rate levels on various hauls, 127–138

Elevations: by central and southern transcontinental routes, 7; railroad contours, 8–9; disadvantages of, 9–14; over Atchison, Topeka and Santa Fe, 10–12; resistance caused by, 14; rates do not reflect irregularities in, 154–155

Ferry trucks, 30
Fertilizers: grouping of points of destination, westbound, 48; of points of origin, 85; articles taking fertilizer rates, 85 n.; minimum carload weights, 85 n.; relative rate levels on various hauls, 127–138

Fresh fruits, destinations of eastbound shipments of, 40. *See also* Fresh grapes

Fresh grapes: grouping of points of origin on eastbound shipments, 41–43, 61–62; of points of destination, 61; minimum carload weights, 61 n.; profile of rates on, 94–96; recent history of rates on, 125–126

Fresh vegetables: destination of eastbound shipments of, 40; grouping of points of origin, 43–45; of points of destination, 59–60; articles taking fresh vegetable rates, 59 n.; minimum carload weights, 59 n.

Grapes. *See* Fresh grapes
Green vegetables. *See* Fresh vegetables

Highways, proportion of transcontinental traffic carried over, 2

Intercoastal steamship service, 7
Interterritorial rates. *See* Comparison of rates
Intraterritorial rates. *See* Comparison of rates

Lettuce: profile of rates on, 93–94; recent history of rates on, 124–125. *See also* Fresh vegetables

Long and short haul: tariff clauses relating to, 33; rates from California to Columbia River points, 59, 72; rates on sugar, 67

Mileage. *See* Distance
Mileage rates, 150–153. *See also* Profiles
Minimum carload weights: on lettuce, 59 n.; on grapes, 61 n.; on citrus, 62 n.; on sugar, 65–66 n.; on canned goods, 69–70 n.; on dried fruits and vegetables, 71–72 n.; on wine, 73 n., 85 n.; on dry goods, 76 n.; on beverages, 78 n.; on steel, 79 n.; on automobile bodies and parts, 81 n.; on clothing, 82 n.; on vehicles, 83 n.; on canned goods, westbound, 84 n.; on wine, 85 n.; on fertilizers, 85 n.; on tin, 86 n.

INDEX

Mixed carloads, rule governing, 30–31
Motor vehicles, proportion of transcontinental traffic carried by, 2
Mountain operation, 6–15
Mountain-Pacific territory: rates in, 25, 30, 115, 133–139, 150–153; carloads originating and terminating in, 40; map of, facing 108; rail distances in, 148

Pacific Freight Tariff Bureau: territory covered by, 21–24; rate groups in, 50–52, 149–150
Profiles: of class rates, 80–93; of lettuce rates, 93–94; of fresh grape rates, 94–96; of citrus rates, 96–99; of sugar rates, 99–101; of canned-goods rates, eastbound, 101–105; of dried fruit and vegetable rates, 104–106; of wine rates, 106–107; transcontinental first-class, Mountain-Pacific first-class, and canned-goods rates compared, 151–154

Railroads, proportion of transcontinental traffic carried by, 2–3
Rate increments: on selected commodities, 88–107; between competitive points, 155–158
Rate levels. *See* Comparison of rates
Rate sheds. *See* Comparison of rates
Ruling grades, 10–13

State boundaries, effect on rates, 131, 155
Steel: grouping of points of destination, westbound, 47; of points of origin, 79–80; articles taking steel rates, 79 n; minimum carload weights, 79 n.; relative rate levels on various hauls, 127–138
Sugar: destination of eastbound shipments of, 40; grouping of points of origin, 45–46; of points of destination, 65–69; minimum carload weights, 65–66 n.; profile of rates on, 99–100; recent history of rates on, 121–123

Tariffs, difficulty in interpretation of, 32–34, 159–160
Tennessee Valley Authority, comparison of intraterritorial and of interterritorial rates by, 109–110

Terminal groups. *See* Western termini
Tin: grouping of points of destination, westbound, 47; of points of origin, 86; articles taking tin rates, 86 n.; minimum carload weights on, 86 n.; relative rate levels on various hauls, 127–138
Traffic: distribution between transportation agencies, 1–2; on transcontinental routes, 17–19; by territories of origination and termination, 40
Transcontinental Freight Bureau, territory covered by, 21–24
Transcontinental rate groups: on class shipments, 51–58; on commodity shipments, eastbound, 58–75; on commodity shipments, westbound, 76–87; history of zones, 52–55; not all points included in, 55–56; advantages of, 140–144; disadvantages of, 144–145; attitude of Interstate Commerce Commission toward rate groups, 145 n.; alternatives to use of, 145–146
Transcontinental shipments. *See* Traffic
Transverse lines, effect on boundaries of transcontinental groups, 142–143 n.

Vehicles: grouping of points of destination, westbound, 48; of points of origin, 82–83; articles taking vehicle rates, 82–83 n.; minimum carload weights, 83 n.

Water: proportion of transcontinental traffic carried by, 2; intercoastal steamship services, 7
Western termini: early recognition in transcontinental ratemaking, 35; grouping of, on class shipments, 36–39; on eastbound commodity shipments, 41–46; on westbound commodity shipments, 46–49; rates to and from, applied as maxima at intermediate points, 49 n.; summary description of, 140
Wine: grouping of points of origin, eastbound, 41–43; of points of destination, 73–74; minimum carload weights, 73 n., 85 n.; grouping of points of origin, westbound, 84; application of rates on, 106–107; recent history of rates on, 123–124

www.ingramcontent.com/pod-product-compliance
Lightning Source LLC
Chambersburg PA
CBHW021709230426
43668CB00008B/781